An Islamic Philosophy

of Virtuous Religions

An Islamic Philosophy

of Virtuous Religions

Introducing Alfarabi

Joshua Parens

State University of New York Press

Published by
State University of New York Press, Albany

© 2006 State University of New York

For information, address State University of New York Press,
194 Washington Avenue, Suite 305, Albany, NY 12210–2365

Production by Michael Haggett
Marketing by Anne M. Valentine

Library of Congress Cataloging-in-Publication Data
Parens, Joshua, 1961–
    An Islamic philosophy of virtuous religions : introducing Alfarabi / Joshua Parens.
        p. cm.
    Includes bibliographical references and index.
    ISBN 0-7914-6689-2 (hardcover: alk. paper) 1. Fáaráabái. 2. Philosophy, Islamic.
I. Title
B753.F34P27 2006
201'.5—dc22   2005014014

ISBN-13: 978-0-7914-6689-6 (hardcover : alk. paper)
ISBN 0-7914-6690-6 (pbk. : alk. paper)
ISBN-13: 978-0-7914-6690-2 (pbk. : alk. paper)

10 9 8 7 6 5 4 3 2 1

Contents

Acknowledgments

I thank the Earhart Foundation, together with my university, the University of Dallas, for generously funding a sabbatical leave (AY 2003–2004), during which I drafted this book. I also thank Cornell University Press for allowing me to reprint words, phrases, and paragraphs from *Alfarabi: The Political Writings: The Philosophy of Plato and Aristotle,* trans. Muhsin Mahdi (Ithaca, NY: Cornell University Press, 1969, 2001) and *Alfarabi: The Political Writings: "Selected Aphorisms" and Other Writings,* trans. Charles E. Butterworth (Ithaca, NY: Cornell University Press, 2001). Even more than in my first book, my debt to Muhsin Mahdi is evident on every page.

I thank my parents for their support throughout my life and for a conversation I had with them, especially my mother, one day that led to this book. To my wife and son, I am most grateful for your patience.

Abbreviations

AH	Alfarabi, *Attainment of Happiness*
Aphorisms	*Selected Aphorisms*
BR	*Book of Religion*
BL	*Book of Letters*
PA	*Philosophy of Aristotle*
PP	*Philosophy of Plato*
PPA	*Philosophy of Plato and Aristotle* (the trilogy of *AH, PP, PA*)
PR	*Political Regime*
VC	*Principles of the Opinions of the Inhabitants of the Virtuous City*

Meta.	Aristotle, *Metaphysics*
NE	*Nicomachean Ethics*
REP.	Plato, *Republic*

AFIPP	Muhsin Mahdi, *Alfarabi and the Foundation of Islamic Political Philosophy*

One

Introduction

Now more than at any time for centuries, Alfarabi, a tenth-century Muslim political philosopher, is especially timely. This book is intended as an introduction to Alfarabi's thought not through a survey of his many writings but through an analysis especially of one of them, one with special relevance to our times. In his *Attainment of Happiness,* Alfarabi envisions the fulfillment of Islam's ambition to spread Islam, as *the* virtuous religion, to the inhabited world. Along the way, however, he raises a few questions: Is one religion suited to the great variety of human communities throughout the world? Is it possible for more than one virtuous religion to exist? If more than one virtuous religion can exist, how and why can they exist? One thing is certain: Alfarabi is not a premodern version of John Locke. Alfarabi's solution to intercommunal conflict, to the extent he intends to offer one, is *not* to pronounce all religions equal as long as they promote a characteristically modern morality and avoid interference in politics. (In this introduction, I will refer to this all-too-brief account of Locke's teaching, not even entertained by Alfarabi, as "tolerance," though I use the term loosely here.) On the contrary, Alfarabi describes a world filled with rank and hierarchy. (Furthermore, he does not separate religion from politics.) He has no qualms about pronouncing one religion superior to another—though he does so without pointing fingers. He describes in challenging ways what makes a religion truly virtuous. Rather than declaring in advance the superiority of Islam to all other religions, he analyzes what it takes to be virtuous and rightly guided and leaves it to his readers to compare existing religions with his account. Most importantly, he does not exclude the possibility of a multiplicity of virtuous religions.[1] For a variety of reasons, Alfarabi was considered too radical for his times. At least to some extent, his time may have just arrived. I do not intend to offer a panacea. Alfarabi does not offer mechanisms or institutions of governance such as the separation of powers, which have the potential, if rightly instituted, to establish a balanced modern government. Rather, he is more interested in educating his reader than in offering institutional solutions. He seeks to explore and illuminate his readers' own hopes and aspirations—through a dialogue of sorts with them—one reader at a time. Such an education, though often difficult to come by in our loud and hurried times, is, I believe, especially important today, for both Muslim and non-Muslim alike.

In his *Attainment of Happiness,* Alfarabi extrapolates from insights that Plato developed in the *Republic*. In the *Republic,* Socrates envisions a perfectly just city (*polis*) as one in which all citizens are devoted solely to the common good. The harm done to the private good of most citizens in that city is familiar to most undergraduates. Alfarabi uses that insight and applies it to his own setting. He wonders what it would take for Islam to achieve its ambition to rule the world justly. He argues that it would require that not only every nation but also every city within every nation should be virtuous. Furthermore, to be truly just, the rulers of each nation would need to be philosopher-kings, and each city would need to have its own peculiar adaptations or imitations of philosophy suited to its particular climate and locale. In other words, a virtuous world regime would require a multiplicity of virtuous religions to match the multiplicity of virtuous nations.

Alfarabi does *not* intend this world regime to be a realistic or even an ideal plan. Rather, he seeks to persuade his reader that the effort to establish a just world regime is an impossibly high, even if a noble, goal. The *Attainment of Happiness,* like the *Republic,* is intended as a cautionary tale promoting political moderation. Above all, it seeks to educate the young and politically ambitious Muslim to temper his or her desire to spread the truths of Islam to the world as a whole. Once again, this form of political education is quite different from the modern focus on mechanisms and institutions of governance. It almost goes without saying that such institutions are indispensable. At the same time, mechanisms alone will not stand a chance in the face of citizens filled with religious zeal for the highest and noblest aspirations of the human heart.

There are obvious similarities between Alfarabi's claim that there can exist a multiplicity of virtuous religions and the liberal democrat's claim that different religions need to coexist in tolerance. Nevertheless, the two claims are not synonymous. The former befits a world in which the primary form of political education is to temper the zeal and ambition of the young; the latter befits a world in which zeal and ambition are directed, for the most part, away from politics toward material acquisition. Could the former be used as a stepping-stone to the latter? Or could the former be used to complement the approach of the latter? There is room for argument, debate, and inquiry into these and related questions. This book seeks to spark such debate and to offer access to the premodern approach to the problem—a premodern approach with peculiar relevance in today's Middle East.

ALFARABI'S LIFE AND HIS INFLUENCE

I need not repeat many of the details of Alfarabi's biography here.[2] Abu Nasr Muhammad al-Farabi (or Alfarabi) was born (in 870 C.E./256 A.H.) and reared on the easternmost reaches of the Islamic world in what is today Central Asia. He was a native speaker of a Turkic dialect, Soghdian. Although before adulthood he received a relatively traditional Muslim education there, he received much of his education, especially in Arabic and logic, from Christian scholars. Eventually he traveled to the heart of the Islamic lands residing in what are today Syria, Iraq, and Egypt, and he is likely to have spent time even in Byzantium. The most striking feature of Alfarabi's education is his deep exposure to a variety of languages, places, and religious and ethnic groups. Although such travels were by no means rare in his time, Alfarabi was clearly a cosmopolitan man. I do not mean to suggest that Alfarabi's biography dictated his philosophy, however. All I mean to suggest is that his life provided him with firsthand experience of the kind of diversity a ruler might face in attempting to establish a virtuous regime of the inhabited world. If any Muslim understood the differences among nations that would have to be reflected in any Islamic effort to spread Islam, that Muslim was Alfarabi.

It could be objected that Alfarabi's cosmopolitanism aside, the world has passed him by. After all, he is a little-studied, tenth-century thinker whose influence, with a few exceptions, seems not to have lasted beyond the thirteenth century. Yet his aborted influence is part of what gives his thought such relevance. The public the world over, including in the Middle East, wants to know what went wrong in the Muslim world. Why has it been left behind? Of course, many in the West leap to the conclusion that Islam is the root of the problem. No one could deny that Islam has played some role. The question is whether the Islam that played a role is truly Islamic. I cannot enter into the details of the debate about whether Islam has an essence and whether that essence cannot be reformed. I have my suspicions that it not only can but also must be reformed. And if one wishes to continue thinking constructively about these matters, then one must assume it can be reformed. In any such reformation, it is essential that Muslims seek to assess where wrong turns were made in the tradition. I hope to persuade the reader that the turn, in the thirteenth century, away from Alfarabi's kind of political rationalism in Islam had deleterious effects. Now that turn was certainly overdetermined. It was not the result of a simple, conscious decision of a few. Rather, factors far beyond the control of individuals such as the Mongol sacking of Baghdad in 1258 contributed mightily to the demise of this rationalism. Obviously the conflict between Islam and Christendom did little to help matters. The rise of mystical and illuminationist philosophy within the Islamic world, however, was not the result solely of events. Rulers, jurists, and ulema made choices in favor of that trend within education. It also did not help that the two staunchest proponents of rationalism, Alfarabi and Averroes (Ibn Rushd), may have been prone to stating their positions too starkly. Above all, Avicenna (Ibn Sina), the most widely known Muslim philosopher in both the West and the Islamic world, contributed to the demise of rationalism by effacing the differences between philosophy and traditional theology.

Yet perhaps the greatest contributing factor to Islam's inability to adapt to the modern world was the relative absence of deep theological differences within the Islamic fold, at least until relatively late in its development. The largest dispute between Sunni and Shi'i was for centuries largely political or dynastic. In contrast, the wars of religion between Catholics and Protestants with their deep theological basis tore Europe apart in the sixteenth and seventeenth centuries. These wars compelled political philosophers to think anew about the proper relation between religion and politics. Furthermore, Christianity's focus on the next life facilitated the separation of religion from politics. Consequently, European thinkers were enabled to give birth to the Enlightenment. These wars of religion, these unwanted spurs to reform, have contributed mightily to Western history. Ironically, Islam's greatest loss may have been being spared the scourge of more profoundly religious warfare within the house of Islam.

To return to Alfarabi, although the Islamic world was incapable for whatever reasons of assimilating Alfarabi's profound rationalism in the medieval period, it may stand to benefit from his instruction now. After all,

Alfarabi is not the purveyor of yet another panacea such as Pan-Arabism or Baathism or Pan-Islamism. Rather, he thinks through the highest ideals of Islam down to their clearest political implications. Unlike a political program or mechanism, this form of political education may be truly timeless.

Alfarabi is barely known in the West because most medieval Christian thinkers were interested in Muslim thinkers primarily as transmitters and modifiers of the metaphysical doctrines of Plato and Aristotle. In the medieval West, then, later thinkers such as Avicenna and Averroes made more extensive and more novel contributions in metaphysics than he and are, therefore, far more widely known in the West. Yet these very thinkers—not only Avicenna and Averroes but also Ibn Bajja and Ibn Tufayl—acknowledge Alfarabi's preeminence among political philosophers in and of Islam.

ALFARABI'S MANNER OF WRITING

Alfarabi is notorious for the caution with which he writes. I, like others before me,[3] have discussed the roots of this need for secretive or esoteric writing elsewhere. In his most explicit statement on the matter in his *Summary of Plato's "Laws,"* he discusses Plato's secretiveness by drawing an analogy between how Plato expresses himself and the actions of an abstemious ascetic who is hated by a ruler. That ascetic seeks to escape the city by imitating a drunk, in other words, by imitating the immoderation of those around him.[4] The arguments for interpreting this as sanctioning secretive writing need not be repeated here.

Rather, we may focus on the issue before us in reading Alfarabi's *Attainment of Happiness,* the possibility of a virtuous regime of the inhabited world, to see whether Alfarabi would not have every reason for treading lightly. The possibility of such a regime, indeed, the requirement that Muslims pursue a highly homogeneous form of such a regime, had come even by Alfarabi's time to be accepted within Islamic jurisprudence.[5] If Alfarabi were to declare openly that Islam's ambition for a virtuous regime of the inhabited world is doomed to failure, then he could be viewed as in some sense heretical. Consequently, he does not declare explicitly that the virtuous regime of the inhabited world is impossible. Indeed, many have read the *Attainment of Happiness* and assumed that it advocates the realization or attainment of such a regime. A philosopher's argument that something is impossible would seem at first to be wholly unnecessary. After all, isn't impossibility self-enforcing? That is, if such a regime really cannot exist, then it never will. And if one attempts to realize such a plan, at best, then one will succeed in bringing into being a pale imitation of it. Why, then, should a philosopher make such an argument, as I am suggesting, between the lines? I believe that Alfarabi makes such an argument to prevent the unnecessary suffering of both rulers and ruled: the former, including the most intelligent and ambitious, run the risk of frittering away their abilities on a pale imitation of what they truly desire, while the latter run the risk of suffering at the hands of ambitious rulers. Alfarabi hopes to redirect these potential rulers' love of things high and noble toward the pursuit of knowledge rather than conquest. In this respect, he takes a page from the book of Plato's Socrates, who made strenuous efforts to prevent extraordinary individuals such as Alcibiades from wasting their gifts on the pursuit of empire.[6]

How, then, does Alfarabi go about communicating subtly his cautionary tale? He does not argue openly for caution. Indeed, if Alfarabi were not identified repeatedly as the leading logician in medieval Islam, and we were not confident that he knows what an argument is, then we might be tempted to suppose that he rarely argues anything, especially in his most renowned political writings. If one expects the explicit back and forth of a Platonic dialogue, Aristotle's *Nicomachean Ethics* (*NE*), or a medieval dialectical disputation, then one will generally be disappointed in Alfarabi. His arguments in his political writings are rarely openly dialectical, let alone demonstrative.[7] Rather, he writes descriptively and rhetorically.

The most prominent parts of his best-known political works, for example, the first parts of the *Virtuous City* and the *Political Regime,* contain his most rhetorical material. When he writes descriptively, he often states the conclusions of arguments without much of the argument leading up to them. For example, in his *Selected Aphorisms,* he offers prescriptions for political life highly reminiscent of Aristotle's *Nicomachean Ethics.* His arguments become evident primarily when one compares his conclusions with Aristotle's. Small differences of conclusion often tell more than detailed and rigorous argument could. In (part ii of) the *Attainment of Happiness* (where Alfarabi turns to his plans for a virtuous regime of the inhabited world) his accounts are also largely descriptive. He describes what a regime of the inhabited world would require to be virtuous. He offers little, if any, argument for why such a regime would be desirable—after all, his religion has already offered the rationale. Furthermore, he does not describe such a regime in detail. Rather, he takes advantage of the universal, philosophic point of view (what is sometimes treated disparagingly in modern philosophy as the view from nowhere) to make the reader responsible for considering the possible details. In what follows, I refer to this aspect of his writing, especially pronounced in the *Attainment of Happiness* and even more so in the *Book of Religion,* as his "schematic" style. In leaving the filling in of details to the reader, he makes the reader responsible for confronting the real challenge of his argument.[8] For example, Alfarabi never specifies how many nations would be part of the virtuous regime of the inhabited world he discusses. But his claim that each component must be virtuous, especially in accordance with the virtuous standard of Plato's *Republic,* boggles the mind when one seeks to envision it in any detail. By leaving the filling in of details to the reader, Alfarabi makes his attentive reader engage in a dialogue with his writings.

Another feature of Alfarabi's writing that will play a prominent role in this book, especially chapter 4, is the way Alfarabi compels his reader to think through shocking omissions. The most obvious examples are the following: In the *Attainment of Happiness (AH)* he is completely silent about prophecy, and in the portion of *Selected Aphorisms,* where one most expects a discussion of *jihâd,* he is silent about it. The former silence is so striking because the inspiration for the entirety of *AH* is surely Islam, especially its ambition to bring virtue to the entire world. But Islam claims to be a revealed or prophetic religion. Yet Alfarabi, though he discusses prophecy in many of his works, is wholly silent about it in *AH.* Does this mean we should suppose that when Alfarabi wrote *AH* he did not have Islam in mind? On the contrary. At least in Alfarabi's time, nothing but one of the revealed religions could have inspired the plan for a virtuous regime of the inhabited world.[9] Similarly, in the opening paragraphs of Alfarabi's discussion of forms of war in *Aphorisms,* sec. 67, when he is discussing a form of war most like *jihâd,* he never identifies it as just or as a form of *jihâd.* As we will discover in the pages that follow, Alfarabi engages in a self-conscious strategy of omitting terms or elements of an argument or a plan that one most expects—to provoke thought.

OVERVIEW

To recapitulate in a more orderly fashion, the three key parts of my argument are the following: (1) To think through Islam's ambition to spread the virtuous religion of Islam to the entire world, Alfarabi compares its ambition to the model of the virtuous city in the *Republic.* Through an analysis of the *Republic,* I show that the virtuous city in that book is intended ultimately by Plato's Socrates to be impossible.[10] I also show that Alfarabi evinces his awareness in our key text, the *Attainment of Happiness,* that it is impossible. (2) Alfarabi adds to this his "a fortiori argument." If Islam is to achieve its ambition of bringing its virtuous religion to the entire world, then every city and every nation must become virtuous in its own right. If it is impossible for one truly virtuous city to come into being, then a fortiori it is impossible for a virtuous regime of the inhabited world to come into being.[11] (3) Alfarabi adds to this his "multiplicity argument." Each religion must be suited in each time and place to the national character of each people, influenced by environmental differences such as climate and food supply and conventional differences such as language. A virtuous regime of the inhabited world, then, would have to include a multiplicity of virtuous religions. Consequently, even if such a regime were possible, each part of the inhabited world would possess a different religion. In other words, a virtuous regime of the inhabited world would not be nearly as homogeneous as many traditionalist adherents of Islam expect it to be.

This book includes these three main arguments and others in the following manner: This chapter, chapter 1, is the book's introduction. Chapter 2 is (1) on the impossibility of the virtuous city in the *Republic.* Chapter 3 is (2) the "a fortiori argument." Chapter 4 expands upon a special thread in the "a fortiori argument," Alfarabi's position on *jihâd.* If virtuous religion(s) is (are) to be spread throughout the world, then virtuous character would seem to need to be spread not only through persuasion but also by force. Although Alfarabi appears at first glance to promote *jihâd,* closer analysis reveals a sophisticated and subtle critique of the traditional juridical justifications for *jihâd.* Chapter 5 is (3) the "multiplicity argument." Chapter 6 on the limits of human knowledge seeks to explain the connection between the inherent multiplicity of religions and Alfarabi's assessment of the limits of human knowledge. If human beings could possess certain and exhaustive knowledge of the causes and grounds of the cosmos, which we cannot, then it might have been possible for one science to take the place of the many religions.

Finally, although Alfarabi's *Attainment* is the main focus of this book, large sections of the book are devoted not only to other Alfarabian texts, especially the *Selected Aphorisms* and the *Political Regime,* but also to Plato's *Republic* and Aristotle's *Nicomachean Ethics.* Without a proper understanding of Plato and Aristotle,[12] much in Alfarabi remains mysterious. At the same time, Alfarabi can only deepen readers' understanding of Plato and Aristotle.

Two

The Impossibility of the City in the *Republic*

Before turning to the *Republic* itself, I must say a word or two about Alfarabi's access to the *Republic*. Alfarabi refers explicitly to the *Republic* in the *Attainment of Happiness* (*AH*) three times. Most of his references there are to *Republic*, bks. 6–7. I will discuss his handling of these references in chapter 3. In his *Political Regime* (*PR*), Alfarabi discusses at great length the nonvirtuous cities treated in *Rep.*, bk. 8. I will devote some attention to this in chapter 5. With the exception of the *Timaeus*, we do not possess any of the Platonic texts that Alfarabi might have had access to in Arabic.[1] Averroes, living just under 300 years later on the opposite end of the Islamic world, wrote a close commentary evincing extensive familiarity with the *Republic*.[2] Averroes cites Alfarabi at least twice in his own commentary. And many more of Averroes's arguments show evidence of debt to Alfarabi in *AH* and *PR*. At least an author with extensive familiarity with the *Republic* saw fit to cite Alfarabi as an authority on it. Little more than this can be inferred about the extent of Alfarabi's familiarity with the *Republic* on the basis of philological data alone.

Leaving aside the scanty philological evidence we possess, we may turn to a more fruitful and substantive approach to Alfarabi's familiarity with the *Republic*. Alfarabi's main basis for interest in Plato is widely recognized among scholars. He is interested in the philosopher-king in the *Republic* as a model for the prophet-legislator of the revealed religions, especially, though not exclusively, Islam. On this basis, he develops a complex prophetology or account of prophecy using elements of Aristotelian psychology and Neoplatonic emanationism to account for the possibility of revelation

9

of the Divine Law to the prophet-legislator. This prophetology based on philosopher-kingship is the core of his political teaching. Although the qualifications of his legislator are not simply identical to Plato's philosopher-king,[3] they are nearly so. The parallels between Alfarabi's and Plato's treatments of the philosopher-king have been discussed at great length by scholars. Although Alfarabi, to my knowledge, offers his qualifications for philosophic rule in only two writings, this theme endured throughout medieval Islamic (and Jewish) political thought.[4] Familiarity has bred some contempt for, or at least scholarly weariness with, Alfarabi's handling of the theme of philosopher-kingship. We must make a special effort to resist such weariness and never to forget just how radical a suggestion philosopher-kingship is. Of course, linking it to prophecy and revelation seems to explain away some of its radicality. Socrates states that it would require some form of divine intervention for kings to become enamored of philosophy (499c). But in the *AH,* upon which we will focus, Alfarabi retains the theme of philosopher-kingship and even combines it with legislation, but he never appeals to revelation or divine intervention for this coincidence. Through his silence about revelation, he is enabled to highlight the difficulties surrounding the philosopher-king (as we will see in chapter 3), however subtly he may do so.

As readers of Alfarabi with a special interest in how he might have read the *Republic,* we must distinguish the task of inferring how he might have read the *Republic* from how he makes his philosopher-king-legislator appear to us at first in his corpus as a whole. Alfarabi goes out of his way to facilitate our acceptance of his radical suggestion. As a philosopher defending philosophy, Alfarabi seeks to foster the acceptance of philosophy within his own community. Could one do better than to make the philosopher into a hero? One could hardly come up with a better way of making the philosopher into a hero than to insinuate that the Prophet himself must have been a philosopher. In doing so, Alfarabi sought to make the unacceptable acceptable.[5] It would hardly have been in his interest to highlight for all to see the doubts surrounding the very possibility of philosopher-kingship. Yet it will be my task (especially in chapter 3) to show that Alfarabi is well aware of just how radical a suggestion philosopher-kingship is.

One way Alfarabi facilitates the acceptance of the philosopher-king premise is to detach it from the other radical reforms Socrates proposes in the *Republic.* Alfarabi's appropriation of philosopher-kingship in isolation contributes to its apparent innocuousness. (Of course, it can be claimed that Alfarabi leaves out the other waves because he is not familiar with them. The bulk of our evidence for just how much of the *Republic* Alfarabi is likely to have known will be given in the next chapter.) Even in reading the *Republic* itself, it is all too easy to forget that philosopher-kingship is the third and highest of three waves. In bk. 5, the other two waves are (first wave) the equal education of female guardians (451c–457c5) and (second wave) the sharing of women and children (457c5–473c). The metaphor of waves is meant to highlight what the reader of the *Republic* might otherwise overlook, that is, that philosopher-kingship is the *most unlikely* of the radical reforms Socrates suggests (473c5–474b2). Readers are so appalled by the second wave and so unfamiliar with what philosophy is that they are likely to ignore just how radical the third wave is.

Briefly and preliminarily, the following are the main reasons the third is the highest wave. Although Socrates succeeds in pressing his interlocutor, Glaucon, to accept the first wave, equal education of women to be guardians, it is at least somewhat unlikely. The contemporary reader is familiar with the debates surrounding women's participation not in the military broadly speaking but in combat units. When one subtracts the use of modern weapons and the return to the simple arms of Greek warfare, it becomes easier to see how difficult such a proposal might be. As we will see, the main challenge is less physical than it is psychological. Indeed, the second wave, sharing women and children, contains within it the most problematic element in the first wave—the assumption that families, especially mothers, can be warriors at the expense of having a family at all. Indeed, the second wave is most appalling to most readers, because they view the family as altogether natural and cannot imagine its destruction in the name of the common good of the city. The third wave, the unification of philosophy and kingship, seems unproblematic in comparison. Ultimately it proves most problematic because it rests upon the consent, if not the successful compulsion, of both the ruled (whose families are being shared in common) and the rulers (the philosophers). It is higher than the previous wave, because both the ruled *and* the rulers will resist it. Why philosophers would not like to rule is not immediately obvious. Furthermore, why they do not object to the destruction of the family is also not obvious. These claims will have to be justified in what follows. Even based on this brief perusal of the three waves, any reader should appreciate why Alfarabi felt it incumbent upon himself to isolate philosopher-kingship from the second wave, namely, to facilitate the acceptance of philosophy in his own society.

Before taking a closer look at the three waves, I must clarify a key source of confusion preventing the contemporary reader from understanding why philosophers might spend so much time making impossible cities and regimes in speech. That is, before showing the beautiful city (*kallipolis*, 527c) is impossible, I must give the reader some reason for being interested in impossible cities.

KALLIPOLIS AS IDEAL STATE OR
TOTALITARIAN NIGHTMARE?

Ever since Machiavelli condemned the ancients for establishing cities on sand and mud,[6] a distortion of the original intention of Plato has crept into the study of the *Republic*. In spite of his frequent condemnations of the ancients, Machiavelli was a devoted student of Aristotle and Plato.[7] Consequently, I do not mean to suggest that he fell prey to this distortion. Rather, he fomented, and intended to foment, such a distortion of the ancients in his readers. Machiavelli put political thought on such a new footing—stressing desirable effects and outcomes more than the philosophical training that occurs along the way—that no one could look back on the ancients with the same eyes. In a sense, he is correct: The ancients' cities, at least their best cities, were founded on sand and mud. They were, indeed, never intended for "use" in the modern sense. In a sense, then, they are useless and worthy of mockery. Measured against the modern standard of utility, ancient political philosophy hardly measures up. In lieu of the ancient submission to the cycles of nature, early modern thinkers championed reason's ability both to refashion "nature" and to envision, albeit within defined limits, new ideas of what man could be.[8] Gradually, man ceases to be a part of nature and ascends to become a product of his own fashioning. Subsequently, various discontents with modernity led thinkers such as Rousseau to look back upon ancient practice, if not ancient thought, for models superior to the low utility championed by early modern thinkers.[9] In the face of the reputedly bleak realism of early modern thinkers, these models came to be known as ideals. Since Rousseau, the *Republic* has often been viewed alternately as laughably (or horrifically) unrealistic and emblematic of man's highest ideals.

Frequently in translating the *Republic*, translators evince this modernity-inspired reading by referring to its city as the "ideal state." Yet the city is far too small to qualify as a state. In modern parlance, this denotation of "state" refers to a large political body—so large that ancient thinkers would have considered it only when discussing empire. Of course, this is one of the claims to fame of the Founders of the United States to have discovered the secret of combining great size with republican principles. Yet as all students of political theory know, modern republicanism is not synonymous with its ancient form. So the city in the *Republic* is by no means a state. Nor, I intend to show, should it be thought of as ideal. It is not ideal because it would not be desirable if it could be realized. The notion of "ideal" as it was developed subsequent to Rousseau suggests something that one should either approach asymptotically—as in Kant's plan for perpetual peace—or realize very concretely—as in Hegel's effort to make the ideal a reality.

Another reason the city in the *Republic* came to be viewed as Plato's ideal city or state is that Socrates refers to it (in the midst of a discussion of geometry) as *kallipolis,* or the beautiful city (527c). Late modern thinkers highlighted the importance of the beautiful and questions of aesthetics to begin with in Kant for morals and progressively in German idealism for politics. Kant links beauty, though its primary significance is aesthetic, to morals.[10] Yet Kant's views on political practice are closer to those of earlier modern thinkers than the more revolutionary or "idealistic" Rousseau.[11]

Although Plato tended to be viewed as an idealist in late modern thought, the ravages of World War II fostered another reading. I refer to Karl Popper's interpretation of Plato as an enemy of the open society, indeed, as a totalitarian. Now there is a sense in which all premodern political thought is totalitarian. I do not know of any premodern thinker who advocates the rights of the individual, made famous by the likes of Hobbes and Locke. All premodern thinkers, in their most "realistic" moments, laid greater stress in their political teaching on the common good than on individual rights. Yet as I hope to show, Plato was well aware of the tension between the individual and the common good—indeed, its explication is one of the central themes of the *Republic*!

Rather than view the *Republic* as an ideal in need of realization or a totalitarian nightmare, I believe that it is more fitting to view it as a cross between a standard and a cautionary tale. True, there is little difference between "standard" and "ideal." Yet I choose "standard" to avoid the misleading connotations of "ideal." Despite the naiveté often associated with idealism in politics, it generally suggests something that one should sacrifice one's last breath in striving to reach, as long as one believes it can be realized. Idealism is underwritten by the tacit assumption that human beings are (almost) infinitely malleable. In contrast to idealism's tendency toward utopianism, I mean by a "standard" a plan that is best viewed as an unreachable model—as is implied in adding to it "cautionary tale."

I admit it seems odd to combine these apparently conflicting elements. After all, the pair sounds like a combination of idealism (standard) and realism (cautionary tale)—a muddy, middle-of-the-road position. The split between realism and idealism, however, is not present in ancient philosophy. It is one of our historical inheritances from the early modern project.[12] This split is absent from ancient philosophy, primarily because ancient thinkers had a lower estimation of what reason could achieve. As we will see, they were more convinced of the challenges desire poses to reason than modern thinkers. Ironically, ancient thinkers were, in a sense, more realistic than either modern realists or idealists.[13] Recall that even the early modern "realists" believed that reason could fashion a new idea of man. They resisted the confines of the ancient view of nature. For the ancients, in contrast, the real task is to determine what, if anything, is natural in human affairs.

Assuming for the moment I am correct that *kallipolis* is impossible, we have stumbled upon at least part of the reason for inquiring into impossible cities—by doing so, we learn about the limits of what can be achieved in public life and about human nature. Still, this is not a complete answer. As we will see in what follows, this question cannot be answered fully without sufficient attention to the characters participating in the dialogue. Until we enter into their desires and aspirations, we will have difficulty making sense of why one should engage in such an apparently futile endeavor.

THE THREE WAVES AND THE PROBLEM OF POSSIBILITY

Now I will seek to justify my claim that the *Republic* is a combination of standard and cautionary tale through a more detailed account of the three waves and the characters involved in them, especially the first two. More importantly, we will focus on the question of whether each wave is possible. Furthermore, we will need to know in greater detail why the waves, according to Socrates, become increasingly high or increasingly unlikely. Of course, these accounts and questions are interrelated. That which makes the waves impossible helps clarify why the *Republic* must serve as a cautionary tale rather than an ideal.

I must sketch briefly the background to the three waves. For the most part, the *Republic* is a conversation between Socrates and Plato's two brothers, Glaucon and Adeimantus. Plato and his brothers were wealthy and well-positioned Athenians. As many interpreters have suggested before me, Glaucon was a politically ambitious young man. Out of concern for the fate of his brother, Plato is known to have sought Socrates' support in discouraging Glaucon from pursuing political prominence.[14] Some evidence in the dialogue suggests that the conversation took place well before the end of the Peloponnesian War—a long and devastating war between Athens and Sparta, lost by Athens. Toward the end of this war, a large group of wealthy Athenians, eventually identified as the Thirty Tyrants, sought to overthrow Athenian democracy, at least in part because they viewed it as the cause of the Athenian defeat. They succeeded temporarily, only to suffer at the hands of those they tyrannized. In the background of the *Republic*, then, is the ever-present possibility that Glaucon will enter politics at perhaps the worst moment in Athenian history, with disastrous consequences for his city and himself.[15]

In bk. 2, Socrates' conversation with Glaucon begins in earnest, in search of a just soul. Socrates suggests that they inquire into a just city as an analogue to the soul. (I will discuss the early stages of his inquiry briefly in chapter 3.) Early in their inquiry, they fill the city they are founding with desire for luxury, at the behest of Glaucon. This luxury leads eventually to war and to the need for guardians to protect the city. In bks. 2–4, Socrates grabs hold of these guardians, turning them into the future rulers of the city. He plans the formation of their character through a complex system of education. He speaks frequently of how he has thereby purged their souls of the excessive desires that led Glaucon to demand the founding of a luxurious city. Their souls need to be shaped so that they serve the common good as if it were their very own (412d–e). To facilitate this devotion to the common good, Socrates sanctions the telling of a noble lie. The noble lie seeks to promote this good by leading young guardians to think of the city and its citizens as if they were their family (414e). Finally, Socrates must withhold private property from these guardians in an attempt to eliminate their desire for private gain (416d–417b).

Already, flags are likely to have been raised in the mind of the contemporary reader. Education focused on character formation rather than on the acquisition of useful information and skills is antithetical to our way of life, no matter how much we might bemoan a decline of public morals. Of course, withholding private property from anyone smacks so of the aspirations of failed twentieth-century communism that it is difficult to avoid Popper's claim that Plato is the enemy of the open society. Such reactions are understandable but anachronistic. The Popperian critique rests on the obliviousness of the grim history leading to our own championing of the private good and private rights. Early modern thinkers became such great defenders of private rights under duress. The premodern pursuit of the common good, combined with monotheism, had eventuated in the wars of religion that bled Europe in the sixteenth and seventeenth centuries. Without these unprecedented historical challenges, it is likely that political philosophers would have remained proponents of the primacy of the common good. Seen in this new, more moderate light, we are able to set aside our assumptions that Plato is a totalitarian out to deprive us of our rights. Could he not just as well be a philosopher thinking through the limits of what can be achieved in the name of the common good?

In bk. 4, Socrates reiterates the centrality of the education he developed in bks. 2–3 for the formation of a united (and thus just) city (422e–427e). In passing, as if a mere afterthought, he announces that the guardians should share "women, marriage, and procreation of children" in common (423e4). Although Adeimantus had allowed this to pass at the time in bk. 4, another character, Polemarchus (whom we will learn more about in chapter 3), grabs hold of Adeimantus in the opening of bk. 5 and enlists him in demanding an explanation from Socrates of this apparently offhand remark.[16] That it is far more than a merely offhand remark is evident from the fact that Socrates' explanation of it will cover bks. 5–7. The suggestion that these things be shared is the basis of the three waves. And their purpose, we can now see, is to follow out the previous efforts to orient the guardian class toward the common good. The three waves and especially the second wave, sharing women and children, bring us closer to the goal of the noble lie. That lie claimed that fellow citizens are one's family. How can the city become one's family without destroying the family? In other words, through the noble lie and the second wave, Socrates seeks to substitute the city for the family. Why he should do so is obvious. The family is a focus of our attachment to our own private good. As such, it is often at odds with the common good. The city, republic, or regime (*politeia*) in the *Republic,* then, is very much the standard of devotion to the common good that all, even modern, citizens recognize as the fulfillment of their highest aspirations for justice. Already, however, we begin to wonder whether Socrates could seriously entertain the destruction of the family in the name of the city. At a minimum, we are now better able to understand why Socrates tried to make the sharing of "women, marriage, and procreation" a merely offhand remark. He sought to downplay a reform he knew would anger many, indeed, most, human beings. Furthermore, he evinces awareness that this anger might be justified because what he is discussing has the potential of misleading others about the truth.[17]

I have not made up the question of whether the three waves are possible. From the start of his discussion of the three waves, Socrates stresses his interlocutors' (especially his immediate interlocutor, Glaucon's) need to determine in the case of each wave whether it is "possible" (*dunata*) and whether it is "best" (*malista*) (450c).[18] As we will see when we get to the second wave, his interlocutors fail to keep him to the task of explaining its possibility. Although Socrates will not declare loudly that the second wave is impossible, he will indicate as much by his evasion of the task he set himself in the beginning of the three waves. Thus Socrates gives the lie to those who would say his plan for *kallipolis* is meant in earnest. This is a fine example of the kind of subtle and indirect evidence we can expect to find in Alfarabi for the impossibility of his planned regime. After discussing the second wave, I will return once more to the question, why discuss an impossible regime? But now I must discuss the first wave, for without it we will not be adequately prepared for the second.

The First Wave

The first wave is that females should receive the same guardian education as the male guardians. Glaucon assents to Socrates' suggestion with the qualification that there is a difference in degree of strength between male and female (457d3–e2). Socrates goes on to wonder out loud what will be most ridiculous in giving men and women the same training. He offers the image of old women exercising in the nude. Yet he reminds Glaucon that for men to exercise in the nude was once viewed as strange but came to be acceptable over time. By this analogy, Socrates raises the question of whether the difference between men and women is merely conventional or a natural distinction. We should not judge things, he suggests, in accordance with what we have become ashamed about by convention (452c4) but in accordance with what is best or the good (452d3). Indeed, he establishes the good or best as the standard not only of the conventional but even of the beautiful or noble (452e). This last step is quite important. Although the good and the beautiful came eventually to be considered to coincide in God in the Western tradition, at least here Socrates treats the one as the standard of the other.[19] When Socrates eventually identifies the city they are constructing as *kallipolis* (the beautiful city at 527c), it is not clear that he is judging it to be genuinely best. From the first moment that Glaucon demanded the luxurious city, he was in hot pursuit of what he took to be beautiful. To say that their city is the beautiful city does not guarantee that it would be best for all human beings concerned if it were to become a reality.[20]

With the underlying exhortation to follow the good in mind, Socrates addresses first the question of whether the first wave is possible (453a ff.).

To answer this question, he must determine whether men and women have the same nature. Earlier Glaucon had insinuated that the only difference was a difference of degree. Often Socrates will engage in conversations with himself so that he might conceal parts of his argument from his interlocutor. Socrates engages in just such a conversation about whether men and women differ only by degree of strength. First he considers what would result if they had different natures. Each nature should mind its own business. Male has a different nature from female. Therefore, male and female must have different jobs (453b–e). Then he encourages the others to sort by "forms" (454a5). He suggests, thereby, that what they need to determine is whether male and female differ merely by degree or somehow by kind. Second, he argues in defense of the first wave by a series of analogies. Along the way, however, he uses problematic analogies that raise the question of whether the differences between male and female are relevant to guardianship. He offers the following analogies: Just as bald versus long haired is irrelevant to being a shoemaker, so man versus woman is irrelevant to being a doctor (454c–d). The difference between the bald and the long haired is certainly a matter of mere quantity of hair. Is the difference between male and female merely a matter of the difference between the quantity of muscles? Or might not the female lack of muscles accompany a nature better suited to doctoring than that of more brawny males? If so, of course, the converse that men are better suited to breaking than setting bones might also be true. Indirectly, by reference to medicine, Socrates raises questions about women's suitability to guardiansip. Just as one begins to wonder, he offers his most suspicious analogy: female : male :: bearing (children) : mounting (to produce children) (454e). This offensive suggestion, that human males and females are different in the same way that animals are, foreshadows a motif that will appear constantly in the second wave, the sharing of women and children. (To make that wave possible, Socrates will have to envision guardians mating with the docility of animals.) For some reason, Glaucon is not disturbed by this analogy between human beings and animals. We will be able to determine why later, in the midst of the second wave. In the meantime, Glaucon assents to these analogies and sticks by his insinuation that the difference between male and female is merely a matter of degree (455b5–e). Thus equal education for female guardians is deemed possible (456c5).

The argument about whether female guardian education is best is quite brief. Just as male guardians are made into the best males by virtue of their special education, so will females be. And, of course, the best citizens make for the best city (456c7–457b4).

The greatest difficulty with Socrates' argument about the possibility of the second wave is concealed within the analogy between human reproduction and animal reproduction, given in the first wave. From a strictly physical or biological point of view, human beings procreate in the same way as other animals. Viewing us through the lens of biology alone abstracts from the possibility that reproduction has a different psychological significance for human beings. The root of this difference is, of course, the human potential for reason. Even if, or perhaps especially if, we never cultivate our reasoning powers, human desire differs from that of other animals by kind as well as degree. (Ironically, uncultivated reason only inflames desire.) With or without the aid of reason, our desires lack the natural or instinctual limits of animals. Glaucon's demand for a luxurious rather than a piglike city (372d) suggests as much.[21] This lack of limits peculiar to human desire tends to manifest itself differently in men and women, especially because of the direction that reproduction gives to female desire. In women, the biological connection with children through childbirth, with its attendant physio-psychological changes, intensifies female attachment to children, in comparison with other animals. In contrast, in men, like Glaucon, unlimited desire combined with spirited frustration with the limits other human beings try to place on desire lead to a desire to be superior to others (symbolized in Glaucon's desire to be raised up on couches and to eat finer food). Ultimately, these desires tend to eventuate in cruelty—cruelty in the name of protection and aggrandizement of what is one's own—far exceeding anything animals are capable of.[22] If what I say is true, and I believe our analysis of the second wave will prove it to be, then the possibility of even the first wave is in doubt.

The Second Wave

Socrates leaves behind the question of the equal education of male and female for guardianship with his first reference to the wave metaphor. Glaucon describes the first wave as high; Socrates assures him that the next will be even higher (457b–c). Indeed, every reader of the *Republic* is more struck initially by the impossibility of the second wave than any of the other waves. Glaucon reminds Socrates, as if he needed reminding, of the need to establish whether the sharing in common of women and children will be both "possible" (*dunatou*) and "useful" (*ôphelimou*).[23] Socrates doubts its possibility, and Glaucon doubts both (457d–e). Socrates reminds the listener of the mock trial that preceded the three waves

(450a–451c) by describing the need to address these two questions (questions he himself established, 450c5) as his "penalty." Yet he just as quickly evades the questions. He recommends that they assume the second wave can exist (or is possible) and then proceed to arrange (*diatassô*) it (458a). This substitution of "arrangement" for "possibility" is all-important. After all, it is all too easy to forget that something can be impossible once one has arranged it (that is, planned its arrangement). Subsequently, Socrates will arrange this wave (458c–461e2), even determine whether it is both "consistent" (*hepomenê*)[24] with the regime as well as "by far best" (461e3–466d4). Like "arrangement," "consistency" could appear to the unwary to be equivalent to "possibility." Just in case we are in doubt about the difference, Socrates will remind us, yet further on, of the question of whether the second wave is possible, only to turn immediately to another topic (466d5–8). Later he will appear to answer the question of the possibility of the second wave, when he merely promises to answer the vague question of whether "this regime" is possible (471c4). In fact, he proceeds once again to evade the question (471c5–473c). In brief, Socrates never answers the question of whether the second wave is possible!

Having peered ahead enough to know where we are headed, we may settle into a closer look at the "arrangement" of the second wave. Socrates begins by envisioning the results of combining the male guardians' common physical education (in the nude) and common mess and homes with the inclusion of female guardians. Males and females in such close quarters are "led by an inner natural necessity to sexual mixing" (458d). Glaucon describes that necessity playfully as "erotic" rather than "geometric" necessity. He thereby anticipates unwittingly a motif that Socrates will develop to the fullest. Of course, by this distinction, Glaucon alludes to the rational necessity of geometry and the irrational necessity of human *eros*. In what follows, Socrates will attempt to use the rationality of mathematics to control, curb, and direct the irrational excess of eros. The most obvious application of this mathematical rationality will be the use of a rigged lottery (460a5). Through this lottery, the best will be, as if by chance, made to mate with the best and the worst with the worst (459e). Ironically, this application of mathematical rationality makes its subjects not more but less rational. Indeed, they participate in a breeding system of the kind human beings impose on domesticated animals, a fact to which Socrates alludes repeatedly (459a–b).[25] Socrates follows out this theme of animalization by placing the offspring of the best (since the offspring of the worst will not be reared, 459d8) in pens (460c). And to prevent the development of the family, he arranges it so mothers will not nurse their own offspring (460d).

He concludes the arrangement of procreation with a comically unenforce-able effort to prevent incest—an inevitable result of having destroyed the traditional family. That it is unenforceable is evident both logistically[26] and by the fact that Socrates develops a divine sanction [!] for incest at least between siblings (461d–e).[27] The real question is how any interpreter of Plato could take these suggestions too seriously.

The difficulties with the second wave confirm my assessment of the difficulties with the first wave. The key to the impossibility of these waves is that they abstract from the special challenges posed by human desire. Only if the difference between male and female is nothing more than a dif-ference of degree of strength or of mounting or bearing as a physical act (the underlying claim of the first wave) would it be possible to destroy the connection between mother and child merely by interfering with breast-feeding (the most implausible aspect of the arrangement of the second wave). Socrates is willing to so abstract from the special challenges of human desire because otherwise he cannot destroy the traditional family and substitute the city's good for the private good. What I have called the "traditional family" all along has the following obvious element of nature speaking for it. Even though the common good—including the most eas-ily shared of all goods, the goods of philosophy—may be highest, our first love is for what is our own or our private good as it is commonly under-stood. Socrates' interest in envisioning *kallipolis* is not to come up with a realistic plan but to display the ineradicable force of the passions for pri-vate goods opposing the pursuit of the common good.

Unlike the argument that the first wave is best for the city, the argu-ment that the second is best is quite long (461e–466d4). We will touch ever so briefly on this argument because it will do little more than confirm what has now become obvious—Socrates seeks to make the city into a family (463c–e, 465b), thereby implying the necessity of destroying the traditional family. Why the destruction of the family should be good for the city should now be obvious. The private good is at odds with the common good. This is obvious when one considers the harmful effects of large and powerful families, such as the various warring Mafia families, on a political regime. The same danger to the city or the state is evident in tribal affilia-tions, which are, after all, merely the expression of very extended families. Affiliations by virtue of language and ethnicity (more broadly understood than tribal affiliation) can, of course, have the same effect of weakening the hold of a larger political unit. This challenge must be kept in mind throughout our discussion of Alfarabi's plans for a virtuous regime of the inhabited world.

The Digression on War

At the very moment Socrates appears most willing to confront the question of the possibility of the second wave (466d5–8), he descends abruptly into one of the longest digressions of the dialogue, the digression on war and the rewards of the guardians. Without reference to Glaucon's character, the reasons for this digression and for Socrates' discussing *kallipolis,* in spite of its impossibility, would be incomprehensible. I begin with the latter. For the politically ambitious Glaucon, the loud-and-clear suggestion that all political regimes are doomed to be more or less unjust—because *kallipolis* is impossible—would have the likely effect of supporting his inclination toward tyranny. We must remember the reason for envisioning such a city in the first place. To begin with, Glaucon is already leaning toward tyranny. Through envisioning a just city, Socrates promised to illuminate a just soul. He could *not* have captured Glaucon's interest in justice through a direct discussion of the soul. If Glaucon were asked at the beginning how he understands the private good of his own soul, then he would likely have given the Thrasymachean answer, to gain advantage over others. After all, that is all he keeps hearing (358c). Furthermore, the initial human preference for what is one's own conspires with those speeches. He had to be led by way of a just city toward a better understanding of his own desire for higher, especially the common, goods. The essential link leading Glaucon from his concern for his own toward the good is his love of honor. Despite all of the bodily pleasures and success in harming others a tyrant might achieve, he cannot achieve the kind of honor a just ruler receives. And although honor is itself a private good, it is usually earned through service to the common good. Through the digression on war, Socrates plays upon Glaucon's love of honor to divert his attention from the question of whether the second wave is possible. Despicable though such diversions may appear at first, Socratic diversions are always in the best interest of the interlocutor. Glaucon could become fully aware of the extent of the second wave's impossibility only once he has ceased being so enamored of honor. If he were no longer so enamored of honor, he then would no longer require belief in the possibility of *kallipolis* to continue his ascent. In the meantime, Glaucon is being led step by step toward what is for him surely the most implausible wave, the wave declaring that philosophers, not young, honor-loving men, would make the best kings.

Aside from his promises of great honor and sexual gratification for exemplary guardians (468b–c),[28] Socrates' main argument in the digression is that *kallipolis* should lead Greece toward a disavowal of inter-city war among the Greeks (469b–471b). Some interpreters have taken umbrage at Socrates' suggestion that they should tell the Greeks to turn their mutual hostility toward barbarians as their "natural" enemies (470c).[29] Some have even suspected that Socrates or Plato is aspiring to dominate "naturally inferior" nations by this Panhellenic alliance. Two different kinds of context must be considered to understand this passage properly, the textual and the historical context. I begin with the far more obvious historical context. A call for Panhellenism at or around the end of the Peloponnesian War was not likely to arouse hopes for great empire. That war had divided Greece into two enormous opposing (Athenian and Spartan) armed alliances. Except for among the most sanguine, such as Glaucon, thoughtful Greeks would be likely to recognize in Socrates' apparent Panhellenism a way of advocating peace among the Greeks.[30] In chapter 4, we will turn to Alfarabi's handling of war in the *Attainment of Happiness* (*AH*). He speaks there (*AH* sec. 43) not only about an association of nations aimed at the attainment of happiness but also even about the possibility of using war to conquer other nations and make them pursue happiness. There we will confront the same kinds of questions we confront now in the *Republic*. Is Alfarabi exhorting his compatriots to an expansionist Islam or enabling them to see what would be required if Islam were to fulfill its promise of spreading happiness and virtue?

For now, we must return to the *Republic*. The textual context is a bit more complicated than the historical. Despite the prominence of the guardians and the centrality of their role as warriors, surprisingly little of the *Republic* is devoted to war.[31] Indeed, one could say that the *Republic*'s focus is almost solely domestic rather than foreign policy.[32] Prior to this digression on war, the only significant discussion of war is the "boxer analogy" (bk. 4, 422a3–e4).[33] Like the digression on war, it is only upon first hearing this analogy that Socrates could appear to be in earnest about promising great martial achievements for this city. And like the digression on war, the intention is the same: to raise Glaucon's hopes of achieving honor by means of this city—even if such hopes prove hollow ultimately.

The boxer analogy is offered because Adeimantus expresses doubts that such a moderate city will be well suited to defending itself. Socrates' analogy is just as one lean, well-trained boxer can defeat two or more fat, luxuriating boxers, so their moderate, well-educated city can defeat two or more wealthy cities (422b–c). Socrates even goes to the extreme of suggesting that their virtuous city might ally with one of the wealthy cities to beat the other wealthy one (422d). When Adeimantus responds, in contrast, by wondering what will happen to the moderate city if the two wealthy cities pool their resources, Socrates shifts abruptly to impugning the unity of the wealthy cities (422d4–e3). (Socrates' quick change in topic signals a weakness in the analogy, namely, money enables cities to hire mercenaries, thus rendering wealthy cities a real threat to "moderate" ones. Unlike money for the city, fat is of no such use to the individual boxer in acquiring allies.) True though it may be that wealthy cities are usually filled with internal divisions between wealthy and poor citizens, Adeimantus's query remains. Will *kallipolis* be fit to defend itself in a world filled with its share of wealthy, nonvirtuous neighbors? Socrates' willingness to offer the misleading boxer analogy reflects his eagerness to make *kallipolis* appear, especially to Glaucon, to be well suited to achieving glory.

Both the boxer analogy and the digression on war appear at first to promise glory to Glaucon. Once again Socrates is willing to bribe Glaucon with hopes for honor only if as a result he can lead him to ascend toward the common good of the city. Socrates averts Glaucon's gaze from the question of the possibility of the second wave with the promise of honor. Glaucon, whose love of honor inures him to the suffering of guardian mothers, is all too willing to oblige. Like most tyrants, he displays his willingness to ignore human nature if only his plans for empire can be fulfilled. But just as Glaucon begins to hope that he has positioned himself well to become ruler of a powerful city, the third wave will dash his hopes.

My analysis of the first and second waves has shown we must not take for granted that philosophers are always serious when they seem to promise empire or perfect virtue. On the contrary, sometimes the best way to deflate hopes for empire or the perfect city is not to discourage the aspiration directly but to show just how costly its achievement would be.

The Third Wave

In chapter 3 we will consider Alfarabi's (and Plato's) treatment of the third wave and its possibility at greater length. Here we must focus on its connection to the previous waves in the *Republic*. I will clarify why it is higher than the previous, despite appearances to the contrary. We make this inquiry now so that when we turn to *AH* we will be better able to see the impediments to the realization of philosopher-kingship. As I argued in the beginning of this chapter, Alfarabi's isolation of the third wave leaves the reader intentionally with the misleading impression that it is not a particularly difficult, not to mention impossible, wave. He does this so that readers will come not only to accept philosophy but also to honor and defer to it. As a result of such honor and deference, philosophers are enabled to guide and shape society through their writings, if not through actual kingship.[34] The philosopher's task of promoting deference toward philosophy must not prevent us from seeing just how doubtful the possibility of the third wave is. Before returning to the *Republic,* I remind the reader that the main reason the third wave is higher than the first and the second is that it gives offense not only to the ruled (as do the first and second) but also the rulers (the philosophers).

As was the case previously, it is impossible to grasp adequately the impediments to philosopher-kingship without attending to Glaucon's reaction to the proposal. By now the dual character of Glaucon's motivations has become amply evident. He is motivated by desires both for honor and for justice. Although he has tyrannical inclinations, he also wants to be a just king.[35] Socrates' task will be to convince him of the following: if he wants to receive honor for excellence as a ruler, then he must become a philosopher. This conditional statement and the whole idea of philosophical rule bring to mind two crucial ironies. Of course, philosophers are suited to rule, precisely because they put little or no store in honor (347a–e, 521b). And Glaucon gives much evidence, including his overweening desire for honor, that he is unfit for philosophy. By arguing for philosopher-kingship with a politically ambitious character incapable of philosophy, Socrates enables us to see one of the most obvious impediments to philosophic rule, namely, the desire of the politically ambitious to rule. Those with a real passion for politics are not likely to sit idly by while philosophers, who would rather avoid politics, rule.[36]

When Socrates announces that the unification of philosophy and political power, or philosopher-kingship, is the only means of achieving public and private happiness (473d), Glaucon's unease is palpable. He announces that a large number of men, "not ordinary ones" (*ou phaulous*), will strip off their clothes and seek to fight or wrestle with him with any available weapon. Glaucon describes this as an imposition of a penalty (once again reminding the reader of Socrates' fate) (474a). It is tempting to jump to the conclusion that Glaucon is describing what other men will do, for is he not even greater than these men? Let us wait and see. Socrates blames Glaucon for the onslaught that has overwhelmed him. Glaucon appears to offer aid, but he does not follow out his own image and offer to defend Socrates with his own arms, as we might expect. Rather, he offers merely "good will and encouragement" (*eunoia . . . parakeleusthai*) (474b). This lukewarm support suggests a reason Glaucon is so capable of imagining other men attacking Socrates: he desires rule for himself. Unless he is confident of becoming a philosopher, he is likely to view Socrates' suggestion, that rulers must be philosophers first, as a threat.

In the pages that follow, Socrates shows Glaucon's remoteness from philosophy by his extensive efforts to introduce him to who the philosopher is (474c5–487a). He begins, as one might expect, with analogies from Glaucon's own experience as a lover of beautiful young men, honor, and music and art. When Adeimantus wonders out loud why philosophers have a reputation for being either vicious or useless (487b–d), Socrates shifts his focus to a defense of philosophy. Subsequently, Socrates is on the defensive. Nevertheless, in a way everything Socrates says from the end of bk. 5 through bk. 7 is part of an effort to introduce Glaucon (and the other auditors) to philosophy. Even by the end of Socrates' account of the philosophic education in bk. 7, Glaucon evinces repeatedly how ill suited to philosophy he is.[37] For one thing, his hopes for a city devoted to military glory are constantly frustrated by Socrates' requirement that the main focus of the philosophic education be more theoretical and less for the cultivation of practical skills useful in war.[38] We are reminded of the conflict between the hopes for military conquest raised by the boxer analogy and digression on war and the real task of Socrates' establishment of *kallipolis,* namely, the formation of a virtuous city. For Glaucon, the beauty or splendor of *kallipolis* derives less from the domestic good of sharing everything in common than from his own overblown hopes for military success.

At the same time, there are important similarities between the philosopher and honor-lover that conceal the absurdity of philosopher-kingship. The most important is the indifference of each to the suffering of the ruled[39] in the second wave. (Of course, this indifference cannot remain—and the second wave cannot succeed or be possible—once the ruled seek to voice their suffering.) Recall that Glaucon did not even notice how implausible the first and second waves are because he was so blinded by the prospect of a splendid, unified city ready to take on all comers. The promise of glory inured him to the total destruction of the family in the name of the unity of the city. Socrates shares this indifference to the family,[40] though not because the brilliance of the beautiful or noble blinds him. Rather, Socrates devotes his life so fully to the search for the good that he has little or no time left over for mundane matters, including making money, acquiring food and clothing, and so on—all matters indispensable if one is to have a family. Furthermore, this devotion to the good leads him to spend all of his time with those in the greatest need of his attention—the talented and dashing young men the city is most likely to take advantage of and corrupt.[41] Only extremely rarely would the best and brightest happen to be his offspring.

Yet equally important as the philosopher's and honor-lover's shared indifference are the opposing bases and spirits of their indifference. In the worst case, they are as opposed as the bestial and divine characters described by Aristotle (*NE* 7). The love of the noble or beautiful can fill the politically ambitious with a tyrannical frenzy for eternity that leads them to trample the ruled. In effect, his desire renders him a beast. In contrast, Socratic love of the good enables him to conjure up the second wave as part and parcel of the philosophic endeavor to pursue the universal to its ultimate conclusion. He is merely conjuring up a city in speech, wholly devoted to the common good. There are only two ways to conjure it up: for everyone to become a philosopher (whose private good happens to coincide with the highest common good of the city), or for those incapable of philosophy to become animals ruled by the only true human beings, namely, philosophers. As long as most human beings have the inflamed desires of a human being without reason limiting and guiding those desires, the only way to make them serve the common good is to wish away their humanity. Socrates' indifference enables him to envision, perhaps even to go along with, the mating of the best with the best. Yet his indifference would never eventuate in political action. Rather, it eventuates in the comic vision of a best city without any typical or "normal" human beings.

Despite the superficial similarity between the philosopher and the political man, their deep differences suggest that far from being the most plausible wave, the third wave is, as Socrates suggests, the highest of all three. Philosophers are ill suited to rule because they refuse the wage of honor, and political men are ill suited to philosophy because they seek honor. Politically ambitious men such as Glaucon can be expected to fight for the right to rule (488b–c); philosophers such as Socrates can be expected to flee rule (521b). Ultimately the only way to make the philosopher a king is to compel or force him to be one. And who can compel the king? Even Glaucon can recognize how unfair this is to the philosopher—indeed, his own desire for rule may very well facilitate his apparent sympathy to the philosopher's plight (519c–520b). The conflict between Glaucon and Socrates regarding rule is itself emblematic of the way in which philosopher-kingship would inspire the loathing of both ruler and ruled.

Three

The A Fortiori Argument

If the *Republic's* virtuous city is impossible, then a fortiori Alfarabi's regime of the inhabited world in the *Attainment of Happiness* (*AH*)—composed of virtuous nations, each of which is composed in turn of virtuous cities—is impossible (cf. *AH,* Mahdi, ed., secs. 44–47; Yasin, ed., 81–85; *VC,* Walzer, ed., 15.3).

After our look at the *Republic,* where Socrates never went so far as to admit explicitly the impossibility of the virtuous city, the reader will not be surprised that Alfarabi in *AH* never states explicitly that the world regime he envisions is impossible. In the *Republic,* Socrates considers it a necessary part of Glaucon's education that he believe this city is possible, at least for the majority of their conversation.[1] After all, Glaucon is a man of action who does not care much for "castles in the sky." Matters are similar, though not identical, in Alfarabi's setting. In his religious community the possibility of a virtuous world regime is assumed—indeed, such a possibility is assumed by all monotheistic communities, even if only as achievable in the end of days.[2] Within such a context, it would be not only surprising but also foolhardy to declaim loudly from the rooftops that a virtuous world regime is impossible. Without an explicit statement that it is impossible, however, it will not be possible to prove beyond a shadow of a doubt that Alfarabi considers it so. Indeed, most scholars assume Alfarabi is in earnest.[3] Nevertheless, I will be able to prove—within the limits of the kind of inquiry we are presently engaged in—that Alfarabi means to suggest, at least to some of his most ambitious readers, that this regime is impossible. If our only purpose were to prove this, then our inquiry might be rather dull. As in the *Republic,* however, an inquiry into this kind of possibility is necessarily an inquiry into one of the deepest problems of all, namely, human nature—its great promise as well as its limits.

An important part of our effort to show that Alfarabi holds that the world regime is impossible will be to show how extensive his knowledge of the *Republic* is. Some scholars will attempt to dismiss the argument of this book because they lack positive evidence about how much of Plato's *Republic* Alfarabi might have had access to. Our discussion of Alfarabi's familiarity with the *Republic* will seek to forestall such a line of interpretation.

At the same time that we inquire into Alfarabi's familiarity with the *Republic,* we will find problems that appeared significant in the *Republic,* such as the tension between being a stalwart king and warrior and a philosopher, grow to enormous proportions in Alfarabi's *AH.* After all, as the regime grows, the need to divide labor and delegate authority only increases. Virtues that might have seemed upon first reading to be in harmony in the *Republic* show just how at odds they can be in *AH.* Alfarabi also has recourse to Aristotle's *Nicomachean Ethics,* in what appears at first to be an effort to draw on the resources of Aristotle to overcome tensions within Plato's account of the virtues. Alfarabi weaves into his Platonic account of philosophic virtues various elements of the Aristotelian account of natural, moral, deliberative, and theoretical virtues. As many undergraduates know, for Aristotle, moral and deliberative virtues are inextricably bound together. In Alfarabi's a fortiori argument, however, even these deep bonds prove to be less than adamantine. An appeal to Aristotle that should have made Plato's philosopher-king more conceivable renders it even more problematic. Alfarabi's a fortiori argument is not, as one might expect, an argument about how Socrates' *kallipolis* when transferred to the world stage is unwieldy—merely a problem of scale. Rather, it is an argument about the heart and soul of *kallipolis,* philosopher-kings.[4] The third wave of the *Republic,* the highest wave, appears in all of its titanic proportions in *AH.* Human nature cannot support the weight of this task, especially when the philosopher-ruler's task is to rule the inhabited world.

ALFARABI ON THE *REPUBLIC* IN THE *ATTAINMENT OF HAPPINESS:* EDUCATING PHILOSOPHER-KINGS TO RULE THE INHABITED WORLD, THE CHALLENGE

We begin our inquiry by considering Alfarabi's more or less direct references to Plato's *Republic* in *AH.* Muhsin Mahdi has identified four references to Plato, three to the *Republic,* and one to the *Timaeus.* According to Mahdi, their exclusive themes are "the proper education of future philosophers and the relationship between philosophy and religion." The first of these two themes is the theme of the passages from the *Republic.*[5] From Mahdi's identification of this theme as our starting point, we may begin our inquiry. The proper education of future philosophers implies the existence of improper forms of education. Of course, improper forms of education contribute to the impossibility, or at least limit the possibility, of philosopher-rulers. Indeed, both Plato and Alfarabi discuss at some length what happens when philosophers are improperly educated, or when people unsuited to philosophy receive a philosophic education. Most of the sixth book of the *Republic* is devoted to an account of why people unsuited to philosophy are rendered "vicious" by it, and why potential philosophers remain "useless" to their cities. Socrates develops an elusive variety of subcategories of the vicious and useless (487b–504a). Alfarabi delineates more clearly four deviations from "true philosophy" (*AH* 54, 60–61). At a minimum, his account of these deviations evinces extensive knowledge of *Republic* 6, which can be counted among the three most important books (bks. 5–7) for grasping why the virtuous city is impossible.

Alfarabi's account of these four deviations from true philosophy is divided into one deviation identified as "defective [*nâqiṣah*] philosophy" and a group of three other deviations (the counterfeit [*al-zawar*], the vain [*al-bahraj*], and the false [*al-bâṭil*] philosopher) grouped under "mutilated" [*bitrâ'*] philosophy, respectively (*AH* M., 54, 60–61; Y., 55, 62–63). Philosophy is *defective* when the philosopher possesses the theoretical sciences but not the power to exploit or use them for the benefit of others.[6] The *counterfeit* philosopher lacks the natural equipment, and the *vain* philosopher lacks habituation in the acts acceptable to his religion or to a generally accepted view of what is noble action (61, 45.13–18). Finally, the *false* philosopher fails to grasp all of theoretical science (61, 45.12–13), or to grasp the purpose of philosophy (61, 46.5–13). He may grasp part or all of the theoretical sciences but tends to believe that happiness is one of the popularly desired goods. The counterfeit and vain philosophers resemble most closely Socrates' account of potential philosophers who become vicious or useless, respectively. The vicious are those who have their great potential corrupted by their own cities and families and are drawn away from philosophy (*Rep.* 494b5). These same cities and families neglect the useless because of one or another superficial flaw, such as sickliness (496b). Socrates has higher hopes of cultivating the useless category, though he expends great effort trying to prevent any potential philosophers from becoming vicious. Perhaps Alfarabi might also single out vain philosophy as being especially close to true philosophy.

A further piece of evidence of Alfarabi's familiarity with bk. 6 is a striking allusion he makes to the *Republic* in the midst of the account of the counterfeit and vain philosopher. The striking allusion is to a relatively minor image from the *Republic:* When potential philosophers so deviate from true philosophy, their knowledge diminishes until it is extinguished more fully than the fire or sun of Heraclitus (*Rep.* 498a–b). A reference to a larger image might evince only casual familiarity with the *Republic*. This reference to a relatively obscure image might suggest more extensive familiarity.

Alfarabi's account of the different forms of deviation from true philosophy is set against the backdrop of an account of true philosophy with striking echoes of not only bk. 6 but also bk. 7 of the *Republic*. Alfarabi's list of the potential philosopher's innate equipment is most similar overall to the account in the opening of *Republic* 6 (485b–487b). To indicate the extensive parallels, I will include citations from the comparable passages in the *Republic* in brackets. After the quote, I will attend to some of Alfarabi's additions drawn both from other passages in the *Republic* and from his own understanding of what his own setting demands.

> He should excel in comprehending and conceiving that which is essential [485b, d, 486c1–4]. Moreover, he should have good memory [486c5–d3] and be able to endure the toil of study [7, 535c]. He should love truthfulness and truthful people [485c], and justice and just people; and not be headstrong or a wrangler about what he desires [486b3–8]. He should not be gluttonous for food and drink, and should by natural disposition disdain the appetites, the *dirhem*, the *dinar*, and the like [485d4–e4]. He should be high-minded [*kabîr al-nafs*] and avoid what is considered disgraceful [*shâ'in*] [cf. 486a4–6 with 486d3–5]. He should be pious, yield easily to goodness and justice, and be stubborn in yielding to evil and injustice. And he should be strongly determined in favor of the right thing. Moreover, he should be brought up according to laws and habits that resemble his innate disposition. He should have sound conviction about the opinions of the religion in which he is reared, hold fast to the virtuous acts in his religion, and not forsake all or most of them. Furthermore, he should hold fast to the generally accepted virtues and not forsake the generally accepted noble acts. (sec. 60, 44.17; Y. sec. 62)

With the turn to piety and religion, Alfarabi adds a theme that lacks prominence at least in the parallel passage of the *Republic*. Rather than in the discussion of the philosopher's virtues, piety appears briefly in bk. 2, where

Socrates revised traditional Greek religion and prepared the way for a new form of education for the common good, aimed at the young guardians.[7] In *AH*, Alfarabi refers to this form of education as "character formation" (*ta'adîb*) (secs. 39, 41–42, 44, 48). He contrasts it with "instruction" (*ta'alîm*) proper (39), though there are significant occasions on which overlap between the two occurs.[8] The hallmark of *ta'adîb* is "habituation" (*ta'awwud*).[9] Character formation is the objective of the young guardian education in *Rep.* bks. 2–4, and instruction is the objective of the philosophic education in *Rep.* bk. 7. According to the *Republic,* the future philosopher-ruler must have received both forms of education. He requires this education both for his own formation and so that he might know how to shape those he rules. (Alfarabi discusses the philosopher-ruler's job of shaping the ruled at great length. See chapter 5, sec. 2.) Of course, in the *Republic,* all philosopher-rulers were guardians first and philosophers second. When one considers the extent to which Alfarabi needs to incorporate in a compressed form both stages of the education in the *Republic,* Alfarabi's inclusion of piety in the innate equipment of the philosopher-ruler is not so profound a departure from Plato. More importantly, an attentive look at the references to piety reveals a highly plastic bit of equipment. In the previous quote, although Alfarabi acknowledges eventually that the philosopher must adapt to the religion of his community, he begins with the claim that the religion must suit the innate excellence of the philosopher.

Perhaps the most important deviation from *Rep.* 6 in this list of the innate equipment of the potential philosopher is Alfarabi's reference to his love of toil. This claim, made for the first time in *Rep.* 7 (535c), is a striking addition to the earlier list. The list in bk. 6 stresses everything pleasurable connected with philosophy. This is part and parcel of Socrates' effort to persuade Glaucon that philosophy and philosophers are as, or rather, more, worthy of imitation than great political actors. Socrates reveals the role of toil, this less attractive aspect of philosophy, relatively late in his discussion of philosopher-kingship. By referring to a discussion of the love of toil in bk. 7 in the midst of a list drawn from bk. 6, Alfarabi demonstrates once again greater familiarity with the *Republic* than might appear at first glance.

We turn to section 62 with section 60 still before us and an effort to flesh out the character of the true philosopher under way. Section 62 demonstrates both Alfarabi's deep familiarity with the *Republic* and his deep awareness of the challenges to the possibility of philosophic rule and the virtuous world regime. In view of how much stress Alfarabi has placed so far on the "realization" of the philosopher's theoretical knowledge in political reality, it is surprising that the philosopher remains a true philosopher, even if the ruled do not make use of him or even acknowledge him (62, 46.13 and 16)![10] Indeed, this comes as such a surprise that the reader is given pause and made to wonder what is the significant difference between the true philosopher and the defective, counterfeit, vain, and false philosophers. At first glance, the true philosopher sounds most like the defective philosopher who lacks the power to realize philosophy in politics, that is, until one realizes that the defective philosopher lacks the power or "faculty" (*qûwah*) within himself (sec. 56). The true philosopher possesses such power, but the ruled do not wish that he should employ it. Of course, the true philosopher is not counterfeit because, in contrast to the counterfeit philosopher, he possesses all of the requisite equipment. And he is not a false philosopher, because he has a better grasp than anyone else of the great rift between his view of life's purpose and that of most of those he would rule. Indeed, this rift accounts for the conflicting facts both that the ruled should want him to rule and that they do not. They should want him to rule because they remain misguided about the true aims of life, and they will not use him as ruler because they remain so attached to their own misguided vision of these aims. A formidable obstacle to the realization of a virtuous world regime indeed! Once again, we realize the vain or useless philosopher comes closest to the true philosopher. And we gain a greater appreciation of why Alfarabi felt it incumbent upon himself to add the virtue or virtues that he did to Socrates' list. This admission that the philosopher might not—or perhaps will not—be used by the ruled is our first strong piece of evidence that Alfarabi intends to raise doubts about the possibility of the virtuous world regime, all the while conjuring up a vision of it before our eyes.

In addition to raising doubts about the possibility of this regime, Alfarabi gives further evidence of his deep understanding of and familiarity with the contents of the *Republic*. His claim that the philosopher remains the true philosopher whether he is asked to rule or not is one of the possible implications of a central image in Socrates' defense of the philosophers in *Rep.* 6, the ship image (488a–489c5).[11] Simply put, the image is intended to explain why philosophers remain useless (487e1–3). This image includes a dull and ungainly shipowner (the regime or ruling part of the city), sailors (politically ambitious men), a man clever at gaining rule for the sailors (sophists), and the true pilot or captain (the philosopher). In brief, the sailors seek to gain control over the shipowner with the help of the clever man. Of course, they deny that the true pilot is better suited to piloting than they. They rule by force rather than by the art of piloting. The pilot or philosopher is identified as "a stargazer, a prater, and useless." Here at least, the main thing preventing philosophers from being used by cities is the ambition of the sailors or men who seek rule for their own gain at the expense of their fellow citizens. Of course, the philosopher would deny that what they hold to be gain is truly useful for them. They are ignorant of their own true good and all the more brazen in their pursuit of it, due to their ignorance. They should want him to rule, but most emphatically they do not.

Leaving aside for the moment the desire of the ruled not to be ruled by philosophers, we must turn to the question of whether philosophers desire to rule. (These two considerations more than any other determine whether philosophic rule and the virtuous city [or regime] are possible.) Socrates and, in turn, Alfarabi argue somewhat indirectly that philosophers would rather not rule. Socrates indicates this indirectly by claiming that philosophers must be compelled to rule (*Rep.* 7, 519c4 ff.). Alfarabi echoes this argument, very much in passing (*AH* 41, 31.11). Indeed, he buries it in the midst of a discussion of obstinate unphilosophic people who need to be compelled to embrace what is right. Neither Socrates nor Alfarabi claims directly that philosophers dislike or hate rule. Yet if they must be compelled, it is because they do not want to rule.

One wonders, then, both why philosophers dislike rule and why they are prone to be secretive about their dislike. I must digress to consider what the *Republic* has to teach us about this; I begin with secretiveness. The politically ambitious but unphilosophic men (sailors) assume that everyone else in the city is a competitor of sorts for the private goods they seek. They cannot believe that anyone else might desire anything but money and honor. Consequently, they view those who claim to lack interest in the advantages of politics as liars out to acquire them behind their backs. If only to allay such suspicions, philosophers such as Socrates and Alfarabi do not declare too loudly their desire to avoid politics. Indeed, they write difficult books that might appear on the surface to indicate their great ambition to rule! For Alfarabi even more than for Socrates, it would be unseemly for him to declare too directly his dislike for politics. After all, if philosophy is to be accepted within the Islamic fold while declaring itself the natural concomitant of the *imam,* legislator, and everything but the Prophet himself, then it must appear unmanly to shirk the duties of the ruler.[12]

That philosophers dislike rule is made all too evident, albeit indirectly throughout the *Republic*. Well before philosophers have been identified as likely kings, Socrates describes certain unidentified "most decent men" (*epieikestatoi*) who desire neither money nor honor as a wage for rule (bk. 1, 347b1). The only wage they seek is to avoid a penalty, to be ruled by a worse man (347c3). Most distinctively of all, a group of such decent men would fight over not ruling (347d2). That is, they would fight with their equals to allow another to rule, because they would trust the justice of their rule, unlike the rule of the worse man. That these men are philosophers is supported by Socrates' reference to the philosophers or true pilots in the ship image in bk. 6 as "most decent men" (*epieikestatoi*) (488a2). One of the most obvious truths and greatest ironies of the *Republic* is that the human beings most suited to rule are those who cannot gain any direct advantage by it. Ruling would interfere with philosophizing.

> For presumably, Adeimantus, a man who has his understanding truly turned toward the things that *are*, has no leisure to look down toward the affairs of human beings and to be filled with envy and ill will as a result of fighting with them. But, rather, because he sees and contemplates things that are set in a regular arrangement and are always in the same condition—things that neither do injustice to one another nor suffer it at one another's hands, but remain all in order according to reason—he imitates them and, as much as possible, makes himself like them. (500b5-c7)

The philosopher's magnificence (*megaloprepeia*), unlike the magnificence of the political man, is evident in his desire to know "all time and all being" (486a7). According to Socrates, seen in this light, human life cannot seem too great.

With the philosophers' distaste for politics in mind, we must consider its implications for the possibility of philosophic rule and the virtuous city or regime. From the side of the rulers, the possibility of philosophic rule seems to hang by a thread. The only thing that can compel philosophers to rule is their desire to avoid the penalty of being ruled by the worse and, perhaps, some sense of indebtedness to their city. Unfortunately for the city, Socrates dispels the danger for the decent man or philosopher of being ruled by the worse. Although *kallipolis* might be of great use in improving nonphilosophic natures, it would not be the best city for a philosopher.[13] Democracy would appear to be better for the philosopher because it contains every kind of human soul, and the philosopher can avoid not only ruling but even being ruled (557d3, e2–4)! Plato's corpus, like a gallery of portraits, displays the centrality of knowledge of the human soul for philosophy. This final point compels us to revise our interpretation of philosophy as presented in the aforementioned quote. Although participation in the day-to-day politics of a city or virtuous world regime might be anathema to a philosopher, an adequate understanding of the human soul proves an especially crucial and elusive part of the philosopher's inquiry into all time and all being. The philosopher, then, combines a passionate dislike for involvement in day-to-day politics with a deep and an abiding interest in where human being fits into the cosmos.[14] As such, the philosopher may be better positioned to teach potential politicians than anyone else. Although philosophers rarely make a direct contribution to politics, their works in political philosophy enable them to engage in philosophy while also serving their communities (earning their wage). The main thesis of this book, that Alfarabi's virtuous world regime is not meant in earnest, must be viewed with these significant matters in mind. Alfarabi is not spinning out castles in the sand pointlessly. He teaches us as much, if not more, about politics by constructing such a regime in speech than he would by laying out possible political mechanisms for a particular country or group of countries.

Before turning to the next stage in my reconstruction of Alfarabi's a fortiori argument, we must turn briefly to the second part of his trilogy, the *Philosophy of Plato* (*PP*). Although *PP* does not discuss directly whether philosophers dislike politics and would need to be compelled to rule, it is still more revealing than *AH* about Alfarabi's understanding of the philosopher's attitude toward the city. It discusses the fate of Socrates, the emblem of philosophy, and its relation to the founding of the virtuous city in speech. In *PP*, as in the Platonic dialogues, Plato engages in a quest for the best way of life, or rather in a quest to confirm that his own way of life is best.[15] After taking an inventory of all of the other competing ways of life (secs. 5–13), Alfarabi's Plato turns to confirm not only the necessary and useful or gainful converge in philosophy (secs. 14–17, 20) but also the most pleasant (sec. 18). Consequently, philosophy must be the best way of life (sec. 19). By philosophy he does not mean the strictly private activity of an Epicurus. Rather, he acknowledges almost from the start of his account of philosophy that philosophy and rule coincide by nature (sec. 22). Indeed, the statesman (*madanî*) appears momentarily (along with prophecy) in the account of the *Phaedrus* as a potential competitor with the philosopher for this best way of life (25, 14.5 [and 18]; Rosenthal and Walzer, ed., sec. 22). Philosophy (as well as statesmanship and perfection!) requires a form of madness for the divine things. This enthralling ascent of philosophy comes to a grinding halt when set against the backdrop of "cities that existed in his time" (29, 16.14). When confronted with the question of whether the philosopher should accept the opinions of his "ancestors" or his fellow "citizens," Alfarabi's Plato or Socrates answers with a resolute no in the *Crito* and the *Apology of Socrates* (29, 17.2–4). He proceeds in the creatively named *Protest of Socrates against the Athenians* and *Phaedo* to describe the choice left Socrates of whether he should adopt the opinions of his compatriots, leading the life of a beast without philosophy, or accept death "as Socrates did" (30, 19.5). This conflict between the city and the philosopher is the occasion for and, at least to a significant extent, the motive behind the construction of a city in speech or the plan for the virtuous city with philosopher-rulers (30, 19.14; 31, 20.1–12; 33, 20.15). After supplementing his account of the *Republic* with accounts of the *Critias, Timaeus,* and, most importantly, the *Laws*,[16] he concludes that the philosopher (or perfect man, investigator, and virtuous man) is "in grave danger." Alfarabi reads Plato's *Letters* as evidence of his efforts to move the cities in his own time into greater harmony with philosophy. Whether Alfarabi's Plato is revolutionary is difficult to determine. And how hopeful Alfarabi might be for real progress in the convergence of popular views with those of the philosophers is even more difficult to determine.[17] Of course, this book as a whole is intended to show that Alfarabi was anything but unrealistic about the prospects for his "castle in the air."[18] For our purposes, however, the crucial fact is that the occasion and possible motive for the construction of the city in speech is the city's animosity toward the philosopher. Like Alfarabi's supreme ruler in the *AH,* whose religion should conform to his excellence (60, 45.6), the virtuous city in *PP*'s account of the *Republic* is constructed to conform to the excellence of the philosopher. This conformity is not facilitated by an inherent tendency of cities to conform to or harmonize with philosophy. On the contrary, according to Alfarabi's Plato, cities and their citizens are inclined to distrust philosophy and philosophers. Given the natural coincidence of philosophy and rule, according to Alfarabi's Plato, this means that the ruled are prone to distrust the rulers. Because the conflict between philosophy and the city can reach a high enough pitch that cities are willing to put philosophers to death, ruling other citizens must engender, at a minimum, unease in the true philosopher or natural ruler.

TENSION IN THE "UNITY OF THE VIRTUES": HARD VS. SOFT

In the previous section, we saw that the possibility of philosophic rule is endangered by the inherent animosity between the philosopher and the city, the ruler and the ruled. For the most part, we focused on how the great risk of improperly educating the potential philosopher could result in a variety of deviations from philosophy or philosophic rule—the defective, counterfeit, false, and even vain philosopher. We turn now to a more positive effort to envision Alfarabi's true philosopher, assuming for the purposes of argument that the ruled would desire to be ruled by him. The greatest challenge to the philosopher-ruler is the requirement that he combine all of the virtues of thought with all of the virtues of action. This is a version of the perennial problem in ancient, especially Platonic, philosophy of the unity of the virtues. As we will see, in Plato's *Republic,* this is a significant problem, which contributes to our doubts about the possibility of philosophic rule. In addition, when Alfarabi tries to weave elements of Aristotle's account of the virtues into Socrates' account, the combination proves weaker, not stronger.

We have already seen Alfarabi's use of Plato's account of philosophic virtues from the opening of *Rep.* 6 in his own portrait of the virtuous ruler. This list is far more extensive than the list of the four cardinal virtues—wisdom, courage, moderation, and justice—set forth and described in the guardian education in bk. 4. Long before the account of philosophy and its virtues, a fissure between wisdom and courage already begins to appear in the *Republic.* Almost from the moment of the virtuous city's inception, the combination of the courage of warrior and statesman and the wisdom of the philosopher is problematic. Simply put, the fissure is between the gentleness and flexibility of the philosopher and the savageness and inflexibility of the warrior, a fissure between opposites.[19]

I review the context within which this problem first appears so that we might grasp the depth of this fissure. To grasp justice in the soul of the individual in *Rep.* 2, Socrates proposes that he and his interlocutors, Glaucon and Adeimantus, construct a just (or virtuous) city in speech. Adeimantus, the brother with less *eros,* joins with Socrates to envision a peaceable, pastoral "city" of necessity—a city that is not yet quite a city because it merely lives in accordance with small appetites rather than living well, as Aristotle puts it. Glaucon, the brother with desires for bigger and better things, repudiates this city and demands one that acknowledges the worth of human beings as dominant or superior, at least to the animals living in Adeimantus's city. This luxurious city requires more jobs and therefore more people to fill those jobs. The increase in population requires more land, leading to war with one's neighbors (372a–373e). The risk of war leads to the development of the guardian class, which from the start is said to combine the warrior's spiritedness, even cruelty, with philosophic gentleness (375c–e). This combination is needed because guardians must be "gentle to their own and cruel to their enemies" (375c1). There are reasons to suspect that this combination is not impossible; however, it is, at a minimum, quite unstable when tested in politics.[20] Socrates indicates the source of this instability by using an unconvincing analogue of the guardian to persuade himself or, rather, his interlocutors that they can be combined. The guardians need to be like noble or well-bred (*gennaios*) puppies who combine gentleness toward friends and cruelty toward enemies (375c1–376a7). Just a few pages earlier, Glaucon had repudiated being on the ground like a sow (372c1–d7). He may not mind the likeness to a nobler animal, but the problem remains, human beings are not animals. The puppy is capable of combining these opposites because he is an animal. Human beings have greater difficulty combining the soft and the hard. Socrates claims that the puppy, like a philosopher, distinguishes friend from foe "by having learned (*katamathein*) the one and being ignorant of the other. . . . And so, how can it be anything other than a lover of learning (*philomathes*) since it defines what's its own and what's alien by knowledge and ignorance" (376b2 ff.). Socrates is taking advantage of his own equivocal usage of learning in human beings and animals to cover up the fissure between the warrior and the philosopher. Yet as always, he does so for reasons that advance his argument and the education of his interlocutors. The philosopher does not limit himself to "his own" when it comes to learning. He desires to know all things and, above all, the good rather than merely his own.[21] He does not hate things he does not yet know but desires to know them![22] In a sense, human beings have the potential of being even gentler than puppies. Ironically and unfortunately, the reverse is just as true. The main problem in producing guardians is not whether they can be educated to be cruel enough to their enemies but whether they can be gentle enough to their friends. In other words, human guardians, unlike well-bred puppies, are prone to cruelty toward those who should be their own, members of their city.[23] In brief, the effort to combine warrior hardness with philosophic gentleness reveals the extremes to which human nature is prone. Far from being harmonious, in human beings the hard and the soft tend in opposing directions.

To grasp this tension more fully, we must consider the problems with Socrates' analogy between guardians and puppies. Of course, human beings possess reason and puppies do not. This is the root of the difference between the philosopher's gentleness and the puppy's. The philosopher's *eros* knows no obvious bounds because the mere potential for reasoning removes the limits present in animal instinct; the puppy's desire or instinct is limited to his pack. Precisely because human desire lacks obvious limits, it is prone to frustration, giving rise to spiritedness (*thumos*). Furthermore, unless desires for lesser goods than knowledge are shaped, molded, and constrained, desire and spiritedness ally in the pursuit of either an excess of high and beautiful or noble things or base and ignoble objects simply. Consequently, the warrior is prone to become a wolf rather than a puppy.[24] In spite of Plato's authorship of the *Republic*, he, like Aristotle, advocates ultimately the rule of law rather than the rule of the wise man, precisely because the dangers of a fall into a mistaken alliance between desire and spiritedness are so great.[25]

Although the fissure between the hard and the soft is not the only tension within the virtues that concerns Alfarabi, it will offer a way into our discussion of the problem of the unity of the philosopher-ruler's virtues in the *Attainment of Happiness*. And though he might appear oblivious of it at first, he indicates subtly but clearly that he is aware of the tension between the need for the philosophic ruler to possess warrior hardness and philosophic softness. We have already come across Alfarabi's distinction between character formation and instruction or education for the common good and private education (*AH* 39). We have also come across his discussion of the need to compel philosophers to rule (41). In that same section, he treats compulsion or force in general as a subdivision of habituation for character formation.[26] He offers the example of the way in which the superintendent of children shapes the character of children both by persuasion with their consent and through compulsion without it. The prince's use of persuasion and force to shape character is similar to the superintendent's. Indeed, the skill in persuasion and compulsion is the "very same skill" (*mihnatin waḥdatin*).[27] Perhaps. But the argument becomes more challenging when he turns from the claim that fellow citizens will have their character shaped through compulsion[28] to the claim that other nations and cities will through war (*ḥarb*) (sec. 43).[29] Although Alfarabi does not use the more strictly Islamic term *jihâd* here, it seems likely that this discussion offers a way of reflecting on that idea, without naming it. After all, the logic of a virtuous world regime would seem to make such war inevitable. One thing is amply evident: this idea lacks precedent in the *Republic*.[30] I will reserve a further discussion of this explosive issue until the next chapter. In the meantime, however, it must be underlined that although Alfarabi here entertains the possibility of using war to shape the character of other nations, it cannot yet be known in what spirit he does so. Is he voicing a personal preference guided by philosophic reasoning? Is he entertaining a possibility he considers ill advised, only to show how problematic it is?

Although we are concerned with Alfarabi's views on the prospects for unity of the various philosophic and ruling virtues in general, we are concerned at present with the combination of philosophic and warrior virtue in particular. When we first discussed the unification of the power to instruct (education for the private good) with the power to shape character (education for the common good) in our preliminary discussion of philosophic virtue, we were not surprised about the idea of their combination. (For one thing, philosophers such as Plato, Aristotle, and Alfarabi seem to engage in these very things in their political writings.) Yet when Alfarabi takes this one step farther and includes within character formation compulsion and even compulsion of other nations, we begin to feel the strain between the philosopher and the warrior. Indeed, the strain increases to the breaking point when Alfarabi states forthrightly that character formation, through persuasion and compulsion, derives from "the very same skill" (42, 32.3). Although he makes this claim in sec. 42, by sec. 48, difficulties begin to emerge. From the beginning of part iii, even before sec. 42, Alfarabi has described how the philosopher ruler should educate and exploit other princes for the rule of the multiplicity of nations and cities under his rule. Even before the claim that persuasion for character formation and compulsion flows from the very same skill, Alfarabi acknowledges the need to use different groups of rulers to shape the character of the ruled through persuasion and compulsion (42, 31.14–17). Nevertheless, when he enters upon the task of delegating responsibility in earnest (47, 48), he acknowledges rather casually that there is a "warlike virtue" and a "deliberative virtue" involved in these activities. It would be best if these were combined in one man. If not, however, the supreme ruler "should add to the man who forms the character of nations with their consent another who possesses the craft of war" (48, 36.3). Obviously the latter requires the "warlike virtue" and the former the "deliberative virtue." If duties can be so divided along the line of these virtues, then Alfarabi seems to have contradicted his claim that the activities of persuasion and compulsion are rooted in the same skill (sec. 42). Before drawing such a conclusion, however, we must wonder what Alfarabi means by "warlike virtue," and why he does not simply speak of courage or bravery as he does elsewhere.[31] If Alfarabi were to identify this warrior virtue clearly as bravery, then he would be identifying it as a moral virtue. Of course, one of Aristotle's most important messages in the *NE* is that deliberative virtue or prudence cannot exist without the moral virtues, and vice versa. This accounts for the distinctively ancient understanding of prudence he advocates, namely, shrewdness without moral virtue eventuates in vice (1144a34–36, 1144b17–18). Not only is Alfarabi all too well aware of this Aristotelian argument, but he also seems to assent to its validity (*AH* 29, 22.18–23.3). Yet the claim that this warlike virtue can be separated from the related deliberative virtue seems to challenge this truism. It should be stressed that this unity of the power to persuade and to compel in war is not an average example of the purported interdependence of deliberative and moral virtue. Rather, it shows that Alfarabi's envisioning of the virtuous world regime places deep strain on the usual unity of these virtues.

Although Aristotle's argument about the interdependence of moral and deliberative virtue was probably meant, at least in part, to overcome this tension between warrior hardness and philosophic softness, it was also intended to counteract the initial impression left by the *Republic*, that only philosophers could be virtuous statesmen.[32] The interdependence of moral and deliberative virtue also enables Aristotle to establish prudence as a distinctively *political* form of intellectual virtue. In lieu of direct dependence on philosophy, Aristotle's prudent statesman relies upon the excellent beliefs (*hupolepseis*) about fitting ends that he has received from his society (1140b10).[33]

Here we begin to see how a combination of the arguments of Aristotle and Plato far from facilitating the unification of the virtues tends to reveal the cracks between the virtues all the more starkly. Aristotle establishes a particularly intimate bond between deliberative virtue and moral virtue in order to be able to separate them from direct dependence on philosophic insight. When Alfarabi lays these distinctions on top of Plato's fissure between warrior virtue and philosophic virtue, in the context of trying to envision a virtuous regime of the inhabited world, even the bond between deliberative and moral virtue is weakened. Although Alfarabi may assent to Aristotle's linkage of these kinds of virtue (for the purposes of everyday political life), he shows that the Aristotelian linkage cannot prevent this Platonic fissure (at least not at the level of the philosopher-king). Indeed, he follows his easy assent to the everyday sense of this linkage (sec. 29) with a striking interrogation of the possibilities and limits of unity within the virtues (beginning in sec. 31).

Let us start over at the beginning of Alfarabi's efforts to discover the unity among the virtues. Having discussed moral and deliberative virtues and their relation to each other so far (secs. 24–30), Alfarabi turns to the question of their unity with a shocking radicality:

> Which virtue is the perfect and most powerful virtue[?] Is it the combination of all the virtues? [O]r if one virtue (or a number of virtues) turns out to have a power equal to that of all the virtues together, what ought to be the distinctive mark of the virtue that has this power and is hence the most powerful virtue? (31, 24.10–14)

Such questions could come as a great surprise had not Alfarabi set forth his argument from the first through the lens of the realization or attainment (*taḥṣîl*) of both earthly and supreme happiness for every nation and every city in every nation (cf. 1, 2.1–5 with 22, 16.19–17.3).[34] Even when he first discusses moral virtues, he discusses them within the context of a wide variety of times and places (24, 18.5–19.5, esp. 18.17–18). Rather than present a detailed account of the moral virtues,[35] he turns almost immediately to what is entailed in "mak[ing] them actually [*bi'l-fi'l*] exist" (24, 19.6 ff.). Because such actualization or realization requires or is guided by deliberative virtue, he hastens to discuss deliberative virtue within the same global context.[36] Alfarabi does not even identify the supreme ruler responsible for attempting to realize or actualize supreme happiness as the philosopher-ruler until quite late in his argument (sec. 58). Yet the demand that happiness be realized potentially for all nations in the inhabited world (24, 19.10–25, 20.3) bespeaks the need for an unprecedented unification of virtues or excellences.

In the previous quote, Alfarabi departs from his usual rhetorical style to engage in some of the most dialectical argumentation in the trilogy, especially the *AH*. He begins by answering the question about the perfect and most powerful virtue as follows (31, 24.14 ff.): This virtue depends upon the possession of all of the other virtues. But if the one who seeks to realize such happiness lacks this virtue, he must possess a moral virtue enabling him to exploit or use the other virtues as possessed by others. Consequently, he must possess either all or merely a moral virtue, which he quickly identifies as the "leading virtue" with unsurpassed "authority" (*ri'asah*). One is reminded of the traditional requirement of prophets, that they possess moral virtue, because whatever knowledge or insight they might possess is revealed to them.[37] Had Alfarabi left matters at this alternative rather than following it out with further argument, we might have had a resolution to the problem of the unity of virtue, albeit not a particularly philosophic one. As an example of this most authoritative, though unspecified moral, virtue, he gives the kind of virtue the general must possess if he is to use the moral virtue of his warriors. Yet even the general, not to mention the city's ruler, requires a "deliberative faculty" to discover what is noble and useful for warriors. In other words, almost before the proposal that moral virtue is most authoritative passes his lips, Alfarabi offers a reservation. Moral virtue, as Aristotle would agree, cannot realize the good ends it aims at without deliberative virtue's grasp of the means. After the brief treatment of moral virtue, Alfarabi turns to the arts (sec. 32). Within the arts the leading art, like the leading virtue discussed earlier, leads by virtue of possessing the art that makes use of the other arts. Rather than appeal to the kind of art one expects, he gives another example from commanding armies—in other words, we would seem to be back at square one, the general requires deliberation, not merely moral virtue. This conclusion is confirmed by asking oneself whether in the arts it is the art itself alone that enables one to lead artists or rather the ability to lead or deliberate along with a mastery of the art. The option of possessing merely one moral virtue by virtue of which one exploits the virtues of everyone else looks less and less promising.

With characteristic gravity and lack of explicit argument (in sec. 33), Alfarabi proceeds to distinguish between various understandings (within one city or nation) of what is noble and what is useful. We recollect from sec. 31, the deliberative faculty discovers what is noble and useful. But here there is the most noble according to "generally accepted opinion" (*mashhûr*), according to a particular "religion" (*millah*), and according to the truly noble. These subtle yet shocking distinctions anticipate the kind of distinction he draws later between the poetic, rhetorical, and theoretical apprehensions of the truth (sec. 46).[38] And one wonders whether the different deliberative faculties that possess these different ranks of apprehension of the noble and useful could do so without the guidance of the theoretical virtues. After all, deliberative virtue relies upon beliefs clarified and set forth by philosophy, which is implied even in these distinctions. Not surprisingly, in the very next section (34) Alfarabi states that the deliberative virtue with the highest authority is itself subordinate to theoretical virtue![39] As he has argued consistently (since sec. 24), deliberative virtue grasps only the accidents (or means) accompanying the realization of voluntary intelligibles (or moral virtues as ends). Here (34) he clarifies, as he implied earlier (sec. 26), that theoretical virtue grasps the intelligible character of these same intelligibles. Consequently, far from the ruler being able to rule by a moral virtue alone, not only are moral and deliberative virtues inseparable but also "*the* theoretical virtue" (*al-faḍîlah al-naziriyyah*) is "inseparable" (*ghair mufârqin*) from the leading (or authoritative, *ri'asah*) moral and deliberative virtues (34, 26.18–20). Here the superimposition of Aristotle's teaching on Socrates' is pushed to the breaking point. Whatever assent Aristotle might give to the interdependence of moral (warrior virtue) and deliberative virtue (as an intellectual or a quasi-philosophic virtue) is compromised by Alfarabi's additional requirement that theoretical virtue come to the aid of these other virtues—in one soul.[40] Alfarabi persists doggedly in requiring that so many different virtues be found in the one supreme ruler if this city is to be oriented toward virtue.

Rather than getting ahead of ourselves, we must linger for a moment to follow out this shocking claim about the different views of what is most noble, according to generally accepted opinion, a particular religion, and the truth (33). Even virtuous ends are not simply virtuous; they are also virtuous according to this rank order. Alfarabi adds to the prior shocking claim another one: "No one can discover what is most noble according to the followers of a particular religion unless his moral virtues are the specific virtues of that religion" (33, 26.7–8). Although we are already shocked by the frankness with which Alfarabi implies the inherent multiplicity of religions, we must try to transcend this shock to wonder about a curious implication with which we will have to deal later (in considering sec. 44 and 46). The prince or supreme ruler will be responsible for mastering the theoretical virtues and sciences and on their basis dispensing the variety of similitudes that will serve as the basis for these religions.[41] Must the supreme ruler possess the moral virtues (33, 26.7–8) and deliberative virtues (34, 26.13–17) of every community in the world to be able to legislate for the whole world? Surely the claim that he requires "the theoretical virtue" and merely the leading or authoritative moral and deliberative virtues suggests otherwise (34). And the conclusion of part ii (sec. 37) confirms the need "merely" for that theoretical virtue and the highest representatives of the other two kinds of virtue. Yet even on the assumption that the supreme ruler need not know every community in profound detail, we now get a sense in advance for what is at stake in the delegation of responsibility to subordinate princes in part iii (secs. 44–48). If any link in the chain of mutually dependent theoretical, moral, and deliberative virtues within any individual ruler or between mutually dependent rulers fails, then the plan for a virtuous regime of the inhabited world will fail. At least it will fail to cover a particular group of nations, a particular nation, or a particular city within a nation. At the same time, we still cannot help but wonder how the supreme ruler will be able to produce fitting similitudes for every nation and every city without intimate knowledge of the accidents accompanying their moral virtues.[42]

In the concluding sections of part ii (secs. 35–37), Alfarabi adds one more piece to the puzzle of the ruler's virtues. In spite of his conclusion in sec. 34, that theoretical, moral, and deliberative virtues are inseparable in the ruler, he remains in doubt that he has solved the problem of their relation to one another completely. He is satisfied that theoretical virtue takes a leading role. Yet he remains troubled about the relation between moral and deliberative virtues, whose interdependence seemed to be the root of the inseparability of the virtues more generally. Although theoretical virtue grasps the intelligible character of the moral virtues, without deliberative virtue's grasp of the accidents accompanying them they could not be realized. So which is anterior or prior to the other, moral or deliberative virtue? At first he argues that deliberative virtue is prior for the very reason I have just given. Yet if the one deliberating lacks (moral) goodness, then he would be incapable of discovering the fitting accidents. We need not follow all of the fascinating twists and turns of his argument here. Let it suffice to say that in a sense the inseparability of moral and deliberative virtue is made possible by the existence of a prior "natural virtue." This natural predisposition toward one or more of the moral virtues makes possible the acquisition of the requisite deliberative virtue and the full development of the moral virtue. Aristotle also discusses "natural virtue" near the peak of his claim that moral and deliberative virtues are inseparable (cf. *NE* 1144b2–18 with 1144a8, a35–b1, and 1145a5). Yet he stresses that moral virtue in the main sense, or what came to be called "acquired virtue," is far more important than natural virtue. After all, one of the central messages of the *NE* is the accessibility of moral virtue to nearly all citizens, in spite of any natural tendency to the contrary (cf. 1099b19 with 1105a1–3, 1109a1–16, b33–35, and 1118b13–20). Although I suspect Alfarabi would agree ultimately that acquired moral virtue is of greater importance for the well-being of individuals than the predisposition for moral virtue, he turns the discussion of natural virtue toward a different end from Aristotle's. He highlights the dependence of all of the other virtues, in their fullest flourishing, upon the presence of this natural virtue. One cannot become a supreme ruler without possessing a natural disposition toward virtue, neigh, toward every significant kind of virtue. Thus he adds one more virtue to his long list of requirements. He uses Aristotle's account of natural virtue to embellish the portrait of such a ruler rather than to stress everyone's access to moral virtue.[43]

THE UNEASY PEACE BETWEEN PRUDENCE AND WISDOM

Plato alludes only subtly to the tension between the opposing warrior virtues and philosophic virtues of his philosopher-king; Aristotle alludes with comparable subtlety to the conflict in the relative rank and duties of theoretical wisdom and political prudence. As we have already seen, Alfarabi makes ample use of the staggering challenges of combining so many and such opposing virtues as Plato discusses, especially in one human being. Now we will turn to Aristotle's conundrum regarding the rank of wisdom and prudence. This latter conflict is closely related to the conflict between philosopher and city (so central to the fate of Socrates in the Platonic dialogues, as we discussed earlier). The problem of rank can be avoided in one human being but cannot in a hierarchy of rule involving extensive delegation of authority. Of course, rule over the entire inhabited world would require extensive delegation of authority. And rarely has any thinker conceived of such an extensive form of "delegation" (*tafwîd*) as does Alfarabi in *AH* (48, 35.18). The problem of rank poses two challenges, "election" and "exploitation." By the "elect" (*al-khaṣṣah*) as opposed to the "vulgar" (*al-ʿâmah*), Alfarabi refers to what Plato and Aristotle refer to by the few (*olige*) and the many (*demos*). In a society organized in accordance with virtue rather than, for example, modern government in accordance with equal rights, distinctions between the elect and the vulgar are an integral part of the political order. But they are no easier to adjudicate for being integral or natural. Indeed, the problem of who qualifies as elect and who as vulgar leads inevitably to the problem of who has not only a right but a duty to "exploit" or make use of (*istiʿmâl*) other human beings as well as nature. Mahdi's choice to translate *istiʿmâl*[44] as "exploit" highlights beautifully the issue we will address.

Before turning to Alfarabi on election and exploitation, I must give a sketch of the Aristotelian background with which Alfarabi is dealing. The conflict between wisdom and prudence or politics is significant, because the inferior, prudence, is better suited to rule than the superior, wisdom (theoretical knowledge). Even if so, how can the inferior rule over its superior? Aristotle's ultimate solution will be to make the inferior rule for the sake of rather than over the superior (*NE* 1145a7–12). This answer is deceptively simple. Ruling for the sake of the wise remains, at least in some sense, rule over the wise. For this reason and others, we are less interested in this deceptively simple answer than the path to it.

Although the conflict between wisdom and prudence is adumbrated in the opening of Aristotle's *NE* and *Metaphysics,* I will limit myself here to *NE*. In the opening of *NE,* Aristotle identifies vaguely either the faculty or science of politics as the architectonic power or science (1094a23–28). After all, what except the city (*polis*) determines the arts and sciences to be practiced and studied? The city itself is the architect of what can be known and thought. The city aims at the good of its citizens as a whole. In doing so, it seems to seek the noblest and most divine end. One senses here all the tension built into the life of Socrates, whose inquiries left him at odds with his city's judgment of what should be studied. Even here (the opening of the *NE*), Aristotle acknowledges ever so subtly the possibility that the common good and the good of the individual might not coincide exactly. Yet here he privileges the common good (1094b10–12). The general structure of *NE* reflects the tension between philosopher and city or wisdom and prudence. Aristotle devotes the first half of his book to developing an account of the moral virtues devoted to the preservation and promotion of the common good. In bk. 6, the first book of the second half, he brings into his discussion, along with a deeper analysis of what "deliberative virtue" or prudence is, brief analyses of other intellectual virtues, such as wisdom.[45] Aristotle need do little more than identify the differing aims of prudence and wisdom (1141a20–b2) to enable the reader to see that prudence, indispensable though it may be to public life, can grasp only changeable (or as Alfarabi says, "accidental") means (1139a5–15) to a given end. Prudence specifies the means to the goods or ends determined by moral virtue (1144a8, 1145a6). In spite of its pedigree as an intellectual virtue, prudence is *the* intellectual virtue that is inferior to moral virtue.[46] Wisdom, another intellectual virtue, far from being inferior to moral virtue, is the higher aim toward which moral virtue, indeed all virtue, strives, however unwittingly!

At the same time Aristotle argues for the superiority of theoretical virtue over prudence, he draws the reader's attention to the relative independence of prudence and wisdom by examples of at least putatively wise philosophers who seemed to lack prudence. Now, Aristotle's declaration of prudence's independence from wisdom can be exaggerated. Alfarabi qualifies this independence when he claims that "theoretical virtue" grasps the moral virtues as voluntary intelligibles (35, 27.1–4).[47] Deliberative virtue merely specifies the accidents accompanying these ends of moral virtue (ibid.). Aristotle alludes to the same qualification of his own claims to the independence of prudence and wisdom in the following way: The prudent man deliberates well about the fitting means (accidents or particulars) to the ends (universals) specified by moral virtue (1140a28). If prudence contributes anything regarding the ends, it contributes certain general beliefs (*hupolepseis*), which really are little more than opinions about what contributes to a morally virtuous way of life (1140b13–28). Prudence appears not to deliberate about these ends (the moral virtues) but merely to have received them from the city (1112b12–21). But not every city will make its citizens virtuous. A truly virtuous city requires a virtuous legislator, who will give laws all of which aim at virtue (1129b15–26). And virtuous legislators, unlike most statesmen, must possess more than received beliefs about what is virtuous. They possess a higher form of prudence, called "legislative prudence," which somehow grasps the universals grasped only inchoately by most citizens (1141b23–26).[48] Of course philosophers such as Socrates, Plato, Aristotle, and Alfarabi grasp the universals of politics with a knowledge transcending prudence or practical or deliberative virtue. They possess political philosophy, which enables them to educate potential legislators and citizens through discursive argument as well as images. With this qualified view of the independence of prudence and wisdom, we come to a rough understanding of Aristotle's claim that the inferior, prudence, rules for the sake of rather than over the superior, wisdom. Prudent political men are unwittingly and indirectly shaped by philosophy. Without philosopher-kings, Aristotle in a way preserves the rule of philosophy.

Although Aristotle's model of indirect philosophic rule offers a desirable and more realizable alternative to direct philosophic rule, Alfarabi is hardly interested in this model because the merely prudent statesman serves as a weak correlate to the legislating prophet. Such a prophet requires at least the virtues of the philosopher-king. Thus Alfarabi turns almost inevitably to the models offered by Plato. Yet when one tries to implement the Platonic model, employing Aristotelian divisions of the virtues, and on a world scale (!), the challenges posed by the tension between prudence and wisdom return with a vengeance. The relative rank of wisdom and prudence and the awkward rule of the superior by the inferior make for an unstable relationship even within the philosopher-king, not to mention any prudent subordinates of the supreme ruler. The larger the scale, the greater the difficulty in getting subordinate rulers and the ruled to follow the guidance of the supreme ruler. Subordinates are bound to question the authority of the supreme ruler to rule. When we turn momentarily to *AH,* this will reappear as the problem of election. In the last section of this chapter, we will turn to the related problem of exploitation. For the supreme ruler to exploit the inhabited world, he must possess consummate theoretical virtue. As we will see, in the *Philosophy of Aristotle,* Alfarabi raises doubts about the hopes for theoretical perfection raised in *AH.*[49]

To my knowledge, Alfarabi discusses the "elect" first at the beginning of *AH,* part iii (sec. 38), when he begins his efforts to realize (if only in speech) the four things leading to human happiness in cities and nations. Here Alfarabi has not yet developed a plan for the delegation of power to subordinate princes (secs. 47–48). The elect are, like their counterparts in the *Republic,* those who are being prepared for "the highest authority," that is, for supreme rule. Referring directly to Plato, Alfarabi confirms that the elect need to be instructed in the theoretical sciences, placed in subordinate offices, and eventually raised to such positions of authority when they are fifty years old.[50] Alfarabi reserves his discussion of the challenges posed by the idea of election, except by implication, until part iv.

   Initially in part iv, it appears as if there should not be any difficulties in the distinction between the elect (rulers) and the vulgar (ruled). After all, the elect are trained in theoretical cognitions by demonstration. In contrast, the vulgar are confined to mere "unexamined common opinion" (*bâdi* al-ra*'y al-mushtarak*).[51] Yet almost at the start, a problem emerges. The vulgar do not confine themselves; rather, they "should *be* confined" (*an yuqtaṣar*) (my emphasis, 50, 36.19). Now, whether they fail to be so confined because they deem themselves worthy of something better than such opinions (the more likely option) or because someone else is likely to expose them to such opinions is unimportant. What is important is that they are prone not to be so confined. Although Alfarabi proceeds to consider the elect and their transcendence of mere unexamined common opinion, the challenge posed by even the vulgar rears its head almost immediately (50, 37.1–5.). Whenever anyone "thinks" (*ẓann*) that he is not limited to unexamined common opinion, then he deems himself part of the elect. If even the vulgar are prone to such visions of vainglory, then one could hardly imagine the competition among the various strata of the elect. In the following pages, Alfarabi seeks to persuade the reader that the truly elect are those suited to the highest authority—finally identified by name as the philosophers (sec. 53). These philosophers possess unqualified wisdom or the "science of sciences" or "wisdom of wisdoms." They are versed in what were identified earlier as "the theoretical virtue, the highest deliberative virtue, the highest moral virtue, and the highest practical art" (37, 29.4–6). Yet he acknowledges along the way that everyone with some form of knowledge departing from unexamined common opinion holds that he belongs to the elect or possesses a title to rule. He includes in this not only those who possess the practical or productive arts (50, 37.7) but also even the wealthy and the well bred (50, 37.13)! Although these lesser claims to rule might compete with the philosopher-ruler, surely the greatest challenge is likely to come from those "with penetrating practical judgment" (or deliberation, *al-nâfid al-rawiyyah*) alone (52, 39.8).[52] Indeed, Alfarabi concludes his promotion of the philosopher's suitability to rule with an acknowledgment of practical judgment's competing claim to the philosopher's wisdom or title to rule.[53] Visions of a titanic struggle between the merely politically astute and philosopher rulers, of the kind we saw glimpses of between Glaucon and Socrates in the previous chapter, appear before our eyes. The greater the prize, here a regime of the inhabited world, the greater the battle.

   Even if we were to assume an absence of competition with philosophic rule from those with penetrating practical judgment, and even if we were to assume that all of the requisite virtues could exist in one human being, another hurdle remains. Leaving aside the extraordinary theoretical virtue this philosopher must possess, it remains to be seen whether he possesses all of the knowledge (not merely the virtue) required for the task of "exploiting" (*isti'mâl*) not only all human beings but also the whole of the Earth.[54] Mahdi has drawn our attention to this difficulty.[55] Ultimately, he concludes that Alfarabi has such a strong sense of the risks involved in the exploitation of all beings on Earth that he leaves as an alternative the private pursuit of contemplation. At least, then, he would be risking "his own life, not all life."[56] I believe that my suggestion that we read *AH* as a cautionary tale more than as a plan to be realized is compatible with Mahdi's observation about this alternative.[57]

The plan to exploit all beings rests upon the conviction that philosophy has acquired wisdom about all beings or theoretical perfection. Yet the evidence for human possession of such perfection is thin. After all, by the end of Alfarabi's *Philosophy of Aristotle,* it appears that man lacks access to the highest metaphysical knowledge about God. If so, then how can the philosophers proffer fitting images for the vulgar? As Mahdi has explained,[58] Alfarabi in *AH* conceives of theoretical perfection in different terms from those of Aristotle. Because Alfarabi includes political science in theoretical perfection (*AH* 18, 20–21), he can distinguish between a lower and higher theoretical perfection, the lower being practical and the higher more strictly theoretical. According to Mahdi, Alfarabi seems to suggest that the lower perfection can serve as "the foundation of right action, even in the absence of a comprehensive knowledge of all beings." Yet Mahdi doubts the possibility that the lower perfection really is possible without making "certain assumptions." If this last claim is conclusive, then Mahdi seems to imply that Alfarabi believes that the knowledge required for the clear-eyed use of all beings is absent, and that the alternative of the private pursuit of knowledge is all that remains. These arguments may account for the fact that Mahdi does not seem to accept the philosopher's claim to be a true philosopher (that is, a true philosopher-ruler) even without having ever been used for rule, that is, without extensive political experience.[59]

I cannot resolve in this chapter the question of whether Alfarabi believes that "sufficient" theoretical insight is available to human beings for the clear-eyed use of all beings to be possible.[60] Rather, here I want to focus on how the limitations that Alfarabi detects in human knowledge fit with my interpretation of *AH* more as a cautionary tale than as a plan intended for realization. Again, I follow out a line of argument first developed by

Mahdi. In his chapter on *AH* in *Alfarabi and the Foundation of Islamic Political Philosophy* (*AFIPP*), Mahdi argues that the starting point of *AH* is the pretechnical understanding of certainty as being already available, without any regard for the differences between the various methods of argument used, and the degrees of certainty present, in different writings. This is the starting point of unexamined common opinion in all places and times.[61] Although Alfarabi proceeds to adumbrate some of the distinctions between the sciences, he fails to specify with clarity what would qualify as true certainty. Indeed, although he alludes to the various methods of argument in *AH* (sec. 4), he does not clarify them either. He offers highly provocative distinctions between the kinds of sciences but not the methods of argument. Without these methods, the reader is placed in the awkward position of accepting on faith Alfarabi's claims that such a variety of arguments exists and should be used to address different audiences. (Indeed, not until the beginning of the *Philosophy of Aristotle* are these methods clarified.) Part i of *AH,* then, is the setting within which Alfarabi argues that political science is part of man's *theoretical* perfection, a setting in which the reader has little idea of what would qualify as certainty.[62] It is also here that he declares such perfection at hand and the virtuous regime of the inhabited world as right around the corner. Rather than *AH* offering an understanding of the relation between the sciences closer to Alfarabi's own, might it not offer an opportunity to think through the realization of Islam's highest hopes, merely with a few gnawing doubts based on a limited understanding of philosophy? These doubts only grow with the interlocutor's increasing awareness of the gaps between his own grasp of the sciences and the ever-burgeoning tasks Alfarabi is assigning him,[63] in accordance with the aspirations of Islam.

Four

Alfarabi on *Jihâd*

Heraclitus ascribed a significant place to war in human life.[1] To my knowledge, however, Plato's Athenian Stranger was the first to claim that human beings desire "to have things happen in accordance with the commands of [their] own soul—preferably all things, but if not that, then at least the human things" (*Laws* 687c1–7). We have already seen just such a desire surfacing in Glaucon in the previous chapters. The significance of this claim is less that it implies the necessity of a war of every man against every man[2] than that it implies something akin to a natural human desire for world rule. This far grander claim may give the reader pause, but reflection on the history of empire building throughout the world suggests the presence of such a desire. Of course, this does not mean that every human being is likely to manifest such a desire. Yet it does imply that one is likely to find evidence of it in the most politically ambitious members of any, especially premodern, society.[3] In the *Laws,* the Athenian Stranger engages in a subtle critique of this desire. As has been shown elsewhere, Alfarabi offers a somewhat less subtle critique of it in his *Summary of Plato's "Laws."*[4] This entire work has been written with that critique in mind.

Although such a desire was present even among the Greeks with their small *poleis* (cities), not to mention the Romans, this desire seems to have taken on a new life and different character in the monotheistic world of Judaism, Christianity, and Islam. Although I will seek to add nuance in what follows, especially to his account of Islam, Majid Khadduri has captured in at least a preliminary way the difference between Judaism, Christianity, and Islam as follows:

To begin with, there is the universal element in Islam which made it the duty of every able-bodied Muslim to contribute to its spread. In this Islam combined elements from Judaism and Christianity to create something which was not in either: a divine nomocratic state on an imperialistic basis. Judaism was not a missionary religion, for the Jews were God's chosen people; a holy war was, accordingly, for the defense of their religion, not for its spread. Christianity on the other hand was a redemptive and, at the outset, a non-state religion. . . . Islam was radically different from both. It combined the dualism of [*sic*] a universal religion and a universal state.[5]

Polytheists tend to view religion more as a means to political ends; monotheists view politics more as a means to religious ends.[6] When one combines a natural desire for world rule with monotheism and a far more intense focus on religious ends, the mixture is likely to result in an unprecedented seriousness about world rule.

In contrast to monotheistic aspirants to world rule, neither Alexander nor any pagan Roman emperor sought to spread paganism. As the very name *Pax Romana* suggests, the main Roman purpose was to reduce war, not to spread the religion of the Romans. Rather than demanding belief in their own gods, pagans usually appropriate the gods of those they conquer. Aside from conflicts with other empires such as the Carthaginian, the most intense conflict Rome faced may have been with monotheistic communities that would not allow the appropriation of the one God into Roman religion—not to mention the worship of other gods in monotheist holy places. From the Roman viewpoint, the monotheist refusal to recognize Roman gods was important for political, not religious, reasons. It implied a divided allegiance in the conquered between their God and Roman political authority.

Of course, world rule suggests primarily political power. Consequently, monotheistic traditions such as Christianity that tend to deemphasize politics can come to view even the use of political means to achieve their religious objectives as suspect, as Christians have come to view it in the modern period. Yet the history of the Middle Ages, beginning with the Emperor Constantine, indicates just how little the frequently anti-political animus of Christian Scripture was to affect ambitious Christian princes. That anti-political animus has no doubt facilitated the modern separation of religion from politics in the West. It must be remembered, however, that Christianity abandoned the pursuit of religious ends by political means in the modern period only after centuries of barely endurable religious conflict. Lacking such deep and enduring conflict, the Islamic world has never had the impetus to such a separation.[7]

Leaving aside for the moment Christianity, let us consider in greater depth the fuel that monotheism, and its focus on religious ends, adds to the natural human desire for world rule. Monotheism seems to require universal obedience. Paganism does not, because if there were a multiplicity of gods, then there would not be any obvious reason for limiting the number of such gods. Paganism reflects the inherent multiplicity of natural forces in the world. In contrast, the most obvious effect of monotheism is the possibility of a created universe. (God demonstrates His transcendent power by having created the heavenly bodies, which pagans so often worship.) If the world is created, then there must be one and only one God. If there are other gods, then that God has limited power. (Rather than other gods, the heavenly bodies must be demoted to the status of divine servants.) Without infinite power, God could not create the world out of nothing. (Even for Jews, whose aspirations to world rule are only indirect, the existence of other gods is precluded.) The requirement that all other human beings accept the one God, and especially "our" understanding of God, gives profound impetus to the hope for God's world rule.

When one combines with monotheism a great stress on religious, especially otherworldly, ends, then life on earth, including political life, ceases to be led for its own sake and becomes a mere means for gaining the appropriate access to the one God. As Majid Khadduri implies, if the greatest act that one can perform with an eye to gaining such access is the giving of one's life for God,[8] then religious war becomes not only the highest but also the only fitting form of war.[9] To many modern readers, the notion that the only righteous war is a religious war must come as a great shock. After all, at least since Grotius, religious war as such has come to be viewed in the West as unjust. I could add little to the extensive work of other scholars on the relation between Islamic law and modern just war theory, nor would it be especially relevant to our inquiry into Alfarabi.[10]

Be that as it may, it could be objected that in relying on Majid Khadduri's account of war in Islam, I am relying on an out-of-date account. Indeed, some might say that his account has been far surpassed by more enlightened authors of today, such as Abdulaziz Sachedina. He, for example, would not accept the notion that there is anything significant about the nature of monotheism recommending the pursuit of universal rule. Indeed, he would not accept the idea that the only proper war is a "religious" war. Rather, he argues that the proper understanding of Islam allows only for a defensive war for "moral" purposes.[11] On the issue of decisive importance for us here, however, Khadduri and Sachedina agree. The prevailing view in the Muslim world *of Alfarabi's time* was that offensive *jihâd* is a duty of the Muslim community (in spite of the Qur'anic verse most frequently cited today about the absence of compulsion in religion [2: 256]). This view prevailed, according to Sachedina, because the jurists of the eighth and ninth centuries sought to justify retrospectively the Islamic conquest.[12] Whether these jurists imposed this view on the Qur'an or interpreted accurately Muhammad's or God's intention is not for us to decide here. I am sympathetic to Sachedina's effort to read the Qur'an in a new light. In spite of my own liking for what has come to be viewed dismissively as "essentialism," I believe modernity has made essentialism in Scriptural hermeneutics at least a problematic position.[13] Nevertheless, we are interested in the prevailing self-understanding of Islam in this period, because it was the context in which Alfarabi wrote. Patient analysis of the relevant texts will show that Alfarabi was critical of the jurists' sanction for offensive *jihâd*. Yet seen within the context of wide sanctioning of such *jihâd*, we should not expect Alfarabi to declare boldly and loudly that it is un-Islamic. Alfarabi was not a revolutionary; he was an educator. Indeed, his message was subtle enough that some authors have argued plausibly that he looks quite favorably on war for the spreading of justice and happiness. I intend to show that this is not the case.

FROM *ÎMÂN* VS. *KUFR* TO *ISLÂM* VS. *ḤARB*

I believe that it is undeniable that each of the monotheistic religions hopes and believes the world will one day accept its interpretation of the path to the one God. I believe that this is too obvious to require any argument in the case of Christianity and Islam.[14] Of course, each views the path differently. These two facts alone are sufficient to account for the greater proclivity of monotheistic communities toward religious intolerance than pagan communities.[15] The most debatable point within each of these communities is what means are appropriate for convincing the rest of the world to accept one's belief. The fitting means is shaped to a large extent by the way each community views the rest of the world. I do not intend to arrive at a final pronouncement about what Muslims believe today is the fitting means for achieving that goal, primarily for the reason that there is no consensus today, if there ever was any. But I am interested in the prevailing Muslim view of the rest of the world and of the appropriate means of spreading Islam in the ninth and tenth centuries, at least as it was expressed by the authoritative jurists.

Scholars writing on *jihâd* often note that the foundation of offensive *jihâd* is the juridical distinction between the *dâr al-islâm* (house or realm

of Islam or submission) and the *dâr al-ḥarb* (realm of war).[16] The realm of
Islam is the realm in which the Muslims have achieved political authority;
the realm of war is the realm in which they have not. We need not descend
into extensive detail here about what constitutes political authority, especially all of the details about the various forms of submission. Contemporary scholars stress often that this is a juridical rather than a Qur'anic distinction. They seem to imply thereby that it is somehow illegitimate.
Sachedina must have some qualms about this distinction, though he does
not voice them explicitly. Nevertheless, he clarifies that although it is juridical, it is based on the Qur'anic distinction between *îmân* (belief) and *kufr*
(unbelief).[17] In other words, he does not dismiss the juridical distinction
as if it were wholly without Qur'anic basis. That the unbeliever (*kufâr*), as
long as he remains one, is doomed to damnation is an oft-stated claim of
the Qur'an (e.g., 8:38 and 39:71). Yet who qualifies as an unbeliever is not
immediately apparent. Does this include anyone who is not a Muslim, that
is, does not accept God and His Prophet Muhammad or the "religion of
truth" (9:29)? Obviously Sachedina cannot accept this. Rather, he offers a
highly nuanced account of what constitutes unbelief, stressing the centrality of a failure to meet certain moral requirements.[18] The jurists eventually
extended protected status not only to the more narrowly conceived People
of the Book (Jews and Christians) but also to the more broadly conceived
(Sabians and Zoroastrians), yet the Qur'an gives some evidence that Allah
views the polytheists, or as they are called "associationists" (*mushrikûn*)—
those who associate other gods with the God—in a special light. They are
taken to exemplify the damnable unbeliever (37:23–38, esp. 36). For our
purposes, whether Christians and Jews qualify as unbelievers in the view of
the Qur'an, then, can be set aside.[19] It may be as Sachedina seems to imply,
that it means to exhort believers to root out only those polytheists who actively harm the Muslim community—as the pagans of Mecca were inclined to (2:190–191). Nevertheless, the early jurists do seem to have
equated associationism (*shirk*) with the gravest of all sins, not merely because it gives rise to what Sachedina would call "immoral behavior," but in
and of itself. After all, should Islam argue that paganism is acceptable as
long as pagans act morally? In the wake of the Enlightenment, we are far
more likely to make such an argument.[20] We may leave aside here the
claim that some, perhaps including Sachedina, would make, that pagans as
such are incapable of acting morally. In the face of the extremely high
moral demands promoted by philosophers such as Plato and Aristotle, I
find this impossible to believe. But if we argue that the God of the Qur'an
would not damn even pagans as unbelievers as long as they act morally,

then much of the incentive for becoming a Muslim is lost. Could the Qur'an have hoped to make its message a winning message without insisting not only on moral actions but also on a minimum of beliefs?[21] Whether the God of Islam has meant to teach this or not, the early jurists were quite clear about the importance of the belief in the one God. Indeed, the underlying justification for the distinction between the realm of Islam and the realm of war is that the latter is filled with unbelievers who need to be shown the error of their ways, whether by force or consent.

Whether or not the Qur'an explicitly sanctions offensive *jihâd* against the polytheists, it does treat polytheists as living in darkness.[22] Indeed, it claims that whereas the believer seeks God's protection, the unbeliever or, rather, the associationist, is an ally of Satan (16:98–100). Polytheism or associationism is linked to a realm of unbelief, which is a threat to the realm of belief. Few things inspire so much spiritedness as the division of the world into a realm of darkness and a realm of light.[23] This kind of division can inspire two kinds of spiritedness: a spirited hostility toward the darkness within oneself and toward the darkness outside. *Jihâd* covers precisely these two senses of struggle.[24] We must conclude, then, for the Qur'an, that the believing Muslim is to struggle not only with immoral actions but also with unbelief: beliefs or opinions matter. In the next section of this chapter, we will inquire along with Alfarabi into the roots of the above two senses of *jihâd,* as he treats them in his *Selected Aphorisms.* This will help us understand both the Qur'anic view of the unbeliever and the means of responding to the unbelievers that the jurists sanctioned, at least in part, because of that view. Furthermore, it will offer an opportunity to consider Alfarabi's response to the jurists.

ALFARABI'S *APHORISMS* ON *JIHÂD*

In Alfarabi scholarship, three basic views have been offered about how we should read Alfarabi, with special bearing on the task of this book and the problem of offensive *jihâd* in particular.[25] First, Ann K. S. Lambton captures well the most widely held approach. We should read Alfarabi as offering a synthesis or harmonization of philosophic and Islamic views.[26] Second, Joel Kraemer has suggested instead that we never fail to hold philosophy and Islam apart, despite Alfarabi's efforts to "accommodate" the one to the other, both lexically and rhetorically. Alfarabi's writings, despite their misleadingly Islamic look, always, or for the most part, express his own philosophic views.[27] Third, Charles E. Butterworth has suggested that

[Alfarabi's] speech, images, and general explanations of the universe as
well as of the human soul all point to great similarity of purpose, even of
general understanding, that exists between the revelation accorded Muhammad and the inquiries of pagan philosophers. By pointing to this
similarity, directly as well as indirectly, al-Fârâbî preserves the possibility
of philosophic inquiry.[28]

Although this view seems to partake of both the first and second, I would
like to follow it out and extend it. But first I must clarify how it differs from
the first and second. Of course, it differs precisely because it appears to combine elements of both of these opposed positions. Butterworth acknowledges the possibility of important substantive overlap as well as accommodation for the purposes of guaranteeing the acceptance of philosophy. I would
like to add to this the possibility that at times Alfarabi entertains views not
because they are his own but because they are Islamic and he seeks to test
them. In doing so, he takes advantage of the similarities between Islamic and
philosophic views precisely to test them.[29] The case I have in mind will be
obvious to many readers already. I believe that Alfarabi entertains the possibility of achieving a virtuous regime of the inhabited world not because it is
his ideal but because he wants to think through what would be required to
achieve it.[30] Indeed, rather than it being his ideal, I hope to show that this
ideal of the jurists is something he seeks to test and prove implausible.

Aphorisms 67 and 79

Although we will return soon to the problem of evil and its relation to
Alfarabi's views on *jihâd,* let us begin with his most obviously pertinent
discussion of war in the *Aphorisms.* A brief look at the differences between
Kraemer's and Butterworth's readings will enable us to see what is at stake
in reading Alfarabi on war. I quote Butterworth's fine translation of the
crucial Aphorism 67.

> War is [a] for repulsing an enemy coming upon the city from outside. Or
> it is [b] for earning a good the city deserves from the outside, from one in
> whose hand it is. Or it is [c] carrying and forcing a certain group to what
> is best and most fortunate for them in themselves, as distinct from oth-
> ers, when they have not been cognizant of it on their own and have not
> submitted (*yanqâdûna*) to someone who is cognizant of it and calls them
> to (*yad'uwahum*) it by speech.[31] Or it is [d] warring against those who do
> not submit to slavery and servitude, it being best for them and most

fortunate that their rank in the world be to serve and to be slaves. Or it is [e] warring against a group not of the inhabitants of the city against whom they have a right, but they withhold it. And this is something shared with two [of the preceding] concerns: one is earning a good for the city and the other is that they be carried to give justice and equity.

Now [f] warring against them in order to punish them for a crime they perpetrated—lest they revert to something like it and lest others venture against the city in emulation of them—falls in general under earning a certain good for the inhabitants of the city, bringing that other people back to their own allotments and to what is most proper for them, and repulsing an enemy by force. And [g] warring against them to annihilate them in their entirety and to root them out thoroughly because their survival is a harm for the inhabitants of the city is also earning a good for the inhabitants of the city.

Unjust war is [a] for a ruler to war against a people only to humiliate them, make them submissive, and have them honor him for nothing other than extending his command among them and having them obey him; or [b] only to have them honor him for nothing other than having them honor him; or [c] to rule them and govern their affairs as he sees fit and have them comply with what he knows of what he has a passion for, whatever it is. Similarly, [d] if he wages war in order to tyrannize—not for anything other than setting tyranny down as the goal—then it is also unjust war.

Similarly, [e] if he wages war or kills only to satisfy a fury or for a pleasure he will gain when he triumphs—not for anything other than that—then that is also unjust. Similarly, [f] if those people have made him furious through an injustice and what they deserve because of that injustice is less than warfare and killing, then warfare and killing are unjust without doubt. Many of those who intend to satisfy their fury by killing do not kill those who made them furious, but kill others who have not made them furious. The reason is that they intend to remove the pain that comes from fury.[32]

The crucial questions are what is Alfarabi's opinion of the kinds of war in the first two paragraphs? And in particular, what is his view of the third kind of war? Of course, we want to know not only his opinion but also his reasons for holding that opinion. Unfortunately for us, Alfarabi is far less forthcoming in his opinions about the kinds of wars in the first two paragraphs than he is in the final two. Yet perhaps we might be able to draw inferences from his reasoning in the final two.

It appears Kraemer infers quite naturally that because the city Alfarabi refers to as engaging in these wars is the virtuous city (that Alfarabi has developed since Aphorism 57), the wars described in the first two paragraphs are necessarily just.[33] As Butterworth notes, however, Alfarabi never identifies the kinds of war in the first two paragraphs as just war.[34] Kraemer's reasoning is simple. The just city as such is incapable of unjust war, therefore, whatever war it engages in must be just.[35] In contrast, although Butterworth accepts that only the virtuous city is capable of just war, he denies that a virtuous city is "impervious to unjust war."[36] By this negation of "impervious," I take him to mean not only is the virtuous city capable of falling prey to unjust war but also is capable of initiating unjust war. Only the virtuous city is capable of just war because unjust cities lack the proper motives for war. Yet the superior ruling motives and character of the virtuous city or its rulers may not be an inerrant guide.

As for the third kind of war, "forcing a certain group to what is best," Kraemer interprets this as the just city's "*mission civilisatrice*" or civilizing mission. He quite clearly identifies this mission as a philosophic mission rather than an Islamic mission. And he seems to claim that Alfarabi offers this mission as an ambitious but desirable philosophical ambition.[37] In contrast, Butterworth recognizes in this account "what *jihād* is usually taken to signify." And he interprets Alfarabi's refusal to characterize it (as just or unjust) or to explain what might justify it, as possible hints of his own reservations about offensive *jihād*.[38] Although an unsympathetic reader might accuse Butterworth of taking Alfarabi's silences too seriously, Kraemer has ascribed to Alfarabi things he does not state explicitly. We have only begun to sort out the proper reading of this passage. Yet an important fact will need to be considered in what follows. Kraemer has assumed that excellence of character guarantees good actions, that is, the virtuous city as such cannot but engage in just wars. An important feature of the *Aphorisms,* I believe, suggests otherwise. Dunlop noticed this feature when he divided it into two parts, immediately following section 67. In Aphorism 68, Alfarabi turns abruptly to a discussion of sound and erroneous opinions. Although both Butterworth and Kraemer have brought some of the following Aphorisms to bear on Aphorism 67 (beginning with Aphorism 77), they have not attended adequately to the riches contained within the intervening aphorisms. The abrupt shift in topic suggests an obvious point. A virtuous or just city can perform an unjust act if it is misled by some erroneous opinion.[39] It may be that engaging in offensive *jihād,* though apparently compatible with a virtuous character, could result from an erroneous opinion, a point we will return to later.

There is a piece of evidence that Kraemer ignores that could perhaps be used to his advantage. As both interpreters well know, Alfarabi refers here (in Aphorism 67) not to *jihâd* but to *ḥarb*. Could he not suggest that Alfarabi's avoidance of the term *jihâd* rules out the possibility that he could have anything Islamic in mind here? Although *ḥarb* came to be used in the Islamic tradition at times as an unjust alternative to *jihâd,* that exact meaning seems unlikely here. After all, then the "unjust war" identified in the last two paragraphs quoted earlier, would be redundant. Kraemer is decidedly uninterested in the significance of Alfarabi's choice of *ḥarb* because he believes that Alfarabi uses words for "war" just as for "law" indiscriminately. As I have already noted,[40] he believes that Alfarabi uses the terms for war and law as indiscriminately as the translators of Plato and Aristotle into Arabic seem to have. In contrast, Butterworth attaches significance to Alfarabi's choice of these words so heavily laden with meaning.[41] Does this not then weigh against his suggestion that the third kind of war (*ḥarb*) alludes to a traditional notion of *jihâd*? Not necessarily. Perhaps what precludes Alfarabi from using the latter, holier term is the conviction that the traditional juridical justification for *jihâd* rests on erroneous opinion.

Both Kraemer and Butterworth attend with care to Alfarabi's subsequent, crucial account of the "virtuous warrior" (*al-mujâhid al-fâḍil*) (Aphorism 79). Although Butterworth draws our attention to Alfarabi's choice of words, he does not draw out explicitly any particular significance to that choice.[42] While Kraemer also notes the Arabic usage, he argues in the spirit of his general claim that such terminological choices are insignificant, that the account of the virtuous warrior is "perfectly Platonic in theme and content."[43] In a sense, he is correct: the account of the virtuous warrior is actively philosophic in spirit. Alfarabi actively resists the notion that warriors should die with an eye to gaining a greater good or life in the hereafter. Instead, they should die only when their death provides a greater good for the city than their continuing life would. Yet the choice of words is an effort to place new wine in old vessels.[44] The necessity of such a transformation in the traditional meaning of *jihâd* only becomes apparent when we see the background of opinion against which this revisionist view of *jihâd* is being offered.

Aphorisms 11–16

Alfarabi draws the reader's attention to the significance of *jihâd* long before his account of the virtuous *mujâhid*. Well aware of the internal as well as external meanings of *jihâd,* or "struggle," he uses the internal sense in the midst of his account of the soul and the moral virtues.[45] Alfarabi's approach to these topics in the *Aphorisms* is more philosophic than in other treatises. According to Butterworth, in the *Aphorisms* Alfarabi approaches topics "from the perspective of what is known in books and treatises."[46] That is, it conveys the views of the likes of Socrates, Plato, and Aristotle rather than more popular ones.[47] Anyone familiar with Aristotle's *Nicomachean Ethics* will find extensive similarities between the *Aphorisms* and that work. Alfarabi's account of internal *jihād* is no exception. According to Aristotle, there are six basic moral types: the bestial, the immoderate, the incontinent (or those who lack self-restraint), the continent (or those possessing self-restraint), the moderate, and the divine.[48] After discussing briefly the lowest and highest ranks in Aphorisms 11–12, Alfarabi turns to a comparison of the four middle ranks, focusing on the top two, continence or self-restraint and moderation. The latter is moral virtue proper (Aphorism 14, paragraph 1). When human beings desire the goods of the body in accordance with what the traditional law (*sunnah*) requires, they are moderate. When, however, they desire in excess but follow the command of the traditional law, they are self-restrained (Aphorism 14). According to Alfarabi's brief and cryptic statement, "Yet the one who is self-restrained may take the place of the one who is virtuous with respect to many matters" (14). Indeed, all other things being equal, the self-restrained and the moderate should act identically. Yet their views of or opinions about the world are not the same. Furthermore, the life of self-restraint is more painful to the self-restrained person than the moderate life. A harmony between reason and desire in the moderate life makes it more pleasant. In the self-restrained life, desires, which should be a source of pleasure, are a source of pain, because they must be constantly combated. This combat between reason and desire Alfarabi refers to as "the virtue of struggle" (*faḍīlah al-ijtihād*). This is clearly and correctly an allusion to the internal *jihād* praised so highly by the Qur'an and the Sufis. How should we read Alfarabi's choice of the word "virtue"? After all, Aristotle deems moderation to be virtue proper and withholds the term from self-restraint. We could assume that Alfarabi does not know his Aristotle, depends on a poor translation, or something else. If we did so, then we would miss the point Alfarabi is making. After all, he clearly identifies moderation as virtue in the opening of Aphorism 14. Without rubbing the reader's nose in the point he is trying to make, he subtly alludes to the problem.

> The person of praiseworthy moral [virtue] [*ṣāḥib al-khulq al-maḥmūd*] whose soul inclines to no vice at all differs from the self-restrained person with respect to the excellence to which each lays claim. If the governor of

cities [*fa-mudabbir al-mudun*] possesses praiseworthy morals [*akhlâq mahmûdah*] and his praiseworthy acts are states of character, then [*fa-*] he is more excellent than if he were self-restrained. Whereas if the citizen and the one by whom cities are made prosperous [*aladhî bihi tu'maru al-madînah*] restrains himself in accordance with what the nomos [*nâmûs*] requires, he is more virtuous than if his virtues were natural. (Aphorism 15, Butterworth, ed.)

First, he merely identifies a "difference" in excellence, rather than stating clearly a rank order, between the moderate and the self-restrained. Second, he argues as if the vaguely identified "praiseworthy morals" (or moderation) were superior to self-restraint, but only if *the ruler* possesses them. (Of course, he, in fact, holds that citizens will mirror the virtues, or lack thereof, of the ruler, as he indicates in the next paragraph.) Third, using a euphemism for the "governor of cities," as if possessing self-restraint were to make him a completely different kind of being, he claims that self-restraint is superior to "natural" virtue. Moderation would appear to be a "more natural" form of virtue than self-restraint. If so, self-restraint would be superior to moderation. Yet what Alfarabi alludes to with "virtue" and "natural" is what he refers to in another writing as "natural virtue." Self-restraint is superior to "natural virtue," because natural virtue is really nothing more than a predisposition toward one or another virtue.[49] Without cultivation, it is likely to become a vice. One thing is certain: although "natural virtue" may be inferior to self-restraint, moderation is not.

The attitude of the self-restrained or possessor of the "virtue of struggle" is one of hostility toward his own desires. Like Aristotle, the self-restrained person identifies those excessive bodily desires as bad desires. For Aristotle, they are bad because they are excessive. But here the paths of Aristotle and the self-restrained part. Alfarabi alludes to the (different) direction that the possessor of the "virtue of struggle" might follow (from that of Aristotle) in his attitude toward these desires in the next aphorism (Aphorism 16). To my knowledge, only two aphorisms begin with the word "evils" (*al-shurûr*) or "evil" (*al-sharr*).[50] In the present aphorism, the theme is how to bring about the cessation of evils by the establishment of virtue or self-restraint.[51] As we will see shortly, on the second confrontation with evil, Alfarabi discusses prevailing views of evil, for example, whether it is something or really an absence of being (Aphorisms 74–76). Alfarabi will advocate for the philosophic and moderate opinion that evil is merely an absence. As we have already seen in our earlier discussion of the two forms of *jihâd,* internal and external, the jihadi and self-restrained opinion is that evil exists externally.

Aphorisms 68–76

As I mentioned earlier,[52] Butterworth and Kraemer attend with significant care to Alfarabi's discussion of war and the "virtuous warrior" (*al-mujâhid al-fâḍil*) (Aphorisms 67 and 79), yet they pay little or no attention to the intervening aphorisms.[53] The connection between these and the previous discussion of war (Aphorism 67) is by no means obvious. In Aphorism 68, Alfarabi begins a highly metaphysical discussion with little or no apparent connection to war. Once again, however, such an abrupt shift is meant to catch our attention. What connection could exist between a discussion of war and a broad survey of, as Socrates calls it, "all time and all being"? We recollect our puzzle by the end of our inquiry into Aphorism 67: can or cannot the virtuous city engage in unjust wars? I suggested then that perhaps a city, like a person with a good character, could engage in bad actions due to an erroneous opinion.[54] Beginning in Aphorism 68, Alfarabi discusses just the kinds of opinions that might lead a city to engage in unjust war, despite its own (or its citizens') good character. One such opinion could be that evil exists externally.

In Aphorisms 68–70, Alfarabi considers the broadest possible metaphysical distinctions. He begins with the oldest and deepest metaphysical distinction between "what cannot possibly not exist" (Being), "what cannot possibly exist" (Not-being), and "what can possibly exist and not exist" (beings that come into being and pass away), revealing his affinities with Plato and Aristotle rather than Parmenides or Anaximander (68). Of course, Not-being really is not at all. Consequently, he redivides the first and last divisions into three genera: beings devoid of matter, heavenly bodies, and material bodies or into three "worlds" (*'awâlim*) the "spiritual, celestial, and material" (*rûḥâniyyah wa-samâwiyyah wa-hayûlâniyyah*). The choice of the word *rûḥâniyyah* or spiritual may be significant (69).[55] In Aphorisms 70–71, he recapitulates the tripartite division given in 68 with the striking addition, "what cannot possibly not exist at a certain moment."[56] For the student of medieval philosophy, the combination of "cannot possibly not exist" and "at a certain moment" gives one pause. I can think of one thing that would fit such a description, a created spiritual being such as an angel or the *jinn*.[57] Now we have greater appreciation for Alfarabi's choice of the word *rûḥâniyyah*. None of the alternative terms would include the *jinn*. Allow me to quote a trustworthy source briefly characterizing the *jinn*. They are "an invisible order of creation, parallel to man but said to be created of a fiery substance, a kind of duplicate of man which is, in general, more prone to evil, and from whom the devil is also said to have sprung."⁵⁸ Does Alfarabi then acknowledge the existence of evil, created, immortal *a parte post* beings (beings that cannot not exist at or from a certain moment) into his account? At first it could appear that he confirms their existence. In Aphorism 71, he recapitulates his division of being one more time, this time vertically ranging from the most virtuous and venerable to the "vilest and most defective," namely, "what can possibly exist or not exist." Alfarabi, as it were, performs in speech the hatred we feel toward evil and injustice. Yet the vilest form of being is not "what cannot possibly not exist at a certain moment" or a created spiritual being; rather, it is merely human beings. We are not surprised, then, when he goes on to argue, "evil does not exist at all," apart from human volition (74). That is, Alfarabi denies that anything is the *embodiment* of evil.⁵⁹ Although the claim that evil does not exist at all is a well-worn, premodern philosophic claim, we will need to attend to Alfarabi's argument with care. Nothing is so important for understanding his assessment of the motive for offensive *jihâd* as his views on evil.

Before getting to evil, Alfarabi deals first with "privation" (Aphorisms 72–73). This is important, because there are many forms of privation, such as the privation of health (illness) and the privation of good in a soul (evil). They are not synonymous, though they are often treated as such. Alfarabi begins with the privation evident in beings that come into being and pass away, that is, beings that must reproduce to perpetuate themselves. Human beings, for example, are members of a species. As such, each member of the species requires another to perpetuate its species. A being unique in its species would not need another to persist, nor could there be another like it (Aphorism 72). Islam does not attach evil, or at least not as directly as Judaism or Christianity, to the notion that human beings need others to perpetuate the species.⁶⁰ Such a privation, then, is not an evil. Much like illness, such a privation would not be caused by the volition of any being.

In the next aphorism, Alfarabi speaks quite schematically (Aphorism 73). Because he does not specify any content, let us follow out the case of human being. He argues that if a being possesses a contrary, then it must also be subject to defect or privation. First we consider an inconsequential example to see how this works. The quintessential quality with contraries in Aristotelian thought is color. For example, the contrary of white is black. As Alfarabi says, white would nullify black (in other words, yield some other color, namely, gray). Colors are qualities in bodies; bodies as such come into being and pass away. In contrast, immortal beings without bodies have neither privations nor contraries. Only a being with a body could be either white or black. Take the case of human being. In us, life is the contrary of death. Death nullifies life in an even more powerful sense than black's nullification of white. Neither illness nor death can properly be viewed as an evil, though one is a privation and the other a contrary.

With this preparation, we turn to the core of Alfarabi's discussion of evil (Aphorisms 74–76). It is essential that the reader not misunderstand the claim that evil does not exist (Aphorism 74). Alfarabi does not mean to suggest that evil is merely relative, as do some thinkers who suggest that evil does not exist.[61] On the contrary, he adds an important qualification of the claim: evil "exists" within the realm of human volition. The evil of injustice in human action may cause untold misery, but such evil does not take on any embodiment or manifestation in separate beings representing evil. To convey this insight, Alfarabi distinguishes roughly between the effects of human volition and what he calls "the worlds."[62] He claims that all things in "the worlds" are good. When he goes on to speak of God or "the first reason" as the good (and thereby the cause of good) in the worlds, he faces the challenge that all who claim only human beings cause evil must face. Even if the good God causes only good in the worlds, then how can evil—even if it has no separate existence—be allowed to "exist" among human beings? Alfarabi argues, apparently self-contradictorily, that God allows evil as just desert. Furthermore, he avoids any effort to account for the suffering of the innocent.[63] Rather, he returns to the question of central concern to us here. How should we view evil? One group distinguishes crudely between existence and nonexistence and good and evil, lumping the pairs together. They marshal their forces, the forces of good on one side and the forces of evil on the other. They avoid all of the nuances of distinction worked out in Aphorisms 68–73, especially between the different sense of privation and contraries. Although Alfarabi does not name the "nonexistences" (or nonexistent beings, *lā wujūdāt*) on the side of evil, he does identify those on the side of good as "chimeric beings" (*mutawahhamah*). With some caution, Alfarabi presents the view of the jihadi who advocates offensive *jihād*. Another group argued quite simply that pleasure is good, and pain is evil. Alfarabi says straightforwardly, "All of these are in error"! He advocates a middle path between the view of the self-restrained and the hedonist.

Alfarabi places so much stress on guaranteeing just deserts in his middle path that his reservations about the jihadi view cannot be interpreted as weakening Islam's promotion of justice or its efforts to promote good habits (Aphorism 74, final two paragraphs). He resists the jihadi conflation of all senses of nonexistence with all senses of evil. In doing so, he appears as the great defender of justice. Only those who deserve it suffer evil and pain; only those who deserve it experience good and pleasure. (Once again, he avoids the problem of the suffering of the innocent.) Above all, this must apply in the spiritual and celestial worlds. Now, even the notion of the *jinn* and Satan or Iblis could be reconcilable with this. Yet Alfarabi has already dismissed at least twice the notion of evil immortal beings. The important thing is that he goes on to extend what he says to the "natural possible [worlds]." In other words, he denies that privation and contraries as such should be viewed as evils. That is, he responds to the question about the suffering of the innocents, at least in part. Privations in the natural realm, such as floods and famines, should not be viewed as punishment.[64]

We must use passages from the opening of Aphorism 74 that I have not yet discussed to clarify its closing paragraph, which serves as an introduction to Aphorisms 75–76. When discussing human volition as the cause of evil, Alfarabi distinguished between misery as an evil, opposed to happiness and the means to that misery. Both the means and the end are in a way evils. An example of an evil means might be an excessive desire for wealth, which leads to pseudohappiness or misery. At the end of this aphorism, Alfarabi clarifies, albeit in a highly schematic fashion, that whereas misery is evil, the desire that is the means to that misery is not inherently evil. Thus he says, "Every natural thing whose principle is a voluntary action may be a good and may be an evil." In other words, our desire to acquire, which is a natural desire for the sake of living, whose principle is a voluntary action, acquisition, can be good or evil. In Aphorism 75, he considers the opposing false opinion. A certain group holds that the appetitive part of the soul is itself inherently evil. The roots of this view in the self-restrained life are not difficult to find. For human beings who find themselves drawn intensely toward sinful actions, it is tempting to view their own desires as inherently evil. Internal *jihâd* lends itself to a hatred of things that are in fact initially neutral and not to blame. Not desire but the formation that desire receives (that is, habituation) is what is to blame.[65] True, human beings are inclined toward excess by the unconsummated partnership of reason and desire. Yet desire as such, not to mention reason, is not to blame.

In Aphorism 76, he considers a related mistaken view. In an even more schematic fashion, Alfarabi argues against those who deny that happiness is the result of human action. Of course, if human desires are inherently evil, and life is nothing but a battle against one's desires, then presumably human beings cannot escape misery. If so, then human action is ineffectual. All apparent happiness in the world, then, is the result of divine dispensation. This leads subsequently to the view that if this world is a vale of tears, then the afterlife must pay us back in kind for the suffering we undergo here. This leads to the self-defeating sight of the human being who forgoes pleasures he desperately desires in this life so that he can acquire them, and then some, in the next. Of course, for Alfarabi, the best option would be to cultivate moderate desires so that life is not a vale of tears. Although promising future reward for rewards forsaken in the present is conducive to self-restraint, it is not conducive to happiness. By degrees, Alfarabi shifts from pleasures forsaken here for pleasures received later to the more convoluted case of acts of courage performed here for rewards of a different kind received later. What Alfarabi is getting at is, I believe, all too obvious. In addition, Kraemer and Butterworth have already discussed these and related matters in their discussions of the "virtuous warrior" (*al-mujāhid al-fāḍil*) (Aphorism 79).[66] Alfarabi has taken over and revised traditional notions of the virtuous *mujāhid*.

In brief, then, self-restraint is conducive to certain problematic opinions. It so reifies its own excessive desires that it is prone to finding them peopling the external world. Internal *jihād* transmogrifies into external and offensive *jihād*. Leaving aside the *jinn*, what human beings are the fitting objects of such *jihād*? Certainly those who sanction excessive desires are the fitting objects. Two terms embody such desires, *fitnah* (temptation and strife) and *shirk* (association). In a text over which much controversy has developed, Muhammad claims that in the Qur'an *fitnah* is worse than murder—thus to slay those who are guilty of *fitnah* is warranted (2:191). *Fitnah* came to be used post-Qur'anically to refer to the early civil wars within Islam that gave rise to the Sunni-Shi'i divide. It has a different primary sense in the Qur'an, however. Some contemporary interpreters of Islam, such as Sachedina, argue that *fitnah* here refers to "persecution."[67] The previous verse lends this occurrence of *fitnah* to such an interpretation. In the previous verse, the Muslims are exhorted to defend themselves. Yet the early juridical tradition dwelt on perhaps the oldest layer of meaning of *fitnah*, namely, "temptation," and interpreted the word as synonymous with *shirk*.[68] In other words, they interpreted this passage as sanctioning offensive *jihād* against those guilty of *shirk*, that is, the polytheists. Because polytheists were believed to give free reign to their excessive desires, their opinion about the divine came to be the manifestation of evil.

We recall the issue that set us on a course through Alfarabi's *Aphorisms*. The question arose of whether the virtuous city or regime could fall prey to unjust war. Although virtue appears at first to be a guarantor that a city will pursue just wars, it appears possible that an erroneous opinion could lead even a just city to engage in unjust wars. At least one earmark of an

unjust war is that it is inspired by the opinion that an entire group of people embodies excessive desires. Alfarabi argues that neither desire as such
nor specific opinions about the divine, but habituation is the key issue
when trying to determine the root cause of bad actions. If, like Sachedina,
a contemporary Muslim holds that *jihâd* is warranted by gross immorality
and not misguided beliefs alone, then it would seem that he must, as Sachedina does, sanction only defensive *jihâd*.

ALFARABI'S *ATTAINMENT OF HAPPINESS* ON *JIHÂD*

The most striking feature of Alfarabi's discussion of war in *AH* (sect. 43) is
his departure from the early juridical tradition. The only warrant Alfarabi
gives for what appears to be offensive *jihâd* is the improvement of a conquered people's habits. He avoids the classic sanction of war for the sake
of the elimination of *fitnah* or *shirk*. We have yet to determine how sin-
cere he is in his apparent sanctioning of offensive *jihâd*. Yet he clearly departs from the juridical view that by dint of their opinions the polytheists
must be eradicated.

Taken in isolation, the relevant section (Mahdi, ed., 43) could be interpreted as a traditional sanctioning of offensive *jihâd:*

> The latter is the craft of war: that is, the faculty that enables him to excel
> in organizing and leading armies and utilizing war implements and war-
> like people to conquer the nations and cities that do not submit (*là
> yuta'âdûna*)[69] to doing what will procure them that happiness for whose
> acquisition man is made. For every being is made to achieve the ultimate
> perfection it is susceptible of achieving according to its specific place in
> the order of being. Man's specific perfection is called *supreme happiness;*
> and to each man, according to his rank in the order of humanity, belongs
> the specific supreme happiness pertaining to this kind of man. The war-
> rior who pursues this purpose is the just warrior (*al-ḥarbî al-'âdal*), and
> the art of war that pursues this purpose is the just and virtuous war.[70]

Yet considered within the context in which it appears, this passage is anything but a traditional sanctioning of offensive *jihâd*. In isolation, it is unclear why the conquered are being compelled, for their opinions or for
their actions. A closer look at the preceding sections will establish clearly
that Alfarabi speaks only of compulsion of character rather than opinion.

Beginning in section 39, Alfarabi distinguishes between two methods of
realizing the four goods conducive to human happiness in cities and nations.

They are "instruction" (*taʿalīm*) and "character formation" (*taʾadîb*), the philosophic, private education and the guardian, common education.[71] Alfarabi proceeds to describe the difference between the two forms of education: one relies on speech alone, the other on habituation. In section 40, he focuses on the former, "instruction." Although the elect members should receive "instruction," even they are educated at first by imaginative methods. The vulgar are permanently limited to that. But in section 41, he subdivides the latter (character formation) into two methods of habituation (with an eye not only to character formation but also to the acquisition of the practical arts): persuasive argument and compulsion. In section 42, the prince or ruler establishes two groups to engage in character formation: one uses persuasion, and the other uses compulsion. As we saw in the previous chapter, Alfarabi claims somewhat surprisingly that the very same skill enables these two groups to shape character. As long as one views this within a domestic context, the idea is not so surprising. Corporal punishment can be used to shape character—though there may be reasons to doubt that it can be used to compel happiness! When the compulsion involved extends to external war, as it does in section 43, it is more surprising. It is less obvious that punishment can be used to shape the character of another people, not to mention compel happiness. Yet we must not lose track of our central concern here, which is to verify that Alfarabi intends such compulsion for the formation of character, not opinion. Thus he concludes in section 42, "The prince needs the most powerful skill for forming the character of others with their consent and the most powerful skill for forming their character by compulsion." The antecedent to "the latter is the craft of war" in the opening of section 43, quoted earlier, then, is compulsion for forming character. Although Alfarabi goes on to argue in section 44 for some slippage between the formation of character by consent and the inculcation of opinions as a part of "instruction," he does not give any evidence of similar slippage between the formation of character by compulsion and the inculcation of opinions or instruction. "Instruction" has little or nothing to do with physical compulsion.[72] At a minimum, then, we may say with confidence that Alfarabi does not allow for traditional offensive *jihâd* for the spreading of the house of Islam and the eradication of *shirk*. To put it bluntly, he refuses all efforts to compel belief.

In a way, that traditional rationale is more comprehensible than the hope of compelling the conquered to acquire an improved character. (It must be remembered that Alfarabi does not believe it is desirable for all nations to adopt one kind of character and set of customs, as we will see in chapter 5.) After all, because the adherence of any individual or group to a particular set of beliefs cannot ever be guaranteed by compulsion, at best early jurisprudence came to require little more than the repetition of certain phrases to indicate adherence.[73] Whenever monotheistic faiths have sought more than words from converts under compulsion, they have descended into inquisitorial practices. Islam can be proud of its rare sanctioning of such practices.[74] One of the main purposes of compelling the polytheist to adopt monotheism is to protect the beliefs of the monotheists. In keeping with the self-restrained understanding, the traditional view considers the unbelievers as a source of temptation to the believers.

Leaving the traditional view aside, Alfarabi's suggestion that compulsion be used to force the acquisition of good character, indeed, to force the achievement of happiness, is more peculiar the more one thinks about it. Perhaps even more than the compulsion of (at least the appearance of) belief, one is led to wonder whether compelling people to acquire good character is possible. Can people be compelled to be moderate and virtuous, for example? Anyone with more than a passing familiarity with Aristotle knows that such a plan is fraught with difficulties. We will consider these difficulties momentarily. In the meantime, it is worth highlighting a hint Alfarabi gives about the difficulty of compulsion. In section 41, the first section in which compulsion appears, Alfarabi's first real example of individuals in need of compulsion is of philosophers who refuse to teach the theoretical sciences. As we have already seen in connection with the *Republic* in chapter 2 and will see in connection with *AH* in chapter 5, the fact that philosophers need to be compelled to rule is one of the first and most obvious indications that the regimes in these two books are impossible. With this hint in mind, we may consider more closely the issue of compelling good character.

Challenges to Compelling Good Character

We return to Alfarabi's *Aphorisms* once more, here because unlike *AH* it is not focused exclusively on the virtuous city. It will be easier to understand the way compulsion functions by focusing on a setting lower than the virtuous, beautiful, or best regime. We hope, then, to shed some light on the question of whether happiness or good character can be compelled. A good indication of the *Aphorisms'* lower focus is its continuous appeal to the analogy between political rule and medicine. Of course, there is little discussion in the *Republic* and, to my knowledge, no discussion of medicine in *AH*. Socrates explains explicitly why this is so. The beautiful city they are envisioning should have little or no need for doctors or judges, for that matter, because it is a city without illness or with a penchant for eliminating every hint of illness, both physical and psychic.[75] At first glance and on a couple of occasions, Alfarabi could appear to argue in the *Aphorisms* as if he were approaching health in the same manner as in the *Republic*. In Aphorism 16, the aphorism on evil we have already considered, he states quite broadly that anyone who cannot be brought around to virtue or self-restraint will be "put outside of the cities." In Aphorism 26, he discusses the need to "amputate" parts of the city when they risk infecting the other parts, like an infected limb. Despite the severity of these two uses of the medical analogy, Alfarabi also discusses something nearly unheard of in the *Republic* and far more relevant to our discussion, physical punishment (Aphorism 19). His reference to punishment is offered in the midst of a highly Aristotelian moment in his discussion. There he discusses the criteria to be considered in choosing the action in accordance with moral virtue. Just as the morally fitting action varies, so the fitting amount of anger and beatings to be used in punishment should vary. This kind of discussion, so prominent in Plato's *Laws,* is nearly unheard of in the *Republic*.[76]

We must recur to Aristotle's basic division of human types—which we have seen Alfarabi employ earlier—into the bestial, the immoderate, the lacking in self-restraint, the self-restrained, the moderate, and the divine.[77] According to Aristotle, most human beings fall somewhere between lacking and possessing self-restraint (*NE* 1150a11–16). The good news about self-restraint is that whether most lack or possess it, they already "possess" (even if only like an actor on the stage) the good beliefs that are necessary for moving from lacking it to possessing it (1146b25–1147b19). The key to moving from lacking to possessing self-restraint or from possessing self-restraint to moderation is implementing or coming to possess those beliefs fully through consistent habituation. When people possess such beliefs, usually all they need is to be exhorted or persuaded to implement them (1179b8–11). Yet one wonders where punishment and compulsion enter the equation. Most clearly, they enter in dealing with the immoderate. The special challenge posed by the immoderate is that they possess not only bad desires (as do those lacking and those possessing self-restraint) but also bad beliefs. If a person has been raised from a young age with bad beliefs supporting his proclivity to fulfill his bad desires or pursue an excess of bodily goods, then he is, according to Aristotle, incurable (1150b33). That is, persuasion lacks a foothold, so to speak, in the soul of the listener. Such a person is most in need of punishment, because only fear of punishment (as opposed to the shame of someone with good beliefs but bad desires) can deter him from fulfilling his bad desires (1179b12–16). The case of those lacking self-restraint is more difficult. Because they act like the immoderate (just as the self-restrained and moderate act alike), it is possible that they may at some time receive punishment. Such punishment would be a warning of the possible danger following upon continued neglect of his good beliefs. It is conceivable, then, that compulsion could play a role in inspiring some individuals to ascend from lacking self-restraint through self-restraint to moderation. But the main role of compulsion is to force the immoderate to act well out of fear of punishment. Above all, such compulsion does not "cure" the immoderate; it merely prevents them from acting on their desires. That the immoderate lack a cure means, above all, that happiness remains permanently out of reach for them.

Upon closer examination, then, it appears that compelling good character and compelling happiness are more difficult than one might expect. Improvement in character occurs as a result of exhortation or persuasion more than the threat of punishment, and those for whom punishment is fitting usually cannot become happy. They can become merely obedient or compliant.[78] Thus the plan to compel good character, and indeed happiness, among other nations through war proves especially problematic from within Alfarabi's Aristotelian evaluation of offensive *jihâd*. Furthermore, as we will see in the next chapter, the variation in character among nations is significant enough that compelling another nation to adopt one's own nation's character is not likely the key to bringing that nation closer to happiness.

Five

The Multiplicity Argument

Alfarabi claims that religion is inherently multiple. Religions must be adapted to the time and place for which they are given (*AH* secs. 24, 33, 46). Each nation possesses a distinct national character (*AH* 45–47 and *PR,* Hyderabad ed., pp. 40–41). If a religious law, which does not suit its national character, is legislated for a nation, it will not give rise to a virtuous nation.

Although I consider the a fortiori argument in chapter 3 a persuasive one against the possibility of a virtuous regime of the inhabited world, that argument need not even be valid for the argument of this chapter to retain its relevance. Even if such a vast virtuous regime were possible, it would be characterized by such internal diversity among its parts that it would inevitably temper the hopes of those who seek a homogeneously Muslim world. It almost goes without saying that views on just how homogeneous the world should be ideally vary widely among Muslims. Our purpose here is not to determine where majority opinion lies on this question by consulting polling data. Rather, we seek to give Muslims, and non-Muslims alike, food for thought about what is possible and what is desirable in human affairs. Furthermore, the purpose of this book is less to advocate for heterogeneity than to follow along while one of the greatest minds of the Islamic tradition thinks through the hopes and aspirations of his community.

In addition to the argument from national character, Alfarabi establishes the claim that religion is inherently multiple on a far more profound, if unnerving, basis. Although he points away from himself to "the ancients,"[1] at least for the origin of the claim, he states quite plainly, that religion is an imitation of philosophy (*AH* 55, 40.14).[2] As all readers of Plato know, imitations are always many, and the original they imitate should be one.[3] The repercussions of Alfarabi's claim were felt throughout Arabic philosophy to Averroes (or Ibn Rushd), and even to the so-called Latin Averroists. Upon first reading it appears to be a version of the so-called double-truth argument, except an imitation is obviously inferior to the original.[4] If anything, Alfarabi's argument appears more offensive to religion than the double-truth argument. Consequently, his claim that religion is an imitation is often taken by the casual reader to imply that he views religion as a sop or an opiate for the masses, not an alternate truth. This hasty likening to the thought of Marx does not do Alfarabi justice, for several reasons: it implies that Alfarabi views philosophy as the possessor of the complete account of the whole (as Marx claimed Marxism was). According to the Alfarabi-as-Marx reading, precisely because they possess such a rare commodity, philosophers willfully and selfishly withhold the truth from the masses. It also implies that all imitations are equally worthless, because all fail to be the original—rather than some imitations being more remote and others closer to the truth, as Alfarabi contends. (As I said in the opening page of this book, Alfarabi discovers hierarchy wherever he looks. To be specific, he consistently stresses hierarchy within the cosmos and within and among human communities.) I will seek to correct the mistaken view that all imitations are equal when we turn to the argument that religion is the imitation of philosophy. In the meantime, let me say in Alfarabi's defense that he offers ample evidence to the effect that philosophers do not possess the complete account of the whole. Indeed, this fact, more than any other, necessitates the existence of a multiplicity of religions.

Before entering into the details of Alfarabi's arguments for multiplicity I must acknowledge that there are moments in the *Attainment of Happiness* when he appears to be arguing for little more than the heterogeneity already present in Islam. That is, in distinguishing national characters and the religions or religious communities (*milal*) that go along with them, perhaps he has in mind little more than the juridical distinctions within Sunni Islam, which to some extent reflect regional differences.[5] At first glance, his few references to habits and opinions shared by all nations might be interpreted to suggest that all nations share the same religion. He exhorts the supreme ruler to identify images suited to "all nations jointly" (*jamīʿ al-ʿumam bi-ishtirāk*) (44, 33.5; Yasin, 82). Of course, we should not be surprised that he holds that there are not only certain opinions but also certain acts that "all or most nations" may share in common (44, 34. 3–5 and 45, 34.11–13). Leaving aside that important qualification of "all," namely, "most," Alfarabi goes on to argue that the basis of these shared acts and opinions is human beings' shared "human nature" (al-ṭabî'ah al-insâniyyah) (45, 34.14; Yasin, 83). Yet it should be obvious that the view that we share some acts and opinions in common need not entail the view that all of our religions should be the same, or that Alfarabi aims at a relatively homogeneous virtuous regime of the inhabited world. On the contrary, he immediately follows up his references to such a shared nature and its entailed shared acts and opinions with references to the ruler's need to attend to the differences between "every group in every nation" (kull tâ'ifatin min kulli 'ummah) (45, 34.15; Yasin, 84). What he says about the things that human beings share is characteristically schematic.[6] He could mean that all or most have common beliefs, such as in one God. It seems less likely that he means that all hold the same basic understanding of that unity, as do the Muslims (and perhaps even the Jews). He could mean that all or most share the view that justice and mercy need to be practiced at least within one's own community, if not toward the enemies of one's faith. Of course, the beliefs and actions that monotheistic religions share are quite extensive, indeed, so extensive that at times each faith must search for ways of distinguishing its own teaching.[7] Though it does not prove it, the very schematic character of Alfarabi's argument suggests that what different communities have in common is likely to be more schematic and less detailed. In contrast, the differences between different groups that he has in mind seem to be somewhat detailed and quite extensive. (In contrast, different juridical schools share far more than they disagree upon.) In brief, I believe that Alfarabi's claims about what religions have in common do not imply that the existence of one religion for the inhabited world would be desirable. But we will return at the end of this chapter to reconsider this evidence, which could be read as contradicting what I believe and will argue for.

In the meantime, I will develop my interpretation of the multiplicity argument. To begin with, I will consider Alfarabi's views on empire or conquest and domination or tyranny, expressed at greatest length in his *Political Regime* (PR). In PR, Alfarabi focuses on a particular form of tyranny or domination, that is, external tyranny or domination of one's neighbors.[8] The inspiration for Alfarabi's discussion is obviously *Republic* 8 and 9. Yet in the *Republic*, Socrates focuses almost exclusively on the threat of internal tyranny, that is, tyranny over one's own citizens or subjects.[9] Apparently, Alfarabi is especially concerned with the possibility that rulers in his community are prone to conquest and external domination for their own sake. Like my analysis of Alfarabi's views on *jihâd* in the previous chapter, my analysis of conquest here further confirms Alfarabi's opposition to wars of conquest of any kind, but especially of the kind sanctioned by the early jurists. After the problem of domination, I will discuss the avenue through which multiplicity enters the regime in *AH*, namely, the task of deliberating about vast expanses of time and place. Founding virtuous cities throughout many nations requires that various levels of deliberation—from those focused on longer periods of time and greater areas of land to those focused on shorter periods and smaller areas—be used to understand the accidents and conditions of a myriad of differences of character among a myriad of groups. Unlike Plato or Aristotle, who both accept and even celebrate the confines of the small Greek cities they concern themselves with, Alfarabi does not have the luxury to dwell solely upon the city—though he notes the perfection of this unit (*VC*, ch. 15). After considering deliberation's contribution to the formation of character, we will turn to Alfarabi's account of the formation of images and opinions about the highest things suited to each place and time. He goes so far as to suggest that every religious community must possess its own store of images or opinions. Finally, we will turn to what may be his most challenging claim: religion is an imitation of philosophy, and as such, it possesses an inherent tendency toward multiplicity.

THE INCREASING TENDENCY TOWARD CONQUEST AND DOMINATION

The primary reason for considering Alfarabi's arguments about conquest and domination in this chapter is to see whether he hints (if he does not state explicitly) that the imposition of one religion on the entire world is a form of domination.[10] As was the case with the a fortiori argument, it is unlikely that Alfarabi would make this kind of argument explicitly. He must do so indirectly, because to do otherwise could be interpreted as a rejection of his own community.

Alfarabi believes that virtuous character, at least on a world scale, is inextricably bound up with multiplicity. If, as we will see shortly, he claims that there is great variety in the character of different nations, then to ignore such differences is to dwell upon a lower common denominator. That is, a religion could only suit all peoples in all places and times if it focuses on what they share. At first, this seems a dim view of our common humanity. Why should we not share that which is highest in our humanity? Further reflection, however, suggests that it is not so dim a view. This dilemma is encapsulated well in Aristotle's discussions of natural justice in the *Nicoma-chean Ethics*. Although Aristotle offers blanket condemnations of actions such as adultery, theft, and murder (1107a13), he also stresses that the only definitive emblem of natural justice is the best regime, which is the same everywhere (1135a5).[11] Otherwise, justice in particular and ethics in general does not lend itself to universal statements about how to act with equal validity everywhere (1104a1–10 and 1134b19–35). In other words, although what is highest may be uniform and certain minimal claims may be considered more or less universal, it appears that universally applicable laws cannot be established to cover the bulk of human life, which ranges between this flooring and ceiling. What is bestial and what is divine in human life are more obvious than the proper way of leading everyday, if virtuous, life in most societies. Here at this middling level the distinctive character of a society must be acknowledged and accommodated if one hopes to give rise to a relatively virtuous city or nation.

Leaving Aristotle aside, in the next section we will consider the positive evidence in Alfarabi's *AH* and related texts for the view that promoting virtue requires recognition of differences of national character. In the meantime, we must consider the evidence in Alfarabi of special concern about, and efforts to counteract, domination and conquest. His most extended treatment of these themes is in the *Political Regime* (*PR*). His discussion of domination occurs in the midst of his most extended discussion of the unsavory alternatives to a virtuous city.[12] This discussion resembles nothing else in previous political philosophy so much as Socrates' discussion of the alternatives to *kallipolis* in *Republic* 8. Yet relative to the length of his discussion of the virtuous city, Alfarabi's discussion of the nonvirtuous regimes is far more extensive and elaborate than Socrates' parallel discussion. Socrates identifies four worse regimes. Alfarabi divides his account of these into three broad classifications and then subdivides the first class into six kinds of cities.[13] This first class, ignorant cities, divided into six parts contains the same elements as *Republic* 8 plus material from other parts of the *Republic*.[14] Although Socrates' account is quite straightforward in beginning with the city closest to the virtues of *kallipolis*, timocracy,[15] and then descending through oligarchy and democracy to tyranny, Alfarabi's account is more circuitous. I will use Socrates' terms to capture the order Alfarabi follows. Alfarabi describes the ignorant cities in the following order: city of necessity, oligarchy, city of luxury, timocracy, tyranny, and democracy. Alfarabi's account does not follow nearly so rigidly Socrates' plan to describe the regimes in order of rank. One should not imagine that Alfarabi diverges from Socrates because he is oblivious of Socrates' reasons for so ranking the regimes. On the contrary, Alfarabi states clearly, in full agreement with Socrates, that timocracy is the best of the ignorant cities (*PR,* Hyderabad, 63), and he highlights the unexpectedly positive things that Socrates conveys about democracy, despite its purportedly low rank (*PR,* 70–71). Alfarabi's most shocking innovation is the juxtaposition of timocracy and tyranny or despotism. This innovation highlights one of the least plausible parts of Socrates' argument. Socrates insinuates that regimes decay one into the other in the same order as their order of rank. This fiction plays a useful role in the *Republic.* It persuades the leading character, Glaucon, that the best and the worst are very far apart indeed. To suggest that they are relatively close could be interpreted to justify pursuing the worst—a proclivity of Glaucon's.[16]

In contrast, Alfarabi is not subject to such dramatic constraints. He implies quite plausibly that not only are timocracy and tyranny quite close, but also that timocracy tends to turn into tyranny! Indeed, tyranny is the result of the excessive pursuit of honor. Now, the love of honor is a significant problem in the *Republic.* Yet matters appear even worse in Alfarabi's world. A small indication of this is that Alfarabi uses a different term to describe excessive love of honor. When excessive, the "love of honor" (*maḥabbah al-karâmah*) becomes transformed into the "love of domination" (*maḥabbah al-ghalabah*). Socrates never describes a distinctive desire to dominate others.[17] I do not mean to suggest that Alfarabi has invented a new desire but highlights a desire that has become a peculiar problem in his own time and place. If anything, the proximity between honor and domination that Alfarabi describes means that Alfarabi's account of honor is also generally less positive than Socrates'. According to Alfarabi, most citizens in the ignorant cities—including presumably even timocracy (!), since the claim is made in the midst of the account of timocracy—give "honor" to those who achieve "domination" (60). Indeed, at one time he goes so far as to collapse the distinction altogether.[18] Leaving aside for the moment this tendency to slide both accounts toward despotism, how can one distinguish timocracy from despotism? In *PR,* the most distinctive feature of timocracy is that the rulers are willing to forgo other goods such as wealth and bodily pleasure as long as their people honor them. Such rulers pursue wealth and other goods only if their society honors those who possess wealth (62). Obviously they must possess significant endurance and control over their bodily desires to hold out for honor alone. They appear, then, to be quite self-sacrificing. In contrast, despots seem to take pleasure only in their ability to overcome others through violent conflict. Indeed, should they acquire any good without resistance from an opponent, they take no interest or pleasure in it (64). Their preference for violent strife with others is complemented by the presence of violent passions for bodily pleasures and booty. Although despots refrain from violence among themselves in order "to survive" or in pursuit of their booty, once their booty is acquired, they tend to fall into violent conflict among themselves (65).

Up until this point, Alfarabi has not departed completely from Socrates' account of tyranny—though he has certainly brought out novel connections between timocracy and tyranny. Yet when he gives an inventory of the kinds of tyranny or despotism, he shifts the focus from Socrates' domestic to his own foreign or external focus. He describes three kinds of despotism, of which only the third resembles Socrates' domestic form of tyranny. The first kind is when all of the members of the city are despots who seek to dominate "those outside the city." The second kind is when one half of the city dominates the other half. I must admit that Alfarabi describes the third, domestic form of despotism at greater length. Yet he offers a disturbing confirmation that the novel attention he devotes to foreign or external domination is especially pertinent. After he has described the kinds of despotism, he turns to an account of regimes in which the pursuit of domination is mixed with other aims, such as wealth and bodily pleasure. Oddly, his first example fits only roughly the description of a regime pursuing mixed ends. He merely alludes to people who pursue other ends and focuses only on those who aim at nothing but the pleasure of murderous subjugation. In one of only two references to a particular people, he notes that some of the Arabs are said to pursue this kind of domination.[19] Although he writes with great reserve, Alfarabi's reason for writing at such length about timocracy and especially despotism is not difficult to decipher, especially when one combines this passage with his account of despotism over foreigners.

Finally, perhaps the most shocking thing about Alfarabi's account of domination (*al-ghalab*) and despotism (*al-taghallub*) is the way the former, if not the latter, permeates the other five kinds of ignorant cities. I am almost tempted to suppose that Alfarabi means little more than compulsion (*ikrâh*) as he uses it throughout *AH*. Yet domination is far less neutral than compulsion in Alfarabi's usage. Domination aims at harming others, often solely for the pleasure it gives us. In other words, force has become almost an end in itself. Wherever domination plays an important role in political life, Alfarabi detects the tendency of human beings to deem themselves superior to others, toward boastfulness, and to a misguided sense of being "high-minded" or to "excessive ambition" (*kabîrî al-himam*).[20] It must not be confused with compulsion or force, which play an indispensable role in all political life, even the virtuous city of *AH*.

We turn briefly to Alfarabi's *Aphorisms* for confirmation that domination and despotism are a special concern for our author. A brief recollection of the kinds of unjust war in Aphorism 67 confirms our suspicion. The main features they include are all present in the account of despotism in *PR*, including the striking overlap with the love of honor. In unjust war, a ruler causes humiliation (*dhull*), submission (*inqiyâd*); he acquires honor (*karâmah*) for himself (not others) or despotism or tyranny (*ghalabah*) over others, or to satisfy his fury (*shifâ' ghayiz*). Interestingly, Alfarabi excludes any reference to the pleasure of dominating over others. Here he makes clear that what might appear an end pleasurable in itself is merely an effort to "remove the pain that comes from fury" (*izâlah al-adhan aladhî bihi min al-ghayiz*).

As befits the *Aphorisms* as a mirror for princes, Alfarabi avoids the kind of descriptive detail in *PR*. Such detail might have the contrary effect of making something attractive that should be repulsive. Like Aristotle, Alfarabi in *Aphorisms* is prone to remain silent on vice rather than to give a detailed anatomy of it. Yet he makes far clearer in the *Aphorisms* than in *PR* just how strongly he intends to condemn despotism and to dissuade his princely reader from pursuing it. Indeed, the specter of despotism is present from the beginning of the *Aphorisms*. Alfarabi begins with a long and an involved analogy between ruling and being a doctor. Lest the potential ruler think of himself as a wolf ready to prey upon his flock, Alfarabi begins with *the* profession that human beings think of as being of service to others, namely, medicine. Similarly, as Alfarabi enters into his account of the "king in truth" (30–32), he digresses to consider the mistaken popular views that rule is for the sake of "honor" (*al-karâmah*) and "domination" (*al-ghalabah*), wealth, or pleasure. The city with the very best of these mistaken views seeks honor through the acquisition of virtue. He descends through rulers who seek the wealth of their city through to those who seek their own wealth at the expense of the citizens. He concludes that the worst are those who seek all of these goods—honor, wealth, and pleasure—by means of the ruled as their tools (*'âlât*).[21] After underlining the fact that the king in truth is king whether he is employed or used by his city or not, he concludes by denying explicitly that being a true king requires being obeyed, acquiring wealth, or "dominion by conquest [*al-tasallut bi-'l-qahir*], humiliation [*al-dhalâl*], terror, and fear" (32). Although these are often mistaken for the true indications of kingship, they are merely sometimes attendant upon being king. As odd as the claim that one can be king without being obeyed may sound, Alfarabi is quite clear in indicating to the potential prince that domination should not be his goal. Rather than domination, the true prince uses compulsion as a mere means and never an end. Alfarabi is far, indeed, from advocating any form of conquest.

THE TASK OF DELIBERATION: SHAPING A MULTIPLICITY OF CHARACTERS

I do not know of any other thinker who has devoted so much attention to the task of deliberating about vast expanses of time and place as has Alfarabi. Part ii of *AH* contains one of his most extensive discussions of this topic.[22] According to Aristotelian usage, we deliberate when we consider the desirable means to a given end (*NE* 1112b12). As we saw in chapter 3, moral virtue determines the fitting end (1144a8). Deliberation, then, chooses the desirable or fitting action by means of which we come closer to the end aimed at by moral virtue. Which action is fitting depends upon a host of criteria (or accidents) that accompany the action—such as the person(s) involved, amount (of, for example, property) involved, time, purpose, and manner (1106b22, 1109a28). These accidents are the material or subject matter about which we deliberate. This kind of deliberation, when performed well, is what Aristotle refers to as (personal) prudence (1141b30–32).

As I mentioned in passing in chapter 3, Alfarabi offers a novel and an especially illuminating approach to moral virtue, which will shape our understanding of deliberative virtue as well. He identifies moral virtues as "voluntary intelligibles" (*al-maʿqûlât al-ʿirâdiyyah*) (*AH* 23, 17.17). Each intelligible, including both voluntary and "natural intelligibles" (*al-maʿqûlât al-ṭabîʿiyyah*), is one in species. How this is true is more obvious in the case of natural intelligibles. For example, all chimpanzees share the same nature or are one in species (23, 17.10–13 and 24, 18.5–8). Each chimpanzee's accidents distinguish it from every other. Alfarabi claims that the same applies roughly speaking to moral virtues such as "moderation" (*al-ʿiffah*) (24, 19.4). All forms of moderation share an intelligible nature in common. The primary difference between natural and voluntary intelligibles is that natural intelligibles are "accompanied by their accidents by nature" (24, 17.18). In contrast, both the intelligible and accidental aspects of moral virtue "can exist outside the soul by will"[23] (24, 18.1). Of course, Alfarabi does not mean to imply that moral virtues are merely conventional constructs generated at will. If they were, then why should they be called "intelligible"?[24] Rather, he is trying to identify the proper cause of moral virtues.[25] In keeping with Aristotle's claim that moral virtues are neither by nature nor against nature (*NE* 1103a25), he implies that their primary cause is the will of the city or legislator that engenders them in its citizens.[26]

Here we have run across deliberation or prudence of a higher order, namely, legislative prudence. In personal prudence, the person deliberates about the fitting means or action in a given setting. He realizes that his action must aim at moral virtue and contribute to the formation of moral virtue in himself. In so deliberating, he must consider a vast host of accidental criteria impinging on the setting. In contrast, the legislator uses his prudence to cause moral virtue in his citizens. Now, like all intelligibles, moral virtues are accompanied by various "accidents" (*al-aʿrâḍ*) and "states" (*al-aḥwâl*) (*AH* 24, 18.4–6). Consequently, the legislator cannot merely will that citizens come to possess various moral virtues (intelligibles). Rather, he must deliberate on the fitting "accidents" and "states" to accompany them. Indeed, like the accidental criteria that are the main concern of personal prudence, these accidents are the central task of legislative prudence.[27] According to Alfarabi, these accidents and states

> vary constantly, increase and decrease, and fall into combinations that cannot be covered at all by invariable and unchangeable formal rules [*qawânîn ṣûriyyah*]. Indeed, for some of them no rule can be established. For others rules can be established, but they are variable rules and changeable definitions. Those for which no rule at all can be established are the ones that vary constantly and over short periods. The others, for which rules can be established, are those whose states vary over long periods. Those of them that come to exist are for the most part realized by the agency of whoever wills and does them. Yet because of obstacles standing in their way—some of which are natural and others voluntary, resulting from the wills of other individuals—sometimes none of them at all is realized. Furthermore, they suffer not only *temporal* variations, so that they may exist at a certain time with accidents and states different from those that accompany them at another time before or after; their states also differ when they exist in different *places*. (24, 18.8–18, Mahdi's emphasis)

The legislator's deliberative task is profound, then, and made more profound the larger the expanses of time and place he intends his legislation to cover. (Here the multiplicity argument lends additional support to the a fortiori argument.) In effect, the legislator cannot cause the moral virtues in his inhabitants merely by legislating the same rules for all citizens in all times and places. The endless variety of impinging accidents and states precludes such uniformity of rules. To make matters worse, there is even variation in the way each moral virtue is affected by accidents. Some are more variable, others less. Furthermore, even if the legislator could possess absolute control over the intelligibles and accidents he wills or causes, these intelligibles (or moral virtues) are impinged upon by other human beings, not to mention natural obstacles. When one nation attacks another, it shapes the moral virtues of the nation attacked. When natural disasters strike, they can shape the character of a nation (even more in Alfarabi's time than in our own). Although Alfarabi does not discuss this here, as we will see shortly, he insinuates elsewhere that national character has natural bases, including not only climate but also, to some extent, physiology.

Although he does not discuss national character here explicitly, he alludes to it in the schematic terms we have become used to in discussing *AH*. Variations due to time and place are "evident in natural things, e.g., Man. For when it [Man as a natural intelligible] assumes actual existence outside the soul, the states and accidents in it at one time are different from those it has at another time after or before. The same is the case with respect to different places. The accidents and states it has when existing in one country [*bilâdin*] are different from those it has in another" (24, 18.18–19.3).[28] He goes on to ascribe the same variability to "voluntary things as well" (19.4). Alfarabi's decision to use "Man" as his example of a natural intelligible is very telling. It lends further weight to my earlier suggestion that his claims about the role of will in shaping our moral virtues should not be taken to imply constructivism or conventionalism. Indeed, it would seem that the intelligibility of voluntary intelligibles is rooted in or based upon our being as natural intelligibles. In the *Virtuous City*, he suggests, "Although the parts of the city are natural, their dispositions [*hai'ât*] and habits [*malakât*], by which they perform their actions in the city, are not natural but voluntary" (ch. 15, sec. 4, end). Because of the intimate connection between natural and voluntary intelligibles in human beings, and because the states and accidents that accompany both kinds of intelligibles are shaped by time and place, we should not be surprised that Alfarabi argues for the recognition of extensive variations in national character. At the same time, we should not ascribe to Alfarabi a romantic notion of national character as rooted somehow in the "instincts" of a people from time immemorial—and therefore unchangeable. On the contrary, for Alfarabi, national character is not purely natural. It is determined to a great extent by the choices of the legislator who shapes the accidents and states accompanying the moral virtues.

I must digress to consider Alfarabi's claims about national character and its connection to climate in *PR* and *BL*. For the student of political

philosophy, the extent to which Alfarabi links climate and national character is unusual. Only Ibn Khaldun and Montesquieu are similar in the spirit
with which they link these two phenomena. Ibn Khaldun followed the
lead of Alfarabi in the link he established in his *Muqaddimah*.[29] I do not
know, though I doubt, whether Montesquieu was familiar with either of
his predecessors on this theme. Why Alfarabi and Ibn Khaldun devoted so
much attention to this subject is not hard to determine. The more severe
climate is the more influence it is likely to have on national character. Both
Alfarabi and Ibn Khaldun were students of a civilization ranging over some
of the hottest terrain in the world.

Before tracing differences in national character to their climatic origins in *PR,* Alfarabi offers one of his most important statements on the
interrelation of nature, national character, and language.

> The absolutely perfect human societies [*al-jamâ'ah al-insâniyyah al-
> kâmilah 'alâ al-iṭlâq*] are divided into nations. A nation is differentiated
> from another by two natural things—natural make-up [*al-khilaq al-
> ṭabî'iyyah*] and natural character [*al-shîmah al-ṭabî'iyyah*]—and by some-
> thing that is composite (it is conventional but has a basis in natural
> things), which is language—I mean the idiom through which men ex-
> press themselves.[30]

We cannot move forward without first clarifying the possible differences
between "natural make-up" and "natural character." Unfortunately Alfarabi does not articulate clearly the *difference* between "natural make-up"
and "natural character" as he uses them here. Consequently, we may shed
some light on his meaning only by drawing parallels with one of his other
works, the *Book of Letters.* As Najjar's translation of *PR* suggests, "natural
make-up" seems to be more narrowly physical in meaning and "natural
character" more psychological or moral in meaning.[31] Based on similar
passages in *BL,* we may assume that Alfarabi means by "natural make-up"
the makeup of the body, which he argues influences, for example, the lin-
guistic conventions a people is prone to adopt. Certain sounds are easier to
make, depending upon the shape of the mouth, tongue, teeth, and lips
prevalent in a particular nation.[32] In contrast, "natural character" seems to
refer to something akin to Aristotle's "natural virtue," by which he means
the predisposition toward the acquisition of certain virtues.[33] Aristotle
seems to refer more to variations in individuals' predispositions toward
particular virtues; Alfarabi refers by "natural character" to the predispositions of nations.

Leaving aside natural make-up and character, we cannot fail to say something about the meaning of "absolutely perfect human societies." Since Alfarabi divides such societies into nations, it is obvious that he means by "absolutely perfect" what he refers to earlier on the same page as his "large society." In *PR* this society is an association of many nations, which "cooperate" [*yata'âwanûn*] with one another. How big, then, is such a society, and what does he mean by cooperation? Here he identifies such a society as being composed merely of many nations. He does not speak of a society of the inhabited world.[34] It is essential to recognize that Alfarabi never discusses his great or large association of nations without including a central reference to "cooperation"—whether that association is supposed to include many or all nations of the inhabited world.[35] In other words, he never speaks of a "world state" in the modern sense of the term.

At last, we may turn to the causes of the differences between nations in natural make-up and character (*PR,* 40). The chain of causality is the following: different parts of different celestial bodies face different parts of the earth[36] (viz., are subject to different climates). Because of these, different parts of the earth possess different soils and vapors. Because of these, differences in air and water result. Because of these, different plants and different species of irrational animals occur in those different parts of the earth. Because of these, human beings have different diets. After giving this obvious chain of efficient causes, Alfarabi states schematically that the differences in orientation of the celestial bodies cause other differences as well. (Obviously diet is only the most concrete and direct effect of climate.) After this, he goes on to the cause of higher perfections among the human species alone, namely, the Active Intellect. This account of higher perfections includes the development of the faculties of soul and intellect (*PR,* 41), culminating in an account of prophetic revelation based on divine overflow to the intellect of the supreme ruler (*PR,* 49–50). This turn to revelation reminds us of our overarching concern to clarify the interplay between natural intelligibles and voluntary intelligibles. Although climate might lend shape to a nation's natural make-up and natural character, revelation and a ruler's legislation play at least as important a role in shaping the acquired character of a people.

At first glance, however, Alfarabi's account of the origins of those differences between nations, what seem at first strictly voluntary differences, appears quite odd. Initially he could appear to be sanctioning some kind of astral determinism. Nothing could be further from the truth. Throughout his writings, he draws parallels between the natural and the voluntary order. In *VC,* where he discusses the opinions of the inhabitants of the virtuous city,[37] he draws very extensive parallels between the orders of celestial bodies, natural bodies (especially the arrangement of their organs), and political bodies. These parallels form one of the central elements of his theologico-political rhetoric—we should strive in politics for the kind of orderly and harmonious arrangement evident in the organs of an animal. Although the drawing of parallels is largely rhetorical, it fits nicely into a highly Aristotelian cosmological scheme. It is not sufficient to relate national character to climate; climate must also be traced back to its ultimate meteorological and astronomical causes. The influence of the celestial bodies is part of what is ultimately an extremely naturalistic account of the origins of national differences.[38]

At the end of this digression, we have a better sense now for the natural bases of national differences. Although climate might shape the body type prevalent in a given nation, the language it acquires, and possibly even certain predispositions toward certain moral virtues, it does not predetermine the character of a whole people. If it so predetermined matters, then Alfarabi would not devote most of his attention to offering guidance about the qualifications a legislator should possess and the tasks he must undertake. The voluntary aspect of human affairs is the predominant one for Alfarabi. At the same time, and more importantly for us here, because of the rootedness of the voluntary in nature, especially natural predispositions, which Alfarabi argues are *not* uniform, legislators also should not imagine that they can render all nations sufficiently uniform to produce a homogeneous world state—at least not as long as they desire a virtuous regime.

Let us turn back to the task of deliberation. The task of legislative prudence is to grasp the enormous variety of different "states" and "accidents" accompanying the moral virtues among all of the individuals who will be ruled by the legislator's legislation. In my discussion of the influence of climate on national character, I could not help but focus on the effect of differences of place on legislation. As we return to consider the task of legislative prudence, we must widen our view to include temporal differences (which we have seen since the beginning of our reading of *AH,* sec. 24), which pose a formidable challenge to the legislator. Not only do the moral virtues of one nation differ in its accidents and states from those of other nations, but also over the history of each nation these accidents and states are subject to wide variation. (Ibn Khaldun develops this aspect of Alfarabi's teaching even more extensively by developing a cycle of stages of development through which tribes, nations, and civilizations pass.) Again, this adds yet another thing the prudent legislator must take into account if his rule is to be truly virtuous. When one considers that different nations are likely to be passing through different stages of moral development at different times, the challenge to the legislator only increases.

The extent of the legislator's challenge is evident in *AH* 24 and 28. We turn to *AH* 24 first. Having established his distinction between natural and voluntary intelligibles and the extent of variation caused by the accidents and states accompanying voluntary intelligibles (or moral virtues), Alfarabi lists the different time spans within which these accidents vary. Some change from hour to hour, others from day to day, and so on and so on, through months, years, decades, and longer periods (24, 19.8–11). Once again, consciously avoiding reference to the legislator (and the philosopher with whom he will be identified), Alfarabi states, "Whoever should will to bring any of [the intelligibles and their accidents] into actual existence outside the soul" must attend to the "specific period" and the "determined place" in which they will exist (19.12). (Here Alfarabi's penchant for writing schematically offers an additional benefit. It enables him to envision an impossible task in all of its difficulty, without its difficulty being too obvious to the casual and inattentive reader.[39]) As if it were not enough to have to keep an eye on all of this variability, amid it there are also cross-cutting commonalities. Some of these accidents are common to all nations, some to more than one nation, and some to one city, and potentially over different lengths of time in each case. We acknowledge merely in passing Alfarabi's reminder (in brief sec. 25) that these changing accidents are not due solely to the willed events of voluntary agents but also to "natural event(s)" (*wâridah ṭabî'iyyah*), presumably well beyond human control.

If one human being were responsible for exerting control over the variable accidents of moral virtue for all times and places, then the task of deliberation would be impossible. (Once again, in the strict sense, the so-called world state or world regime is shown to be impossible.) The only hope must be for deliberation about all of these details to be divided up among different rulers responsible, at least, for different countries. As early as *AH,* section 28, Alfarabi prepares the way for the delegation of power that comes to full fruition in section 48.[40] He does this by adapting in a quite striking way Aristotle's analysis of prudence at *NE* 1141b20–35. Aristotle distinguishes between prudence of the individual, the household (or economic prudence), and the *polis.* He then subdivides that of the *polis* into legislative as opposed to the properly political (including deliberative and judicial).[41] Of course, in the vast majority of the *NE* Aristotle is concerned with individual moral virtue as it relates to the city, not the virtue of the *polis* proper. In contrast, from the beginning of Alfarabi's discussion of deliberative virtue (24, 19.10), he is concerned first and foremost with Aristotle's political deliberative virtue—especially as it relates to the problem of knowing such a wide variety of accidents and states accompanying the moral virtues. Consequently, when Alfarabi divides deliberation, he leaves personal prudence until the end. He begins instead with the political deliberative virtue and subdivides it into a legislative and an unnamed kind, and then he tacks on a variety of deliberative virtues concerned with smaller groupings within a city, including economic, and military forms (28, 21.10–22.7). Of course, here he diverges from Aristotle in treating deliberation about the household as if it were a subdivision of political deliberative virtue, though he does distinguish between the faculty used in the unnamed kind of political deliberation and the faculty used in economic deliberation. These somewhat tacked-on deliberative virtues can be further subdivided in accordance with the periods of time they cover, long or short (28, 22.8–14). Aside from the political forms of deliberation, he distinguishes between a personal and consultative form of deliberation. The former is excellence in deliberating about one's individual affairs, the latter about the affairs of another.

We are most interested in the higher political forms of deliberation: the legislative and unnamed kinds. I must interpret with greater precision than I previously used. Alfarabi does not speak of a legislative form of deliberative virtue but merely of something "more akin to a legislative ability" (*kânat tilka ashbah an takûnu qudrah 'alâ waḍ' al-nawâmîs*) than the kind of prudence concerned with shorter periods and greater variability. The quasi-legislative kind is concerned "exclusively with the discovery of things that are common to *many nations, to a whole nation, or to a whole city,* and that do not vary except over many decades or over longer periods of determinate length" (28, 21.18–22.3, my emphasis). The unnamed kind of political deliberation is a subordinate form. It concerns shorter periods of time; strangely, however, it covers a wider spatial expanse, not merely what is common to many nations but even "events that affect *all* nations" (22.3–5, my emphasis)! Leaving aside the obvious divergence between the legislative and unnamed deliberative virtue, longer periods and less varied versus shorter periods and more varied, the most striking difference is that Alfarabi only dares to speak of deliberation about all nations when discussing short periods of time. Alfarabi seems to be saying that only matters of short duration affect all nations the same way. At a minimum, the quasi-legislative prudence appears to need far greater supplementation by other forms of prudence than we might have expected, based on the near omniscience required of the person responsible for bringing the voluntary intelligibles, with all of their variable states and accidents, into being. Once again Alfarabi prepares us for the necessity of very extensive delegation of rule. Furthermore, the great variability in the states and accidents accompanying moral virtues implies that variability of character between peoples in different nations is likely to be the greatest impediment to a regime of the inhabited world. We are reminded here of our previous chapter on *jihâd*. According to Alfarabi in *AH, jihâd* needs to compel virtuous character. Yet even more than beliefs or opinions, character varies from one community to the next. Compelling virtue, especially compelling the adoption of foreign forms of character or mores, through war appears doomed to failure.

THE TASK OF THEORETICAL VIRTUE: SHAPING A MULTIPLICITY OF OPINIONS

The legislator's task in shaping a multiplicity of characters in different cities poses major challenges (*AH*, part ii); his task in shaping opinions poses its own challenge (*AH*, part iii). One might expect that in principle everyone in the same city should share the same opinions. According to Alfarabi, matters are not as we might expect. Within each city different members of society will gain access to different levels of insight, and, therefore, not only different opinions but different kinds of opinions or arguments. When one combines this with the fact that each city must have access to religious opinions suited to its own setting, one can see a recipe for profound complications. With the turn to opinion, the role of religion becomes far more prominent.[42] As I mentioned at the end of chapter 3, Mahdi has shown that whether opinion, especially religious opinion or belief, possesses certainty is the opening problem of *AH*. I also mentioned that the distinction between the methods of argument sketched in *AH* (sec. 4) is hastily sketched. Alfarabi withholds a proper discussion of the various methods of argument until the opening of the *Philosophy of Aristotle* (*PA*) (sec. 3, end-16).[43] Consequently, the more explosive implications of Alfarabi's treatment of religious opinion, especially its rank among the methods of argument, are made available to most readers only after they have read the whole trilogy, if then.

AH begins by questioning the perspective of the religious believer. According to the believer, his religious opinions possess "certainty" (*al-yaqîn*).[44] Alfarabi wonders whether those who believe they possess certainty are even aware of the variety in methods of argument (secs. 3 and 4). He quickly identifies, though he does not name, four of the methods of argument that

Aristotle identifies: demonstrative, sophistic, rhetoric, and poetic.[45] After identifying these methods of argument, Alfarabi engages in a long and an often complicated excursus on the sciences (secs. 5–21).[46] Although this discussion grows increasingly relevant to the status of the sciences most relevant to religious opinion, especially metaphysics and politics (secs. 17–21), he studiously avoids clarifying the role of these methods of argument in religion. Indeed, he does not even clarify the possible role that rhetoric (not to mention dialectic) might play in the science of politics. Not until Alfarabi has begun his descent from the sciences and demonstration to the problem of how to realize the four things needed for the attainment of happiness (in part ii) does he allude to the status of religious opinion and the subdemonstrative methods of argument. We ran across this first reference to opinion in chapter 3, when discussing the problem of the unity of the virtues. At the time, we focused on the connection Alfarabi draws between our grasp of opinions of the noble and base and our possession of moral virtues. We were surprised to see that Alfarabi suggested that one could not know a religious community's opinions about the noble and base without possessing its moral virtues. This seemed to imply that the supreme ruler would need to possess the moral virtues of every community he rules over. We return to the assertion that serves as the basis of that argument: "What is most useful and noble is in every case either most noble according to generally accepted opinion [*ajmal fī'l-mashhûr*], most noble according to a particular religion [*ajmal fī millatin*], or truly most noble [*ajmal fī'l-haqîqah*]" (sec. 33). However, one thing is certain. What is most noble according to a particular religion falls short of what is truly most noble. In this respect, this passage merely anticipates the claim that religion imitates philosophy, which we will consider shortly. We suspect but cannot show based on this passage alone that Alfarabi locates the opinions of particular religions *between* the truth and generally accepted opinion. That he has offered these different forms of access to the noble and base in the present order suggests an ascent from the lowest form of access to the highest. Here in part ii Alfarabi is concerned only with opinions that inform moral virtue. He ascribes the adequate grasp of moral virtues as voluntary intelligibles to theoretical virtue (*AH* 34, 26.12). That is the reason opinion is discussed here at all. We must turn to part iii with its treatment of religious opinions, including ones only indirectly related to action, to see the full task of theoretical virtue and to clarify the rank of religious opinions.

Theoretical virtue's task is what we identified in chapter 3 as "instruction" (*ta'alîm*). Alfarabi discusses first the instruction in theoretical sciences when they are taught to the elect, the future rulers of the virtuous regime. At the least, the elect need not ever be exposed to "unexamined common opinion" [*bâdi' al-ra'y al-mushtarak*]. Even the elect, however, must first be instructed in using persuasive (or rhetorical) methods. Furthermore, even the poetical methods of producing "similitudes" (*mathâlât*) or "imagining" (*al-takhkhayîl*) incorporeal, divine things (using corporeal images) should be used at first with the elect. These two methods are the ones to be used with the vulgar at all times. The elect graduate to more demonstrative forms of argumentation (*AH* 40, 30.12–17). Here we receive further evidence that the hierarchy of generally accepted opinion, a particular religion, and the truth can be linked to the hierarchy Alfarabi establishes here between poetic and rhetorical as opposed to demonstrative argument. Perhaps the particular religions of section 33 are composed of a mixture of rhetorical arguments and poetic similitudes and images.

When the various methods of argumentation are referred to next (sec. 44), Alfarabi moves to the first stage of the supreme ruler's or prince's legislation. This stage employs similitudes and images suited to "all nations jointly." This is the moment at which the difference between demonstrative arguments, on the one hand, and poetic and rhetorical arguments seems smallest. Indeed, Alfarabi alludes to this lack of distinction when he says, "[The prince] ought to make these similitudes produce images [*yanbaghi an yaj'ula tilka al-mathâlât mathâlât takhayyul*] of the theoretical things for all nations jointly, so establish the similitudes that persuasive methods can cause them to be accepted, and exert himself throughout to make both the similitudes and the persuasive methods such that all nations and cities may share in them" (44, 33.4–8). Not only is the line between similitudes and images quite hazy here,[47] but also the exact relation between similitude and persuasive methods is less clear than elsewhere. All similitudes could become the same for all nations only if similitudes could be the truth. In a manner of speaking, this could be considered the vision of most religions when they take their religious certainties for the demonstrative truth. Alas, though Alfarabi allows this vision to culminate in a Book of Opinions and a Book of Acts shared by all nations, this shared vision is merely a preliminary stage.

Shortly, Alfarabi begins to anticipate the divisions among nations regarding the kinds of sciences or methods of argument used to convey the sciences (44, 34.7–9). He goes on to acknowledge the differences between nations but mixes this admission with a continued stress on common opinions and actions (45). The stunning extent of multiplicity connected with opinions only begins to emerge toward the end of section 45. Every nation must possess two or more groups of "instructors," those fit to preserve the theoretical sciences (or demonstrative methods) and those fit to preserve the "popular" *(dhâ'i')* or "image-making theoretical sciences" *(al-naẓariyyah al-mukhayyilah)* (45, 35.1). The very notion of "image-making" sciences will come as a surprise to any reader who knows little more than the names of the different methods of argument, alluded to in the opening sections of *AH*. Presumably, different nations have different popular sciences. This unprecedented division of the sciences is merely a prelude to an even more striking multiplication of sciences in the next section.

> If [*fa-idhâ*][48] all of these groups [of instructors] exist in nations, four sciences will emerge. First, the theoretical virtue through which the beings become intelligible with certain demonstration. Next, these same intelligibles acquired by persuasive methods. Subsequently, the science that comprises the similitudes of these intelligibles, accepted by persuasive methods. Finally, the sciences extracted [*muntaza'ah*] from these three sciences for each nation. There will be as many extracted sciences as there are nations, each containing everything by which a particular nation becomes perfect and happy. (sec. 46)[49]

How the sciences suited to each nation are drawn from the three preceding sciences is unclear. Perhaps such extraction is meant to allude to the role of the imagination in formulating "popular theoretical sciences" (section 45). The "sciences" may be the same as the plethora of extracted sciences envisioned in sec. 46. A few things are obvious, however. In accordance with his initial adumbration of the methods of argument, Alfarabi envisions a stunning proliferation of layers and levels of opinion. He multiplies layers of opinion both vertically ([a] certain demonstrations about intelligibles, [b] persuasive arguments about same, [c] similitudes of these intelligibles; [a1] extracted versions of certain demonstrations, [b1] of persuasive arguments, and [c1] of similitudes of intelligibles) and horizontally (for nation 1: a1, b1, c1; for nation 2, a2, b2, c2; for nation 3, a3, b3, c3). The vertical multiplication increases significantly the distinctions he already drew in the shocking section 33: He adds layers of mediation between the demonstrative truth and the lowest kind of opinion we saw earlier ("generally accepted opinion" [*al-mashhûr*] [sec. 33], or perhaps even lower "unexamined common opinion" [*bâdi' al-ra'y al-mushtarak*] [sec. 40]).[50] In section 33, the opinion of the noble and base in a particular religion was the one level of mediation between the truth and this lowest layer. Now he increases the vertical multiplicity of layers of opinion, both through additional layers of mediation and the addition of extracted sciences mirroring these multiple layers. Of course, the horizontal multiplication of extracted "sciences" or opinions introduces a diversity of opinion that grows dramatically with every increase in the number of nations for which the supreme ruler is responsible. Although Alfarabi does not identify similitudes or extracted sciences as religion here (part iii), the definition of religion he develops later (part iv, 55, 40.9–12) confirms my inference that this discussion of extracted sciences is actually an elaboration of the particular religions (alluded to in sec. 33).[51] The implied proliferation of "sciences" or opinions or religions here is dizzying. Within two sections, Alfarabi elaborates upon the necessity for extensive "delegation" of the responsibility for instruction (in the plethora of opinions discussed earlier) and character formation to groups in each nation. One supreme ruler cannot legislate the same opinions and program of habituation for every people everywhere.

RELIGION AS AN IMITATION OF PHILOSOPHY

The claim that religion is an imitation of philosophy is so bold that Alfarabi is unwilling to assume full responsibility for it. As I said earlier, he credits his predecessors, "the ancients," with this idea. Of course, there is a precedent for this claim in Plato, though he never renders it into a principle as Alfarabi does. Plato's characters merely employ tacitly the principle Alfarabi articulates. Articulating a shocking, tacit principle of another author is far more shocking than employing such a principle tacitly. Yet ascribing the principle to that other author can take away some from the initial shock. According to Alfarabi, religion uses corporeal imagery to imitate incorporeal principles.[52] In Plato's *Timaeus*, political offices are used to imitate incorporeal principles, political actions to imitate incorporeal actions, and human faculties of will are used to imitate "natural powers and principles" (55, 41.2–4).[53] (By the way, this characterization of religion describes quite aptly the kinds of persuasive arguments and images regarding the divine that Alfarabi himself provides in the openings of *VC* and *PR*.)

Alfarabi's claim about religion's imitative character offends our modern sensibilities. His claim presupposes the principle that different audiences are capable of different levels of insight. The popular mind has difficulty rising above corporeal imagery. Because we have been educated in the egalitarian spirit of the Enlightenment, we find Alfarabi's reliance on this principle appalling. Of course, this reaction is only natural considering the circumstances. Yet our emotional reaction leads us to oversimplify his point. We tend to oversimplify as follows. If religion is an imitation of philosophy, then religion is a lie. Most people must be made to accept this lie as a sop or an opiate. As I alluded to in the introduction to this chapter, we jump to the conclusion that Alfarabi is using religion in much the same way as those who despise religion. Marx argued that his predecessors used religion as a tool to make the downtrodden more compliant with their own oppressors. Their oppressors knew the truth of human affairs, which is that those who possess the means of production also come to possess the product of (and profits from) the workers' labor. They used religion to cow the laborers into accepting the predations of their bosses. Of course, Marx sought to dispense with the lie of religion once and for all. How could Alfarabi be so dull as to use a line of argument that only someone who despises religion could use?

Alfarabi is neither so sanguine about his knowledge of the whole nor so disdainful of religion as an imitation of philosophy, as is Marx. The latter was so sanguine about his knowledge of the whole because he eliminated all incorporeal principles. If the whole is nothing but bodies in motion, then modern science should at least in principle come to possess absolute knowledge of the universe. In contrast, Alfarabi follows the lead of Aristotle in searching for both corporeal and incorporeal principles, especially final causes. In his *Philosophy of Aristotle* (the third part of the trilogy), Aristotle is shown repeatedly attempting to establish whether each part of the whole, including its smallest parts or elements, possesses its own end, and more problematically, whether all ends are linked in a hierarchy.[54] This is part of the problem of "exploitation" we considered in chapter 3 and will attempt to resolve in the next chapter. If human beings fail to know the final cause of the whole, then how can they order any of the subordinate purposes? In brief, Alfarabi is far less sanguine about human knowledge of the whole than, for example, Marx.

In chapter 3, I considered some of the effects of Alfarabi's reservations about human knowledge of the whole. There I inferred that at least that lack of knowledge should dampen hopes for a virtuous regime of the inhabited world. Without such knowledge, how could the philosopher-ruler know how to "exploit" all beings properly? Here I would like to focus on a more positive result of these tempered hopes for knowledge of the whole, namely, the inherent multiplicity of religions. If human beings possessed comprehensive knowledge of the whole, then there should be one scientific philosophy (to use a late modern phrase) or one religion adequate for the entire world. If, however, we lack such knowledge, then we lack a firm footing when we attempt to repudiate various religions as obviously false. This should not be taken to imply the validation of any and every religion, however. As we will see, Alfarabi argues that some imitations of the truth are, in fact, closer to it than others. He is not an advocate of contemporary forms of easygoing relativism. Permit me to digress briefly before clarifying this crucial point and concluding this chapter.

It is essential that the reader not confuse Alfarabi's reservations about human knowledge of the whole with modern and especially late modern disavowals of interest in such knowledge. Beginning with philosophers such as Machiavelli, Bacon, Descartes, Hobbes, and Spinoza, a concerted effort was made to overcome the tendency toward theologico-political conflict in Christendom by skirting the issue altogether. All of these philosophers repudiated the search for first or formal or final causes. These causes either were God or were too closely linked to God to be acceptable objects of attention. Consequently, these philosophers limited themselves to a narrow range of causes, material and proximate efficient causes, whose usefulness in fostering the human mastery of nature has been unprecedented.[55] Eventually, late modern thinkers such as Kant codified the avoidance of formal and final causes by shunting them off to a noumenal realm to which human beings lack objective, scientific access.[56] Alfarabi's attitude toward theoretical philosophy is altogether different. He does not renounce interest in formal and final causes. As we will see in the next chapter, he acknowledges limits in our knowledge of the interrelation of all final causes. He does not deny their existence altogether (as does Spinoza, for example). He does not identify all such knowledge (or formal and final causes) as being inaccessible to human beings in principle (as does Kant). To be more precise, Alfarabi does not repudiate the very existence of natural and voluntary intelligibles[57] merely because human beings lack adequate knowledge of the ultimate final cause and the ways in which final causes of various species might be related to one another. For our purposes, "voluntary intelligibles" are the more pressing concern. He supports the claim that moral virtues are voluntary intelligibles when he writes a work such as his *Selected Aphorisms,* which contains extended discussions of the moral virtues in a spirit highly akin, if not identical, to Aristotle's *NE*.[58] Yet as we saw in the previous chapter, even Mahdi has raised some doubts in his revised introduction to the *Philosophy of Plato and Aristotle* (*PPA*) about whether Alfarabi acknowledges the ability of political science (as he conceives of it, as a part of theoretical philosophy) to achieve political insight without comprehensive theoretical knowledge. Once again I believe that we must distinguish the reservations Alfarabi has about the possibility of a theoretical science (including political science) that could lay the ground for the exploitation of all beings from any reservations he might have about any other, lesser tasks he might assign philosophy, especially political philosophy. Perhaps political philosophy is possible without comprehensive knowledge of the whole, though it must be far less ambitious, especially about realization of its plans, than it would be with such knowledge.

For the moment, we still need to clarify why there should be a multiplicity of virtuous religions and how those religions, rather than just any religion, can be identified as virtuous. I will not repeat the citations of Plato showing that for him originals (such as the truth or the idea) are one and imitations of them are inherently multiple.[59] Alfarabi has already appealed to a similar principle in *AH,* when he argued that intelligibles are one in species but not in number (23, 17.11–24, 18.8).[60] The individuals who are members of a species would be one if it were not for the accidents that distinguish each from the other. Something similar may be said about religions. If they were the complete and comprehensive or absolute philosophic truth, then they would be one. But especially because of our limited access to philosophic truth, religions must only approach the truth. As imitations of the truth, they can only approximate to it. In approximating to it, each must be characterized by the accidents peculiar to its own place and time.

Here we may also have stumbled across one of the secrets of the persistence of religion even in the face of modern efforts to minimize its relevance. As long as human beings lack access to the truth, we will persist in adhering to imitations and anticipations of that truth. This is made necessary both by the demands of everyday life and the continued appearance of ambitious human beings. The latter believe their imitations of the truth to be the truth itself. Indeed, love of honor and spiritedness lead the most ambitious to embrace an account of the whole that supports their sacrifices, even without the extensive inquiry of the philosopher.[61]

Now that we have an appreciation for why Alfarabi views religion as inherently multiple, we may turn to the basis for distinguishing good religions from bad. Immediately after announcing that religion is an imitation of philosophy, and Plato's *Timaeus* exemplifies this principle, Alfarabi goes on to discuss not the theoretical truths or opinions imitated in religion but the more basic and practical question of imitating happiness (*AH* 55, 41.7 ff.). He begins by admitting the necessity of imitating true happiness (as found in the philosophic way of life) with things popularly believed to be happiness. Alfarabi could be referring to the philosophic penchant to characterize the best life as if it were the most intensely pleasurable life.[62] He also seems, however, to be alluding to the religious legislator's need to promote the ways of life closest to true happiness, namely, the life of an honor-loving, if a nonphilosophic, ruler. Honor-loving rulers are popularly believed to be the happiest of men. Of course, Alfarabi has tried to show that the way of life closest to the possession of the truth, philosophy, is the best way of life.[63] Subsequently, he argues that religion attempts to bring its similitudes "as close as possible to their [true] essences" (55, 41.11). The closer to the truth a similitude or an imitation is, the better it is. The best religions are those that promote the best way of life, not only by protecting and promoting the philosopher but also by cultivating and promoting those ways of life that approximate most closely to it. That there are few religions existing in the world that promote philosophy does not undermine Alfarabi's argument, for he adds a corollary to the principle that religion imitates philosophy, namely, "philosophy is prior to religion in time" (55, 41.13).[64] This jarring claim makes perfect sense when properly understood. True religion, or philosophically informed religion, is preceded by philosophy in time. Only such a religion will imitate philosophy well. Certainly many a base religion has preceded philosophy in time.

In conclusion, I believe that the depth and extent of attention Alfarabi devotes to the differences between nations and religions are quite striking and likely unprecedented in the history of early medieval philosophy. When set against this strong emphasis in his thought, I think that we should not interpret his few references to the things that "all or most" nations share (cited in the introduction to this chapter) as evidence that he advocates one religion for the entire inhabited world. Rather, writing in what had rapidly become a predominantly monotheistic world, Alfarabi acknowledges some commonality especially in the beliefs, if not the actions, held to be virtuous by most people in the world. Yet as the world became more homogeneous in its devotion to one God, its disagreements about the proper understanding of that God only increased.[65] (If Alfarabi is correct about the present factual limits on human knowledge, then we should not be surprised by this increase in disagreements, in spite of the hopes for agreement monotheism nurtures.) In the face of monotheism's mounting expectations of consensus, Alfarabi persists courageously in showing why a homogeneous virtuous regime of the inhabited world is a self-contradiction. Such homogeneity is incompatible with virtue. Differences of place and time, climate, national character, and language justify Alfarabi's championing of religious multiplicity.

Six

The Limits of Knowledge and the Problem of Realization

Muhsin Mahdi's felicitous translation of the *Attainment of Happiness* (as well as his revised introduction) has served as our greatest aid in understanding *AH* throughout. If I take issue with the translation of a key word here, then, I do so only because of the myriad of other things his translation has enabled me to see. Of course, in the title, *Taḥṣīl al-saʿâdah*, Mahdi renders *taḥṣīl* as "attainment." Yet on many occasions he renders it as "realization."[1] Of course, both meanings are within the range of denotations of the Arabic word. Mahdi stresses that he has not stuck to a rigid literalism in his translation, because the text does not lend itself to one. And he acknowledges that all translations engage to some extent in interpretation.[2] He cannot possibly be faulted for a "mistaken" translation. Indeed, I do not intend to fault his choice of the word "realization" so much as the interpretation underlying it. Even more than in his introductions to and translation of *PPA*, Mahdi has dwelt at some length on Alfarabi's focus on "realization" in his authoritative interpretation of Alfarabi in *AFIPP*.[3]

I question the choice of "realization," because I doubt Alfarabi's intention to realize the regime of the inhabited world described in *AH*. I believe it is more accurate to think of *AH*, like the *Republic*, as a standard and cautionary tale. The difficulty with "realization" is that it has too much of the air of "reality" or concreteness about it. Comparison with Mahdi's choice to use "attainment" or a cognate word in other instances will clarify my reservation. For example, consider the opening sentence of *AH*: "The human things through which nations and cities attain earthly happiness in this life and supreme happiness in the life beyond are of four kinds." It is readily

apparent why Mahdi chooses "attain" here rather than "realize." The suggestion that supreme happiness in the life beyond is capable of "realization" would strike any reader as perverse. Since time immemorial, that life
beyond has been contrasted with this "reality." The choice of "attain" here
as in the "attainment" of the title suggests an important connotation to
taḥṣîl at least as it is used in some passages in *AH:* attainment is more
something we aim toward than a reality we expect to realize here and now.[4]

As we saw at the end of chapters 3 and 5, the realization or attainment
of the virtuous regime of the inhabited world would entail the "exploitation" (*isti'mâl*)[5] of untold numbers of beings, both human and nonhuman.
Such exploitation would require comprehensive knowledge of the whole.
According to Alfarabi, such knowledge eludes humankind. We need to explore and clarify here the connection between the limits of human knowledge and the problem of exploitation or, more broadly, of realization of the
virtuous regime of the inhabited world.

I have already mentioned an important area of human ignorance or
uncertainty, our lack of knowledge about the extent and interrelation of
various final causes. The other significant area of ignorance concerns particulars, especially future particulars. Islam as a monotheistic faith attributes knowledge of every particular to God, who can reveal them miraculously in turn to His Prophet. In contrast, Aristotle, in part because of his
reliance on reason alone, limits human knowledge of particulars to the ex-
trapolations or guesses of prudence. Alfarabi's account as a philosophic one
seeks to make sense of the conflict between the certainty of revelation and
the uncertainty of philosophy. Although Alfarabi does not refer explicitly
to the problem of universals and particulars in *AH,* it is a crucial source of
the divergence between philosophy and revelation regarding certainty,
which he does refer to explicitly.

Knowledge and Exploitation

To begin with, I will clarify the connection between knowledge of final
causes and the exploitation of human and nonhuman beings. Then we will
inquire into the details of Alfarabi's views on and arguments about the limits of our knowledge of final causes. At the same time, we will consider
whether Alfarabi's views are similar to or different from those of other philosophers, especially Aristotle.

So far I have devoted little attention to part i of *AH.* It is here that the
themes of certainty of knowledge and exploitation of beings first appear.

The initial impression this part leaves the reader with is that the certain knowledge needed for the virtuous regime is within human grasp. Indeed, *AH* as a whole seems to give such an impression. I remind the reader of this although this part highlights the lack of certainty attaching to some methods of argument, it barely begins to explain what those different methods are. Without an adequate understanding of these different methods, it is difficult to assess the degree of certainty that we should attach to Alfarabi's inferences about the virtuous regime. By now in our inquiry, it seems evident that there is less certainty than first appears. I also remind the reader that those methods are clarified only in the third part of the trilogy, the *Philosophy of Aristotle* (*PA*). In contrast to *AH*, *PA* is far less sanguine about the extent of human knowledge. Seen against this background, part i of *AH* will appear less confident about human knowledge than it did upon the first reading.

Attainment of Happiness

After a brief allusion to some of the various methods of argument and an account of the relation between what is first for us (the principles of instruction) and what is first by nature (the principles of being), Alfarabi takes an inventory of the sciences. He begins with mathematics (sec. 10), the science characterized by the greatest certainty (because in it what is first for us is the same as what is first by nature).[6] Then he ascends to physics (sec. 13). Already a divergence between what is first for us and first by nature gives rise to limitations in our knowledge of and certainty about physics.[7] In a rush to ascend to the divine, Alfarabi turns to the heavenly bodies and an inquiry into metaphysics or beings beyond nature (sec. 16). Without explanation, but presumably because the inquiry is premature, he descends immediately to consider beings with souls or, at least, animals (sec. 17).[8] Almost immediately, he turns to rational animals or human beings as beings guided by metaphysical principles. His treatment of living things, like his hasty ascent to the heavenly bodies, is in the spirit of *AH*'s concern with supreme happiness beyond this life. The metaphysical principles "never were or ever will be in bodies" (17, 13.8). In the rational soul, the closest thing to such a principle is reason or intellect. Whether it can or cannot be said to "be in bodies" is unclear. One thing is clear, however: human beings need more than natural principles to achieve their perfection. Whether that perfection is achieved through the separation of intellect from the body or through our voluntary intelligibles is not settled here. Be that as it may, Alfarabi turns to voluntary intelligibles in the next section (18), though without identifying them as such. Instead he gives an account of human or political science far more extensive and clear than anything he has said so far about heavenly bodies or metaphysical beings. Here he launches the program of exploitation (*isti'mâl*). Rather than discuss immediately the necessity that the wise ruler should exploit other human beings (since the need for such a ruler has not yet been felt), he speaks vaguely of man's need to exploit "a large number of natural beings." He adds that human individuals are not self-sufficient and require other human beings or are naturally political. Before following out the theme of exploitation in *AH*, I must sketch briefly the conclusion of part i. Abruptly, Alfarabi turns to begin (anew) the inquiry into metaphysical beings. This inquiry leads to the first principle, which transcends all categories.[9] His account is extremely brief and sketchy. Above all, Alfarabi speaks here only of what human beings should come to know, never of what they do know about these topics.[10] And it is followed immediately by a recapitulation of the task of political science. The primary addition to this recapitulation is the enlistment of the metaphysical realm in support of political order. Throughout part i, Alfarabi has manifest the kind of haste in the search for the divine so evident in the pretheoretical certainty that he describes in the opening of *AH*. Such haste and excessive certainty lend themselves to abuse. Preestablished metaphysics in hand, human beings are prone to set out on a journey of exploitation of other beings.[11] The cost will become evident only as we proceed to consider the exploitation of human beings. Most shocking of all, Alfarabi gives little or no evidence that human beings possess adequate knowledge (of final or any other causes) to exploit other beings appropriately.

In part ii of *AH*, Alfarabi shifts his focus on exploitation from man's exploitation of (other) natural beings to the exploitation of the virtues (31, 24.18) and arts (32, 26.2) of other human beings. With a slowly growing awareness that the one thing needful is a prince or ruler with a stunning array of virtues and kinds of knowledge, part ii touches on the matter of exploitation quite obliquely. Although sections 24 and 25 raise hopes about a regime, including the inhabited earth, part ii hardly draws the connection between the array of virtues and the task of exploitation at hand.

Part iii, without naming the philosopher-king, announces Plato as a guide and his educational plans in the *Republic* as the inspiration for the formation of an immensely complex educational and governmental hierarchy (sec. 40). Here the connection between knowledge and a hierarchy of exploitation becomes more obvious.[12] The end of part iii is the end of the main argument envisioning the virtuous regime.[13] Here Alfarabi returns explicitly to the theme of exploitation. "Delegation" (*tafwîḍ*) is the mechanism by which a higher level of the hierarchy is enabled to "exploit" its subordinates (cf. 48, 35.18 with 48, 36.9).

Only after the argument about how to realize or attain supreme happiness has come to an end, at the end of part iii, can the relation between knowledge and exploitation be made fully explicit. After all, only in part iv is Alfarabi willing to broach explicitly the theme of the philosopher-king. And the philosopher-king embodies, above all, the problematic relation between knowledge and exploitation. In section 54, the decisive feature of the "defective philosopher" is not that he succeeds in but that he fails to "exploit" his knowledge! The true philosopher possesses both the theoretical sciences and the faculty for exploiting that knowledge. (Here we leave aside the problems surrounding the unification of the virtues, especially theoretical knowledge with political acumen, considered in chapter 3.) Lest we confuse Alfarabi's (or Islam's hopes for the) exploitation of all human beings (in God's cause) with a debased late modern vision of exploitation, it must be underlined that the exploitation of "theoretical matters [is] for the benefit of all others" (54, 39.14). The reader may ask himself or herself whether this differs from exploitation in a modern setting. It must.[14] At the same time, exploitation of knowledge for the benefit of others is one thing and exploitation of human beings, even if for the sake of others or the common good is quite another. Not until the last reference to "exploitation" in *AH*, section 57, does Alfarabi state the meaning of philosopher-kingship or his own intention in discussing this clearly.

> Only when all other arts, virtues, and activities seek to realize his purpose [*gharaḍ*] and no other [!], will his art be the most powerful. . . . For with all of these powers he will be exploiting the powers of others so as to accomplish his own purpose. This is not possible without the theoretical sciences . . . and the rest of those things that are in the philosopher.

Of course, the philosopher's purpose is the common good. There is no question of domination of others solely for one's private good here. Yet, or at least so it appears, the common good can be fully realized, that is, every human being can be properly exploited for the common good, only if the philosopher's knowledge of theoretical science is adequate.[15] How can we know what the common good is unless we first know the final cause of the cosmos within which human beings appear? For is it not the philosophers who declare that the highest manifestation of the common good is knowledge of the whole, including, above all, the relation of the causes of the parts to the cause of the whole? And if that theoretical knowledge eludes us, then how can we orient the city toward its good? The philosopher's "purpose" for the city requires knowledge of the final cause of the cosmos, that is, God.

The *Philosophy of Aristotle:* The Limits of Our Knowledge of Final Causes

These questions, with which *AH* concludes, reappear toward the beginning of the *Philosophy of Aristotle* (3, 67.13–69.7).[16] Alfarabi's Aristotle is far less sanguine about achieving knowledge of the highest things than is either Aristotle as he has come to be interpreted in the Christian tradition or Alfarabi's persona in the *Attainment of Happiness.*[17] The most obvious indicator of these lowered expectations is the closing remark of *PA,* denying human possession of metaphysical science (99, 133.1–2). Of course, here we are more interested in the contrast between Alfarabi's Aristotle and his own persona. The reader needs to take seriously the possibility that Alfarabi might allow his Aristotle to be more aware of the limits of human knowledge than he appears to be himself, because these limits cast a pall over the political aspirations of *AH.* Alfarabi might consider it unwise to sound too pessimistic in *AH.* After all, *AH* is "written in his own name" and is likely to be interpreted by the reader as more in the spirit of Islam than *PA.* Medieval authors, however, often express their own views more freely in their commentaries than in texts written in their own name.[18] Furthermore, Alfarabi's ordering of the trilogy raises doubts that he views *AH* as his own last word. If *AH* were the last word, then why not place it last? Perhaps, then, the lowered hopes and expectations of *PA* may reflect more honestly not only Aristotle's but also Alfarabi's own views.[19]

Final causes play a central role in the traditional sanguine portrait of Aristotle's philosophy. Before considering Alfarabi's reservations about this sanguine view, we would be well served to consider briefly that view itself.

Aristotle offers perhaps his most sanguine portrait of teleology, as well as of human knowledge of that teleology, in *Politics* 1.8 (1256b15–23).[20] According to this account, plants exist for the sake of animals, and animals exist for the sake of human beings. Aristotle acknowledges, only to pass over quickly, the challenge posed by the existence of wild animals. He argues that most, if not all, exist for man—for food, clothing, and so on.

He concludes by affirming one of his most famous dicta. Since, or rather if, nature makes nothing in vain or without a purpose, then it has made all of this for man. This passage more than any other would seem to buoy our hopes for the success of what Alfarabi calls the "exploitation" of natural beings.[21] This account resonates most loudly with two related views, the views of the revealed religions and those of the political actor. The revealed religions stress the centrality of human being within the broader scheme of creation.[22] Both Genesis (1:27–32) and the Qur'an (2:30–34, 95:4) are quite clear that human beings are the crown of creation.[23] Of course, both Scriptures also take great pains to remind human beings that they are merely creatures whose purpose is to serve God.[24] I believe that Alfarabi's inquiry into "exploitation" is intended as a grand reflection on the ambition on the part of the revealed religions in general and Islam in particular to exploit all beings with an eye to the perfection of human life. We will return later to this prevailing revealed view.

Let us return to Aristotle. His claim in *Politics* 1.8, that everything else exists for man's sake, is precisely the kind of view one might expect from an ambitious political actor.[25] It is only proper that the *Politics* should echo, at least at times and to some extent, the views of political actors more than those of philosophers. Yet Aristotle seeks to temper this view elsewhere as a philosopher and in a spirit akin to the revealed religions—but by very different means. Of course, he does not demand humility before the Creator, nor even before a pantheon of gods. He argues that human beings are not the highest beings in the cosmos, nor is politics the greatest human activity. The heavenly bodies, or the underlying order for which they stand, are far higher than human beings, and contemplation of them is the highest human activity.[26] Now human inferiority to the gods, for Aristotle, is not necessarily incompatible with the idea that human beings are the peak of the animals, or even that all plants and animals exist for man's sake.[27] Yet it gives one pause. Perhaps Aristotle is not expressing his own ultimate view about the interrelation of ends in the *Politics*. Is the higher purpose of all other parts of nature the benefit of human beings? Of course, political actors view the world as "their" world. The question is whether Aristotle believes it and has good arguments for it.

With the aforementioned issues in mind, we turn to the reservations about human knowledge of final causes in Alfarabi's *PA*. Although the extensive material on the need to know the purpose of the whole to know the purpose of man is well worth reading more closely, here I quote merely the most telling passages.

> [Aristotle] explained that the proper human activity becomes known only after one knows the purpose [*gharad*]28 for which man is given a place in the world as a part thereof and as that by which the totality of the world is perfected. . . . It is also impossible to know [man's] purpose without knowing the purpose of the whole of which it is a part, and his place within the whole and among all the parts of the whole. . . . For the purpose of every part of a sum is either a part of the total purpose of the whole, or else useful and necessary for realizing the purpose of the whole.29
>
> Thus if man is a part of the world, and if we wish to understand his purpose and activity and use and place, first we have to know the purpose of the whole world so that we may see clearly what the purpose of man is, and also that man has to be a part of the world because his purpose is necessary for realizing [*an yahsûla*] the ultimate purpose [*al-gharad al-aqsâ*] of the whole world. (3, 68.8–69.2; Mahdi, p. 67)

Two features of this passage are most striking. First, in the second sentence, Alfarabi does not settle on whether there is an ultimate purpose or a totality of purposes. For if a part has a purpose that is part of the purpose of the whole, then it does not exist merely for the sake of something else. In other words, being a part does not mean necessarily that a part is merely a means to the whole. Second, in the second paragraph, he stresses the necessity of knowing the purpose of the whole (the cosmos) before one can know the purpose of the parts. One wonders how necessary it would be to know the purpose of the whole if the whole proved to be a looser totality or affiliation rather than a rigid hierarchy in which each part serves its superior.30 More obviously, the necessity of knowing whole before part places enormous weight on first knowing the highest cause. But because we do not have immediate experience of the highest incorporeal causes, these principles of being are far from first for us. Even before beginning, the project almost seems doomed to failure.

Alfarabi's first occasion for extending the aforementioned comments on final causes is in the midst of his first account of the first science proper, natural science or physics. In section 22, he explains that motion, the theme of the *Physics,* itself indicates the purposiveness of all things. All bodily beings move with a purpose. This will lead to one of Aristotle's most problematic claims, namely, that everything, even the elements, has a purpose. This leads to the notion, especially strange to us in our modern world of inertial motion, that bodies have a natural place. Yet Alfarabi adds an important clarification. "Everything that is a bodily substance is either for a purpose and an end, or is a concomitant of, and adheres to a thing that is for a certain purpose [*gharad*] and end [*ghâyah*]" (22, 92.21). In ad-

vance, Alfarabi opens up an important option. Even if many or most com-
posite beings have purposes, does this mean that even the constituents of
bodies must also have purposes?

At the end of his discussion of the *Physics,* Alfarabi turns to *On the Heavens.* There he surveys all of the parts of the cosmos, dividing them into five,
the substance of the heavenly bodies and the four sublunar elements (sec.
38). He quickly turns away from *On the Heavens'* grandest of views to the
humbler view from Earth, as captured in *On Generation and Corruption*
(secs. 39–53).[31] Near the end of the discussion of the four elements in *On
Generation and Corruption,* Alfarabi returns to the theme of final causes (sec.
52). The heavenly bodies are singled out as agent principles (or motive or efficient causes) of the motions of the sublunar elements (sec. 49), but Alfarabi
omits any answer to the question of the final causality active in or acting
upon the elements. In characteristically Alfarabian style, he limits his remarks to the claim that Aristotle "investigated" (*faḥaṣa*) final causality here.

After *On Generation and Corruption,* Alfarabi turns to Aristotle's *Meteorology* still on the theme of the four elements (secs. 54–66). He punctu-
ates a shift from his discussion of books 1–3 to book 4 of that work with another stab at whether the four elements manifest final causality (sec. 63).
Contemporary scholars view Aristotle's answer as clear and decisive. Not
only are the elements constituents in animate beings, but they also possess
their own purpose. Indeed, early modern attacks on Aristotle's supposed
claim to demonstrate that each element has its natural place have only re-
inforced the idea that he was convinced of the truth of such claims.[32] In
contrast, Alfarabi continues the lack of decisiveness we saw in section 52.
Again, Aristotle merely "investigated" (*faḥaṣa*), albeit in an increasingly
complex fashion, whether the elements possess their own final causes or are
merely constituents, or both.

Before turning to animate beings, Alfarabi touches one more time on
the theme of final causality in his next Aristotelian text, *On Minerals* (secs.
67–68). Here he discusses the mixed bodies composed of a mixture of elements, such as rock formations. I add to what he states explicitly. It is by
no means apparent what final cause might be served by most rock formations. Even more so, and like many wild animals, it would be even more
difficult to say how such formations might exist for the sake of human
purpose.[33] Consequently, in this final discussion of final causes among inanimate beings, he reiterates explicitly perhaps his most troubling claim
about ends. Aristotle cannot achieve resolution in his various "investiga-
tions" into final causes so far, "since it is not easy to give an account of
the ends unless one knows beforehand the end of the totality of the world,

he postponed the inquiry into their ends to the science in which he would investigate the ultimate principles of the world" (viz., metaphysics [68, III.11–13]). Again, we already know what his final pronouncement will be on metaphysics.

Once he turns to animate beings, Alfarabi turns almost immediately to one of the analogues that served as the inspiration of the search for purposes in the cosmos, namely, the relation between an organism and its organs.[34] The whole/part relationship depends on some form of final causality, if only within the living individual. Unfortunately, such final causality has little or no bearing on the broader question of whether some natural beings exist for the sake of others. Beginning with the pseudo-Aristotelian *On Plants* (secs. 69–71), Alfarabi's Aristotle does not merely "investigate" final causes in plants but "he proceeded to state (*shar'a fī an yudhkaru*) the end for the sake of which each organ of every species of plant is generated" (sec. 70). He reasserts this same point in connection with animals in the *Parts of Animals* (secs. 72–74, esp. 74, 113.5–20). And he adds more explicitly that not only are various organs for the sake of the whole animal, but the body (as matter) exists for the sake of the soul (as form) (viz., the soul is the final cause of the body). Yet again we remain within the confines of the individual rather than concern ourselves with the relations between various beings, either within the same species or across species. Of course, the latter is our real concern—about which Alfarabi is shockingly silent.

Having broached the topic of the soul in his discussion of *Parts of Animals,* Alfarabi turns to *On the Soul* (secs. 75–78, 117.12) for a far more penetrating and problematic discussion of the soul. *On the Soul* soon proves to be *the* pivotal text for Alfarabi's discussion of Aristotle.[35] Alfarabi repeats his discussion of the relation between body and soul, but here he generalizes it into a discussion of the relation between the natural and the psychic. Broadly speaking, Aristotle divides the cosmos into the natural (*al-ṭabī'iyyah*), psychic (*al-nafsāniyyah*), and intellectual (*al-'aqliyyah*) powers (90, 122.15–20). Each of these in turn serves as potency for the higher genera of being. Thus here, during the first discussion of soul, nature in the narrow sense of physical nature is the potency for the soul (psyche or *nafs*) as form or actuality (76, 115.13–16).[36] Even before announcing this, Alfarabi prefaces it with a discussion of "ruling (*ra'īsah*) nature(s)" and "subservient (*khādimah*) nature(s)" (76, 115.3–8). Of course, body is, in some sense, subservient to soul within an individual being. Does this mean, however, that merely natural or inanimate beings are subservient to psychic or animate beings? In other words, the broad division that emerges gradually within

Aristotle between nature, soul, and intellect suggests or implies a hierarchy *within* each intellectual being, such as human beings. Yet does this same division also necessarily entail a hierarchy among beings in which animate beings "exploit" inanimate beings, because the latter exist for the former's sake? In the remaining paragraphs of section 76 (115.16–116.14), Alfarabi goes on to discuss the various capacities of the soul (such as nutrition) in general terms, highlighting the hierarchy among them. The questions just asked only grow more insistent. Do such hierarchies within individual beings imply, then, the existence of such a hierarchy among different beings? Alfarabi's conclusion is stunning and, to my knowledge, unique among medieval Aristotelian commentators.

> Then he investigated whether the species of bodies that have become nourishments are at the outset made by nature for the nourishment of animals and plants; or whether such bodies are generated for their own sake as parts of the world, but as they become suitable for the nourishment of animals and plants they are used as nourishment merely because they happen to be suitable, or whether it is not by chance that these things are nourishments for animals and plants; or whether their generation for their own sake or as a part of the world is such that their perfection and purpose consists in their being for the sake of the things nourished by them. He investigated closely; for this investigation of these things is similar to the preceding investigation of whether the elements are for their own sake or for the generation of other bodies.
>
> At first he made an imperfect investigation here of these things. For it was denied him to go beyond this in the study of the world. Hence he abandoned them and proceeded to other things. (78, 117.1–12)

From this point he turns to a discussion of texts concerned with illness and death, in a word, the problem of mortality, and then on to even more marginal issues, such as divination and understanding the souls of animals or beings without intellects (78 [117.13]–88). It is little wonder that the theme of immortality should play such an odd, yet a prominent role in Aristotle's *On the Soul*.[37] Uncertainty about the purpose of the things before us in this earthly life must be dwarfed by the kinds of uncertainty human beings are prone to about our supreme end. An inadequate answer to the question of whether we are warranted in exploiting other beings is likely to make the politically ambitious wonder about the justice and honor their great actions will elicit from the divine. As if to confirm the conclusion of section 68, section 78 drives home the same essential point: without an adequate grasp of the end of the whole cosmos, it is extremely difficult to say that

human beings are justified in "exploiting" other beings, even inanimate beings, not to mention human beings.

Should the reader expect Alfarabi's Aristotle to resolve the problems
surrounding final causes and exploitation in later discussions (for example,
of beings that possess intellect in addition to soul and body), then he or she
will be disappointed. After his brief turn to mortality, Alfarabi returns to
On the Soul (sec. 89, or 90–99, 130.24). Alfarabi's Aristotle has little difficulty establishing that in the individual nature serves soul, and soul serves
intellect (secs. 90–94). The intellect shows its superiority to the soul by its
focus not only on things that are useful for existence (practical intellect)
but also things that are not useful for anything else (theoretical intellect)
(91).[38] At last, the relation between what rules and what is subservient
within the individual can come to an end. Because theoretical intellect[39] is
not useful for anything else, it must be the ruling power in man or "the
substance of man" (secs. 93–94). At least in section 93, it is unclear whether
this substance is not achievable for man here in earthly life.

Yet when Alfarabi turns to the relation between human being and other
beings, with the additional powers of intellect in mind (sec. 95 ff.), he acknowledges that this is a mere continuation of his earlier discussions of the
relations between the final causes of various beings (cf. 96, 126.21–127.3).
And he states, rather vaguely, the results of his investigation: "When he investigated these matters, however, what he was looking for became clear to
him only in part; he encountered a difficulty with respect to the rest (*wa-
ʿusr ʿalayhi baʿḍahu*) because he had not yet pursued another investigation."
What, if anything, about the interconnection of final causes became clear is
not stated. Perhaps we will gain some insight by considering the subsequent
or "another investigation" he pursued, at least in part, to answer these questions. Much as he followed his previous discussion of *On the Soul* with an
inquiry into mortality, here Alfarabi turns to that most problematic section
of *On the Soul,* 3.4–6, on immortality. We do not have the space to cover
this section of Alfarabi's argument (97–99, 130.24) in any detail. The usual
players are involved, potential and Active Intellect, practical and theoretical
intellect, the human intellect in act, and even the heavenly bodies—though
he seems at pains to avoid the complex proliferation of souls and intellects
for each heavenly body.[40] The Active Intellect is called upon to resolve the
problem—where does theoretical intellect acquire its objects, since it does
not from its subordinate power, practical intellect? The forms or species, if
not the forms as "in" individual beings, seem to require some "place" of res-
idence (99, 130.1–8). Unfortunately, because *On the Soul* is supposed to approach the soul from within "natural theory" (*al-naẓar al-ṭabīʿī*),[41] that is,

study it as it exists *in* matter or the body, these inquiries into the Active Intellect stray beyond the proper confines of natural science (99, 130.11–23).
Alfarabi properly accuses Aristotle of straying beyond his own mandate in
On the Soul in those most problematic chapters. The very fact of having so
strayed should have given others in the medieval tradition greater pause.[42]
Be that as it may, it appears that we may not view this "other" investigation
as having solved the remaining problem. As Alfarabi suggests, Aristotle has
argued persuasively for a hierarchy within the powers of the individual soul
(99, 130.18–24), but evidently he remains unable to resolve the conundrum
of the relation between the ends of various beings. At a roadblock in his inquiry into the theoretical intellect, he turns back to practical intellect as it
is treated not in natural philosophy but in ethics (99, 131.1–23). Rather
than resolving our conundrum, political or human science merely ascends
to the same problem without adequate resolution. Of course, "we do not
possess" (*idh lam yakun ma'anâ*) the science that could resolve all such co-
nundrums, metaphysics.

In conclusion, the implications of the *Philosophy of Aristotle* for the *Attainment of Happiness* can hardly be underestimated. Our lack of adequate
knowledge of the interrelation of the final causes[43] flows inevitably from
the inadequacy of our knowledge of the highest cause. Yet without adequate knowledge of the interrelation of final causes, how can we justify the
exploitation of one kind of being by another? Of course, the opening part
of *AH* leaves us with the impression that we possess adequate knowledge of
the whole. For without such knowledge, how could one justly exploit one
part of humanity with an eye to establishing a virtuous regime of the inhabited world? Even an adequate grasp of political or human science cannot justify such a universal scheme, because it presupposes comprehensive
knowledge. We must be careful to avoid falling into an unlimited form of
skepticism. At a minimum, political philosophy is up to the task of recog-
nizing the limits of human knowledge. It is fully capable of warning us of
the dangers of presupposing greater knowledge than we possess. Without
such knowledge, Alfarabi could not have composed such an impressive
standard and cautionary tale as *AH*.

CERTAINTY AND THE KNOWLEDGE OF UNIVERSALS AND PARTICULARS

Another limitation of human knowledge is apparent from the opening pages
of the *Philosophy of Aristotle* with significant implications for "exploitation."

This is the limitation in the extent of our certainty about the highest things. In contrast, the *Attainment of Happiness* reflects a pretheoretical confidence in the degree of certainty attaching to our beliefs, and it mentions different methods of inquiry without ever explaining what the different methods might be.[44] The *Philosophy of Aristotle* follows out the subtle challenge posed by *AH* to outline the methods Aristotle employs (3–15, 70.15–85.19). When Alfarabi displays these methods, he is challenging the views of those who conflate all methods.[45] Whereas those who conflate all methods ascribe the same kind of certainty to everything they believe, an essential purpose of sorting these methods is to identify which methods, if any, offer certainty. To highlight how crucial the clarification of these methods is, Alfarabi speaks, at least twice, as if demonstrative method were the or an essential part of "certain science" (*al-ʿilm al-yaqîn*) rather than a mere propadeutic or method employed in science (cf. 15, 84.6 and 13, 78.15[46] with 3, 70.15–20). Alfarabi's discussion of logic, including the arts falling short of demonstration, does nothing so well as to highlight how stunningly high Aristotle's standard of science is (in clear contrast to the pretheoretical understanding of what is certain). In Alfarabi's account of the *Posterior Analytics* (secs. 7–12), he alludes to the interesting paradox often noted but almost equally often misunderstood about Aristotle's view of demonstration. Demonstration with true certainty (or "simple" or "unqualified," *haplos,* demonstration) is possible only in the study of things about which universal, necessary, and eternal propositions can be made (cf. 7, 75.17–25 with *Post. Anal.* 75b23–27). Yet the vast majority of Aristotle's theoretical works about (earthly) nature are filled with propositions about what is true only "for the most part." The last, best hope for true demonstrative certainty would seem to be theoretical works about things "above the sphere of the moon," as the medievals often put it. Of course, the ultimate conclusion of the *Philosophy of Aristotle* is that these theoretical works, or at least the *Metaphysics,* fall short of demonstrative science. These limitations of the theoretical sciences no doubt contributed to Alfarabi's conviction that political science or political philosophy may offer a superior frame for philosophy as a whole than metaphysics. No matter what we may conclude about the degree of certainty achievable by political science, it remains obvious that Alfarabi frames his entire philosophy within political philosophy.[47]

Initially in the *Philosophy of Aristotle,* Alfarabi appears quite hopeful about the kind of certainty the practical sciences can provide.[48] He claims that once one has achieved "certainty" (*al-yaqîn*) in one's practical inquiries, one has achieved "the perfect science" (*al-kamâl fî ʿilm*), and "he can hope for no better assurance [*al-thiqah*] or reliability [*al-sukûn*]" (3, 62.20–24). I, like other authors, have considered this a promising declaration about the kind of certainty attainable in practical science, until I began to see this statement more clearly in its context. Most importantly, this passage appears both before Alfarabi has differentiated the various methods of argument (beginning at the earliest at 3, 70.15) and especially before he has identified the kinds of propositions that can be certain (7, 75.17–23). Practical science does not employ propositions that are universal, necessary, and eternal. At least this version of practical science cannot achieve certainty.[49] Furthermore, it appears in the midst of what can be deemed at best a preliminary discussion of science that began in the opening of *PA*. Its preliminary character must give us pause in assessing the definitiveness of this claim for the certainty of practical science.

I must sketch briefly the preliminary character of the context in which the claim about practical science occurs. Alfarabi opens *PA* by identifying four things "that everyone pursues from the outset," soundness of (1) the human body and of (2) the senses, (3) the capacity for knowing what leads to the soundness of the former two, and (4) the sound power to labor toward the first two (1, 59.8–15). Rapidly, Alfarabi's Aristotle acknowledges our desire for knowledge beyond these four useful things and even divides the sciences into the useful (practical) and the useless (theoretical) sciences. And he notices that all people somehow recognize the superiority of the latter kind of knowledge over the former (sec. 2).[50] Finally, Alfarabi identifies cognitions in addition to those from sense experience that are innate and by nature (sec. 3). It is at this point that he identifies practical science as the "perfect science." Yet almost immediately thereafter (3, 63.11 ff.) he raises doubts about this assessment. It is one thing to show vaguely that useful things are engaged in for the sake of useless things; it is quite another to establish with certainty the ultimate ends of these useless inquiries. In other words, this preliminary form of political science does not resolve the problem of ends. I will not add anything to our already extensive discussion of final causes here, except to note that Alfarabi goes on to wonder whether this search for knowledge beyond the useful is the result of "overreaching, . . . an intemperate appetite, and an infirmity attached to him by nature" (3, 65.13–16 and 66.12–14). If this proved true, then it would be tempting to jump to the conclusion that practical science is adequate without theoretical science. Perhaps there is some truth to this.[51] Yet Alfarabi's Aristotle does not cease his inquiry because of these gnawing doubts; rather, he turns undaunted to develop the tools for and to pursue unrelentingly the theoretical sciences.

Plato and Aristotle seem to be in agreement that despite the risks posed by (theoretical) philosophy, it must be pursued. Indeed, Alfarabi's

Plato establishes an intimate connection between the *mania* of philosophy, prophecy, and politics (*Philosophy of Plato,* sec. 25). He seems to imply thereby that one cannot possess an adequate understanding of human life, even political life, without seeing it against the background of (to speak un-Platonically, theoretical) philosophy. The pursuit of certain knowledge about the highest things, even if it can never be achieved, is itself an essential phenomenon for political philosophy to understand, as this book (especially in chapters 3, 5, and 6) has sought to illustrate.

Be that as it may, we may say with confidence that the rudimentary practical science deemed certain in *PA* is unlikely to measure up to Aristotle's standard of certainty. Yet a political science with a wider and deeper grasp of the human pursuit of knowledge of the divine can, at least, deepen itself into political philosophy.[52] Such a science truly rises to the level of being "human science" or "human wisdom," even if it fails to be demonstrative or certain.[53]

Alfarabi's persistent shattering of our hopes for certainty is not intended to destroy our love of wisdom. When combined with a deeper awareness of the methods of science, it is meant to chasten our political ambitions far more than our theoretical ones. Leaving aside theoretical science's search for ends and political science's hopes for certainty, there is one thing Alfarabi, like Aristotle, seeks to rule out as a possible object of certainty, namely, our grasp of future particulars. For these *falâsifa,* the notion that certainty could attach to propositions concerning universals, but not particulars, is fundamental. It provides the groundwork for an all-important distinction, the distinction between a prudent grasp of particulars and scientific knowledge of universals. Because of Aristotle's conception of certainty, no prudent political actor should ever suppose that certainty could attach to his or her forecasts of events. This has become such a commonplace for us that we fail to appreciate the deep implications of this claim.[54] We need only attempt to reconstruct the pretheoretical view that certainty attaches equally to all of one's beliefs to understand these implications better. In pretheoretical settings, the politically prudent often possess unchecked, even apparently divinely sanctioned, authority.[55] After all, their insights, or lack thereof, seem to make the difference between life and death. The distinction between knowledge of universals and particulars has implications beyond the distinction between science and prudence.

There is another important implication of this distinction for the relation between philosophic and revealed views of God—that implication underlies the philosophic penchant to deny God access to particulars, and the revealed assertion that God does have such access. Despite Alfarabi's heavy reliance on the quasimystical imagery of Neoplatonism, his God is the First Cause, not a mystical "good beyond being."[56] True, the First Cause, in a sense, transcends the categories by failing to belong to a species.[57] Yet Aristotle himself never insinuates that discursive, as opposed to intuitive, knowledge of the divine is possible.[58] Alfarabi also acknowledges such limits to our discursive powers.[59] Nevertheless, he seems to be as confident as Aristotle that the First Cause is the cause of substance, not of privation. He causes what we can know, not the accidents that elude knowledge altogether.[60] Such a being is unaware of privation, accidents, and evil. Truly a cause only of good, this being does not grasp those particulars of human life subject to the whims of mere fortune.[61] If this God knows anything other than Himself, He knows only the universals, not the particulars.[62] In keeping with the relative rank of prudence and science, Aristotle views prudence as being beneath the dignity of his God.

In contrast, revelation is quite adamant about God's knowledge of particulars. Indeed, His knowledge of them is often singled out as an indication of the superiority of the revealed God to the God of the philosophers. After all, if He did not, then it would appear that He is inferior to human beings who can, in some sense, know particulars—even if not scientifically. Yet Aristotle might counter that we possess knowledge of particulars because we live in a realm of coming into being and passing away (or generation and corruption). Although the changeable character of this world is an indelible aspect of it, this also dictates that our knowledge of this world not be limited to its unchanging underpinning but should include its variable aspects. As we saw in *AH,* deliberative virtue grasps states and accidents that accompany the essence of things. Those states and accidents are dependent upon or inhere in the substances that theoretical virtue seeks to know. Once again, from Aristotle's viewpoint, theoretical virtue's focus upon the necessary, universal, and eternal (or what is for the most part) is superior to deliberative virtue's focus on accidents.

Yet rare is the human being who does not put greater store in the prudence of great rulers than the theoretical insight of the philosopher. Alfarabi has captured beautifully the contrast between the austere realm of universals and the more livable one of particulars in his *Book of Religion* (*BR*). This book is, bar none, Alfarabi's most schematic work.[63] Ironically, the opening theme about its object, religion, is the fact that religion is "determination" (*qaddar*). While philosophy offers the universals of theoretical science and practical science, some other power facilitates the determination of those particulars. As Mahdi has shown, Alfarabi gives different answers in his various works as to what makes determination possible, prudence or imagination. However that may be, Alfarabi exemplifies the determined or particularized character of religion in the first half of his *Political Regime* and *Virtuous City*. Against the backdrop of *BR*, one can see why works such as *VC* and *PR* have received greater attention.[64] They offer worlds in which one can reside. The austerity of *BR* offers a barely livable setting. As we know all too well from Alfarabi's claim that religion is an imitation of philosophy, religion's reliance upon images makes it a more hospitable medium for most.

Not only is religion more appealing, but its readiness to render concrete that which is merely universal in philosophy reflects the view of religion that the divine must concern itself with particulars. After all, if the divine does not concern itself with particulars, then how can we be confident of the rectification of injustice? In contrast, if God knows particulars, then we are compelled to confront the notorious challenges of divine foreknowledge and its relation to divine omnipotence. Can an omnipotent God possess an infinite foreknowledge of all events without His power playing a role in shaping, even determining, those events?

In spite of his lack of direct contact with the revealed tradition, Aristotle offers a response to revelation's notion that particularity is what counts. Human beings find prudence so impressive because, caught in our web of particulars, accidents, privation, and evil, we long for an escape from the vagaries of fortune. At first glance, nothing would seem to insulate human beings so fully from misfortune as prudence. And it is precisely the great political actor's ability to extricate us from the threat of misfortune that leaves us so enamored with political power. According to Aristotle, however, there is something that does a superior job of insulating us from misfortune, namely, moral virtue.[65] We recall from our discussion of moral and deliberative virtue in chapters 3 and 5 that despite deliberative virtue's being an intellectual virtue and moral virtue being a virtue of the appetites, that is, despite the expected inferiority of moral virtue, it is ultimately superior to deliberative virtue. Moral virtue fixes the ends; deliberative merely selects the means. The ends are, of course, superior to the means. Moral virtue enables the actor to endure misfortune, even more than prudence. It is not flexible prudence but rigid moral virtue that offers the best armor against misfortune. At the same time, it must never be forgotten that, according to Aristotle, what he means by prudence cannot be had without moral virtue, and vice versa. Yet the real issue is whether *someone else's* prudence, that is, the prudence of the ruler, is our best shield from misfortune. Aristotle seems to answer "no."[66] As long as we remember this, we are less likely to succumb to the illusion that great political actors, or the most powerful, lead the best life.

In brief, then, Alfarabi acknowledges significant limits on human knowledge of God and the interrelation of final causes. Nevertheless, he does not declare all such knowledge permanently off limits to human beings as, for example, Kant does. Alfarabi also challenges the pretheoretical assumption that certainty attaches to our most cherished metaphysical claims. Political philosophy, even if it lacks the kind of certainty metaphysics would require to call itself science, offers a more secure basis for the sciences than the typical metaphysical basis. Alfarabi also seems to suggest, however, that the limits on our knowledge only become more overawing as we ascribe knowledge of future particulars to God. Whether ascribing such knowledge to God is not in fact demeaning to God, as Aristotle seems to suggest, or the *sine qua non* of transcendence, as revelation seems to suggest, cannot be settled here. Yet as long as human beings lack knowledge of future particulars, it is difficult to see how we could have great success in achieving the ambition of establishing a virtuous regime of the inhabited world.

THE LIMITS OF KNOWLEDGE AND THE INHERENT MULTIPLICITY OF RELIGION

The limits of human knowledge are at the root of Alfarabi's claim that there can be a multiplicity of virtuous religions (*PR,* Hyderabad ed., 56). Leaving aside the diversity of national or natural characters among the nations, that is, even if, contrary to chapter 5, human character were highly homogeneous, the inadequacy of our knowledge would make the imposition of one religion on all of humanity a great injustice. No philosopher-king exists whose knowledge of final causes or prudent grasp of particulars could match the variety of human experience. Once again, we receive further confirmation that the *Attainment of Happiness* is not an ideal but at best a standard and, perhaps above all, a cautionary tale. In chapters 3 and 5, I have shown that the plan for the attainment or realization of happiness hatched in parts i–iii of *AH* rests upon the account of the sciences in part i. In this chapter, I have shown that part i of *AH* merely *appears* to ground the formation of a virtuous regime of the inhabited world necessary for the attainment of happiness. Above all, *AH* speaks frequently of the "exploitation" of other human beings and other species of beings. Yet without knowledge of the ends of the whole, a philosopher-king, in spite of his many virtues, could not be guaranteed to "exploit" others with an eye to their own highest possible good. Furthermore, part i's outline of the sciences fails to offer an adequate account of the various methods of argument in the sciences. Without such an account, we cannot judge whether Alfarabi's own arguments in *AH* offer certainty or mere surmise. In *AH*, we receive mere hints of the impediments to the achievement of certainty. Not until *PA* does Alfarabi make the reader fully aware of the near impossibility of attaining certainty about the highest objects of theoretical virtue, not to mention practical science.

Admirable though the ambition to bring virtue to the whole globe is, surely it presupposes that human beings are capable of far more than we really are, at least when left to our own devices. Of course, revelation does not rely on human ability alone. The *Philosophy of Plato and Aristotle* envisions what it would take for human beings to achieve the ambition of Islam and the other revealed faiths. Perhaps we should not be surprised at the less-than-stellar results. Yet Alfarabi's inquiry is surely useful, even for those believers who presuppose divine aid. Such believers must believe not only that the Prophet received divine aid in the form of Scripture, they must also believe that such aid is ready at hand today. The Shi'ah appreciate the full challenge of the appearance of a miraculously supported human ruler on Earth. One wonders whether Sunni Muslims have not become complacent in the conviction of the medieval jurists, that there need be nothing miraculous about a ruler for him to be able to achieve a virtuous regime of the inhabited world.[67]

At a minimum, one need not even be a Muslim to admire Islam's ambition to spread virtue throughout the Earth. Of course, some in the West will object that virtue does not exist. It is merely a subjective value dressed up in the premodern clothing of *the* truth. Perhaps this book will have given such readers pause. No doubt some of them will embrace Alfarabi's apparent advocacy of a multiplicity of religions but reject his recourse to virtue. Yet those who view virtues as merely subjective values are not likely to take religion nearly as seriously as did Alfarabi. In doing so, they embrace an illusion, the illusion that religion, like virtue, is merely a passing fetish. Constant technical progress seems to offer science as a substitute for premodern and pretheoretical hopes for certainty. Religion was supposed to go the way of the dinosaurs. Yet the two regimes that have most fully embodied anti-religious, especially anti-monotheistic, forces, communism and fascism, have gone the way of the dinosaurs. Whether they will remain extinct, knowing human nature, is by no means guaranteed. But their demise gives hope to those who continue to believe that virtue and religion can, neigh, must, play a positive role in human affairs.

Yet even if non-Muslims share the ambition of achieving a virtuous world, they need not accept Muslim means, especially not the means of the traditional jurists. For this reason, Alfarabi could be of value to both Muslim and non-Muslim alike in thinking through how virtue is to be spread.

Notes

CHAPTER 1

1. See Alfarabi, *Political Regime* (*PR*), Hyderabad edition, 56.

2. For a brief version of his biography, the reader should see the preface to Charles E. Butterworth's *Alfarabi: The Political Writings: "Selected Aphorisms" and Other Texts* (Ithaca, N.Y.: Cornell University Press, 2001), ix–x. As Butterworth indicates, this brief sketch is based on Muhsin Mahdi's more detailed accounts in "Al-Fârâbî," in *Dictionary of Scientific Biography*, vol. 4, ed. C. C. Gillispie, 523–26 (New York: Charles Scribner, 1971) and "Al-Fârâbî's Imperfect State," *Journal of the American Oriental Society* 110:4 (1990): 712–13.

3. Most notably, Leo Strauss, Muhsin Mahdi, and Charles E. Butterworth for Alfarabi and Leo Strauss, Stanley Rosen, and Charles Griswold for Plato.

4. See Joshua Parens, *Metaphysics as Rhetoric* (Albany: State University of New York Press, 1995), introduction, sec. 2. A translation of parts of the *Summary* already exists in Ralph Lerner and Muhsin Mahdi, eds., *Medieval Political Philosophy* (Ithaca, N.Y.: Cornell University Press, 1972), and a translation of the whole is forthcoming in the Cornell series, *Alfarabi: Political Writings*, edited by Charles Butterworth.

5. In chapter 4 I discuss the roots of these views. What I claim here about homogeneity is implied in Abdulazziz Sachedina's admission, discussed in chapter 4, that early Muslim jurists sought to justify the early expansionism of Islam by sanctioning offensive *jihâd*, that is, the duty of Muslims to spread Islam by the sword.

6. See Plato, *Symposium* 212c4–223d, and *Republic* 491b–e, 494b–e, 496b–c. Cf. Thucydides *Peloponnesian War*.

7. For an exception, consider my later discussion of Alfarabi's dialectical presentation in *AH* sec. 31 of an argument about the unity of the virtues (chapter 3, Tension in the "Unity of the Virtues").

8. I do not mean to suggest that the schematic character of the *Book of Religion* necessarily plays exactly the same role there as it does in *AH*. In fact, *PR* and *VC* are in their own ways examples of what a filling in of the details of *BR* might look like. Still, the comparison of *PR* and *VC* is left to the reader. See my review of Muhsin Mahdi's *Alfarabi and the Foundation of Islamic Political Philosophy* (*AFIPP*) (Chicago: University of Chicago Press, 2001) in the *American Political Science Review* 96:2 (2002): 410–11.

9. For a justification of this claim, see the beginning of chapter 4.

10. I am not the first to make this argument. Readers who are already convinced of the impossibility of the virtuous city in the *Republic* could skim chapter 2, though I appeal to arguments made there in the rest of the book, especially chapters 3 and 5.

11. This key premise is never stated explicitly. For the reasons it is suppressed, review the beginning of this chapter. As I will seek to show in the body of this work, this premise can be inferred from what Alfarabi does say, however.

12. I do not assume the reader's knowledge of the *Republic* and *NE*, or of what I call a "proper understanding." I have sought to strike a balance between assuming scholars' understanding of the relevant texts and the need to inform a wider public about the meaning of Alfarabi as well as Plato and Aristotle.

CHAPTER 2

1. See Paul Kraus and Richard Walzer, eds., *Plato Arabus*, vol. 1, *Galeni compendium Timaei Platonis allorumque dialogorum synopsis quae extant fragmenta* (London: Warburg Institute, 1951). Also see Alfarabi's *Philosophy of Plato* in *PPA* for some evidence of what dialogues he seems to have had greater and less access to. It has often been suggested that some of his accounts of dialogues are whimsical (especially in comparison with his more straightforward discussion of Aristotelian texts in the *Philosophy of Aristotle*). It may be more reasonable to suppose that Alfarabi chose to take liberties with the originals he knew. See Strauss, *What Is Political Philosophy?* (New York: Free Press of Glencoe, 1959; reprint Chicago: University of Chicago Press, 1988), 154. Finally, for the discussion of his background and likely access to texts, see Parens, *Metaphysics as Rhetoric,* introduction, sec. 3.

2. See Averroes, *Averroes on Plato's "Republic,"* translated by Ralph Lerner (Ithaca, N.Y.: Cornell University Press, 1974) and Hebrew ed. in *Averroes' Commentary on Plato's "Republic,"* edited by E. I. J. Rosenthal (Cambridge: Cambridge University Press, 1960).

3. Consider, for example, the addition of eloquence as a qualification.

4. For Alfarabi's direct treatments of philosophic qualifications for rule, see *AH,* Mahdi ed., sec. 60, and *VC,* Walzer, ed., ch. 15, esp. sec. 12 ff. To begin to trace the extensive influence of Alfarabi's adaptation of Socrates' list of philosophic virtues even beyond the Islamic tradition, see Abraham Melemed, *Philosopher-King in Medieval and Renaissance Jewish Political Thought,* edited by Lenn E. Goodman (Albany: State University of New York Press, 2003).

5. Alfarabi's procedure should be compared with Plato's effort to portray Socrates as the new Achilles in the *Apology* (28b4 ff.) and the new Odysseus in the *Republic* (620c). Of course, Socrates transcends the virtues of both Homeric characters—but as such, he is in a sense the new embodiment of them.

6. Although Descartes uses the phrase "sand and mud" to describe the foundations of the "magnificent palaces" erected by the ancients, Machiavelli condemns the "republics" of the ancients more directly as merely "imagined." Cf. Descartes, *Discourse on the Method,* pt. 1, with Machiavelli, *The Prince,* ch. 15.

7. His devotion is evident both from the brilliance with which he subverts the old teaching—the greatest warriors know their formidable opponents better than anyone else—and his famous letter to Francesco Vettori of December 10, 1513. See Vettori's letter in Harvey Mansfield, trans., *The Prince* (Chicago: University of Chicago Press, 1985), appendix.

8. For the seeds of idealism, even within Locke and Spinoza, see Locke's discussion of archetypes in moral knowledge in the *Essay Concerning Human Understanding* 4.4.5–8 and Spinoza, *Ethics,* part 4, preface. For an insightful contrast between the modern effort to escape the cycles of nature accepted by thinkers such as Plato, Aristotle, and Alfarabi, see Mahdi, *AFIPP,* ch. 11.

9. Consider, for example, Rousseau's praise of Sparta, if not Plato's *Republic,* in the First Discourse, the *Discourse on the Sciences and Arts.*

10. Immanuel Kant, *Critique of Judgment,* sect. 59, "On Beauty as the Symbol of Morality."

11. Consider Kant's late political writings, including "An Answer to the Question: What Is Enlightenment?," "On the Proverb: That May Be True in Theory, but Is of No Practical Use," and "To Perpetual Peace: A Philosophical Sketch."

12. See Harvey C. Mansfield Jr., *Taming the Prince: Ambivalence in the Modern Executive* (New York: Free Press, 1989), introduction.

13. At the same time, ancient thinkers appear less realistic than modern realists, because they advocate the cultivation of virtue. But virtue is, to a great extent, reason's effort to constrain desire. Rather than limit desire, modern thinkers sought ever-changing objects and horizons for it, as well as a state with far greater force with which to constrain it (in extreme cases) than the ancient city.

14. Their suggestion is based on a report from Xenophon's *Memorabilia* 3.6.

15. For evidence supporting this reading internal to the dialogue consider, in addition to the extensive discussions of tyranny in bks. 1, 8, and 9 (and to some extent the end of bk. 10) in general, the direct allusion to the tyranny of the Thirty Tyrants, in particular at 564d–565d. Glaucon's proclivity toward tyranny is evident, for example, in his susceptibility to Thrasymachus's praise of tyranny, to which Glaucon alludes at 358c–d. At the very same moment, one sees his desire for justice, however. Glaucon is emblematic of the tension between desires that draw us toward injustice and the service of our own private good in the lowest sense, and those that draw us toward justice and the service of the common good.

16. That it was in fact not intended as merely offhand but intentionally buried by Socrates is evident upon a closer examination of the material surrounding this comment in bk. 4. Immediately prior to it in 423e, Socrates discusses the need to stick with the education discussed in bks. 2–3, and immediately following it in 424b4 ff., Socrates reiterates the same claim, as if he were given to repeating himself. The consummate artist, Plato could not allow his model of precision and insight, Socrates, to repeat himself meaninglessly.

17. For an indication of his awareness of this anger, consider his characterization of being made to discuss the sharing as a form of arrest (450a4–451b6). This playful talk of arrest and trial should be compared with the mock arrest in the opening page of the dialogue

as a whole. Both should be compared with Socrates' actual trial and execution in *Apology* and *Phaedo*. For Socrates' awareness that he might be misleading others about the truth, see especially 450d4–451a4. This passage alone should have given Popper greater pause.

18. Socrates does not announce the metaphor of the three waves until he ends the first and begins the second (457c).

19. At the end of bk. 6, when Socrates engages in his most extended discussion of the good, he offers an image in which the true, the good, and the beautiful tend to become merged with one another (508e–509c). This image, along with the statement that the good is beyond being (509b8), has come to be viewed as the precursor of all of Neoplatonism. I believe that full attention to the context of this image (beginning in 504a3) suggests that it must be viewed as an image, and an image especially well suited to a committed lover of the beautiful, Glaucon. For evidence that Socrates puts greater store in the good, consider *Symposium* 204d4–205a4. The difficulty with the beautiful is that it seems to promise immortality and endless pleasure, which may transcend the merely human. The good, though humbler, is somehow "truer."

20. To gain an appreciation for the ambiguities inherent in identifying something as beautiful in the *Republic,* consider the recurrent motif of the beautiful painting, sculpture, or statue as an emblem of the city and to a lesser extent the soul. See 361d4, 420c4 ff., 472d3, and 540c.

21. Despite their reputation for excess due to their rotund shape and where they find their food, pigs have no difficulty "knowing" when to stop eating. Grazing animals, such as horses, are notorious for not knowing when to stop eating. Indeed, horses can eat themselves to death when eating oats. I do not view this as a significant piece of contradictory evidence. As grazing animals, horses are "programmed" to eat constantly, because to acquire enough nutrition from their natural food, grass, they must eat constantly. Death by eating among horses is the result of human intervention through domestication.

22. Regarding male cruelty, I believe that I am fleshing out points that Socrates implies in his treatment of the guardians as well-born puppies who run the risk of becoming wolves (cf. 375a–376c with 416a–c and 565d5–566a4), something I will discuss in chapter 3. Aristotle makes the same basic point about human desire, when the proper cultivation of reason is lacking. See *NE* 1150a1–8.

23. Of course, what one understands by the "useful" depends upon whether one grasps what things should be used for. When Socrates employs the term in the best sense, one can be confident he aims at the good. One cannot be so confident that Glaucon has the proper good in mind.

24. Middle voice of *hepô*.

25. Socrates furthers this humorous critique of applying mathematical rationality to human affairs later, for example, when he argues that *kallipolis* decays into timocracy because it fails to follow the so-called nuptial number (546a–547a), and when he argues that the just king leads a life that is 729 times as pleasurable as the life of a tyrant (587d–588a). Although Socrates never develops a sense of rationality that is not only nonmathematical but also nontheoretical, like Aristotle's *phronesis* (prudence), he obviously alludes to the need for something like it here. Of course, he never argues that mathematics plays anything more than a propaedeutic role in his account of philosophic education in *Rep.* 7. Cf. the

Eleatics Stranger's exploration of the various senses of rationality, especially about politics, in Plato, *Statesman* 283c–285c, 303e5–305e.

26. How can one know who one's siblings and parents are (or who was born or gave birth at what time) once the family has been destroyed, unless guardians are somehow branded?

27. On the one hand, once the family has been destroyed among the guardians, there is little rationale for incest prohibitions. Prohibited sexual relations develop in human societies precisely to control the human proclivity toward sexual excess. That proclivity is intensified by constant close proximity. Without the family, the occasion for the excess is removed. See Maimonides, *Guide of the Perplexed*, III 49, 115b. On the other hand, among the guardians, everyone is part of one large family. Consequently, all relations are, then, in a way sanctioned incest. And every time guardians are thrown together repeatedly with the same people, the intensity of "erotic necessity" is likely to be inflamed even more than in a traditional society, because no sexual relationship is prohibited in principle.

28. This in itself is a departure from the objective of producing guardians who come to view the common good as their own. It is yet another concession due to the tension between private and common good.

29. For example, Averroes criticizes what he takes to be Plato's implied denigration of non-Greeks, and he praises Aristotle's putatively favorable view of endeavors such as Muhammad's mission to the Red and the Black, that is, his aspiration to world empire. See Averroes, *Averroes on Plato's "Republic,"* 46.20–23, and Lerner's note referring to the spurious "Letter of Aristotle to Alexander." It should be underlined that despite Averroes's apparently favorable view of world empire, he seems to embrace Alfarabi's requirement that such a regime be composed of virtuous parts, which reflects the natural diversity of peoples (46.18–20). In effect, Averroes seems likely to have accepted at least the argument of chapter 5, if not chapter 3, of this book. On whether Averroes deems *kallipolis* possible, see his suggestion that even without the appalling exile or murder of everyone over the age of ten (541a), it would be possible as the result of a continuous succession of virtuous kings until "the end of time" (which presumably for Averroes means eternity)—a dubious defense of possibility.

30. For a bit of Platonic argumentation against world rule, see the discussion of the origin and nature of the human desire to rule the world at *Laws* 687c (in Parens, *Metaphysics as Rhetoric*, 65–66).

31. A similarly small part of the *AH* is devoted to war, indeed, small enough so that some manuscripts contain variant readings that nearly eliminate the discussion of war.

32. See the discussion of the relative prominence of war and foreign policy in Plato's *Laws* as opposed to his *Republic* and in modern as opposed to ancient political philosophy (Parens, *Metaphysics as Rhetoric*, ch. 6).

33. There are no significant subsequent discussions of war.

34. The cultivation of deference toward philosophy abounds in the writings of Plato and Aristotle. For example, Socrates cultivates such deference in Glaucon in the *Republic* by arguing that only a philosopher could be the kind of ruler he should want to be. Aristotle cultivates such deference through his frequent appeals to the superiority of the theoretical life, even in works such as *NE*, where he does so little to explain that life directly.

Indeed, Aristotle facilitates philosophy's influence over politics in large part by stressing—and perhaps even overstating—its purely theoretical character. As purely theoretical, it appears less of a threat to the politically ambitious.

35. I lack the space to illustrate in detail Glaucon's hovering between pursuit of just and unjust rule. Yet the most obvious evidence for this is a passage near the opening of bk. 2, to which I have referred the reader repeatedly (358b–362d, esp. 361d5). It displays *both* his passionate demand for a defense of the goodness of justice, without any appeal to consequences, *and* his ability to paint the potentially pleasurable consequences of injustice.

36. On the desire to avoid politics, see 500b5–c5. I will discuss the strange wages that Socrates promises philosophers in chapter 3. Yet even here it should be obvious that the most natural wage of politics, to the extent any wage for it exists, is honor. If one rises to the level of engaging in politics only for itself, not its wages, then one has come to recognize that it itself or virtue itself is its highest wage. Cf. *NE* 1095b23–32.

37. For further evidence that Glaucon lacks philosophic potential, consider his preference for the short road [mere opinion] rather than the long road [the laborious philosophic search for knowledge] to a proper understanding of the soul (cf. 435c–e, 504b [Adeimantus] and 506b–d [Adeimantus] with 535c).

38. *Rep.* 525b ff., for example, 527c–e.

39. My discussion of two oppositions, philosopher as ruler (Socrates) versus honor-lover as ruler (Glaucon) here and ruler versus ruled, as discussed heretofore, runs the risk of appearing contradictory. Previously, when I have used ruler versus ruled, that is, in my discussions of the first and second waves, I have meant philosopher-guardian or golden class versus auxiliary guardian or silver class. (In a sense, the lowest class, the farmers and craftsmen, is left to its own devices, except insofar as its members are prevented from straying into matters of rule. That is, in a sense, the lowest class is not ruled.) Furthermore, I was treating the older guardians as the rulers of the younger guardians (in keeping with *Rep.* 412c). The claim to rule of the older guardians is, of course, that they have been properly exposed to philosophy when mature (539b). In contrast, the younger guardians are ruled because they have not yet graduated from the love of honor.

In my present discussion of the third wave, we are confronted by an honor-lover, Glaucon, who does not seem capable of graduating to the philosophic class, with longings for rule. In other words, he seeks to become a ruler while in fact being suited to nothing more than being ruled. Although Glaucon can imagine himself as ruler and does not mind the suffering of the ruled, if he were to live in *kallipolis,* he would himself be, at best, a member of the ruled class, suffering at the hands of his indifferent rulers!

40. For mere hints of his indifference, see *Apology* 41d and *Phaedo* 60a. For an obvious self-portrait displaying Socrates' indifference more fully, see his account of the aristocratic soul that engenders a timocratic one (*Rep.* 549c3–e).

41. Cf. *Rep.* 494c with 496b–c. Glaucon and even more so Alcibiades exemplify his concern for those who are most vulnerable. Contrary to modern expectations, the beautiful and well heeled, not the poor and ugly (like Socrates), are the most vulnerable to their corrupt family and city's flattery.

CHAPTER 3

1. See Socrates' strongest explicit doubts about the possibility of *kallipolis* at the end of bk. 9 (592a–b). The last lines indicate that Glaucon does not fully accept the impossibility of the city, even when Socrates is willing to acknowledge it.

2. For more on this, see the beginning of chapter 4.

3. See Joel L. Kraemer, "The *Jihâd* of the *Falâsifa,*" *Jerusalem Studies in Arabic and Islam* 10 (1987): 287–324, esp. 303–304, 319 and his citation in 303n41 of E. I. J. Rosenthal's *Political Thought in Medieval Islam* (Cambridge: Cambridge University Press, 1962), 126.

Richard Walzer evinces his belief that Alfarabi intends his talk about an association of the "virtuous inhabited world" (*al-maʿmûrah al-fâḍilah*) as an ideal (he hopes to realize) by rendering this phrase as "the excellent universal state" and entitling his translation of *VC*, from which this phrase is taken, *Al-Farabi on the Perfect State* (Oxford: Clarendon Press, 1985), ch. 15, sec. 3.

4. It is worth recalling Socrates' famous dictum here: "There is no rest from ills for cities, my dear Glaucon, nor I think for human kind" (473d3). In it Socrates comes close to arguing that philosophic rule is not only the necessary but also the sufficient condition for this rest from ills or happiness—as if all other conditions would follow inevitably upon its coming to pass.

5. Muhsin Mahdi, *Alfarabi and the Foundation of Islamic Political Philosophy* (*AFIPP*), 192–93. Mahdi's three *Republic* citations are *AH* sec. 40, 30.7; 61, 45.17–18; and 61, 46.2. The first and third citations mark the beginning of a passage referring to the *Republic*. The second citation marks the end of a passage. It is meant to set off the second citation from the third because they appear so close together. Because we have even more reason to be interested in these references to the *Republic* than did Mahdi in his chapter on *AH*, I will give the citations inclusively here (*AH* sec. 40, 30.7–11; 60, 44.17–61, 45.18; 61, 46.2 ff.). It is unclear whether Mahdi intends his final reference to go on beyond section 61 into section 62. One thing is certain, however: section 62 contains one of Alfarabi's key arguments in the *AH*, which is a reasonable inference to draw from an important image in the *Republic*. Alfarabi's inference is that the philosopher is the true prince or *imam* whether he ever holds office. (Note parallels between *AH* 62 and *Aphorisms* 32.) The ship image, from which he draws this inference, is Socrates' account of why philosophers have not yet come to rule in cities (*Rep.* 488–489). We will return to this later.

6. The exact meaning of "theoretical science" in *AH* is a challenge. See *AH* esp. 20–21. Alfarabi's understanding of theoretical science there encompasses political science or its "theoretical" part. As Alfarabi knows all too well, Aristotle seems to preclude theoretical science from having any use! See *PA* 2, 60.19–61.3; 91, 123.16–124.7. Whether Alfarabi develops this expanded view of theoretical science because it is part of a plan to develop a political science that is an extension of natural science (Mahdi, rev. intro. to *PPA*, xiv–xvi), because it is part of a discussion of the methods of the sciences that is pretechnical (Mahdi, *AFIPP*, 174–83, esp. 176), or because Aristotle makes more use of theoretical science than is commonly believed cannot be settled here.

7. See *Rep.* 391d and 393e. Piety plays a far more prominent role in Plato's *Laws*. Alfarabi's reliance on written legislation in *AH* makes it, in this respect, more akin to the

Laws than the *Republic*. For the relation of the *Laws* to the *Republic* in both Plato and Alfarabi, see Parens *Metaphysics as Rhetoric*, ch. 4.

8. Cf. within sec. 44, 32.18–33.8 with 33.9–34.3, and look more generally at secs. 44 and 45.

9. Alfarabi's understanding of habituation is at once deeply indebted to Aristotle's discussion of the same in the *Nicomachean Ethics* and at times appears quite different. For a discussion far more similar to the *NE*, see *Aphorisms* secs. 9–13. At first, Alfarabi's *AH* 23–24 presents a shockingly new perspective. Not only are moral virtues treated as "voluntary intelligibles" (an impressive but unprecedented interpretation of Aristotle), but also Alfarabi acknowledges a shocking degree of variability in the states and accidents accompanying moral virtues, depending upon differences of time and place (esp. *AH* 24, 18.17–18) (see the discussion of sec. 24 in the next section of this chapter). Once one takes into account the vast periods of time and areas of geography or, rather, peoples that the virtuous world regime is supposed to encompass, it becomes readily apparent that only a fool could ignore the different forms these virtues are likely to take. The obvious temptation then is to infer that Alfarabi views moral virtue as wholly conventional or mutable. To see that that is not what he intends, one needs to attend with great care to everything he says about the relation between the natural and the voluntary throughout the trilogy. At a minimum, Alfarabi's decision to characterize the moral virtues as "voluntary *intelligibles*" gives them greater fixity than would those who embrace pure conventionalism.

10. See note 5 in this chapter for my first mention of this claim.

11. Ibid.

12. Although Alfarabi stops short of including prophecy among the credentials of the supreme ruler in the *AH,* he does so elsewhere. See *VC,* Walzer, ed., chs. 14 and 15, sec. 8 ff.; *PR,* Hyderabad ed., 49–50; *Book of Religion* (*BR*) secs. 26–27.

13. I say this in full awareness of the existence of at least one passage that seems to imply the virtuous city is necessary for the full flourishing of the philosopher (497a2). Note the ambiguity in Socrates' reference to the "suitable regime" and to his "growing more and more." He could mean that only in *kallipolis* will the philosopher be celebrated and acknowledged for what he is worth. Such growth is not central for philosophic development in the most significant sense.

14. On the centrality of the soul for philosophic inquiry, consider *Rep.* 434d–436c, esp. 435c–d and 504a3–505a4. Socrates implies that there is a longer inquiry into the soul, even longer than the *Republic*. I take this to be an allusion to the Platonic corpus as a whole, which is the "gallery of portraits" I had in mind previously. Most of Plato's dialogues are named after the character whose soul is displayed most prominently in the dialogue.

15. Despite the similarity between the itinerary mapped out by Alfarabi's Plato and the itinerary of Plato's Socrates, Alfarabi does not mention the character Socrates until his account of the *Symposium*. Alfarabi describes the *Symposium* as a dialogue in which Plato shows the superiority of philosophic pleasure to any other. In conclusion, he attributes the dialogue (or perhaps this view) to Socrates. Although this is not a prevalent view of the theme of the *Symposium,* it highlights a key aspect of its drama. While displaying his own *eros* for the wrong things in a drunken stupor, Alcibiades describes Socrates as a man whose bodily desires are so moderate, perhaps even somewhat ascetic, that when they receive normal satisfaction Socrates derives extraordinary pleasure from them (219e4 ff.). (On the ap-

pearance of asceticism, see *Rep.* 485d3–e4.) This scene and Alfarabi's interpretation of the dialogue help explain one of the better-established themes of the dialogue, namely, Socrates' claim that the only thing he really knows is *eros* (*Symp.* 177e). He has unlocked the secret of *eros* sufficiently to lead the most pleasant, if not the most debauched, life.

16. On the relation between the city in the *Republic* and the city in the *Laws* (merged in the *PP*), see Parens, *Metaphysics as Rhetoric*, ch. 4.

17. Cf. Christopher Colmo, "Theory and Practice: Alfarabi's *Plato* Revisited," *American Political Science Review* 84:4 (1992): 966–76, esp. 970–74.

18. On the question of Plato's (and, by implication, Alfarabi's) realism, see the first section of ch. 2. Also see chapter 6 on the status of "realization" or "attainment" (*taḥṣīl*) in Alfarabi's thought.

19. For the characterization of courage as savage (*agriotes*) with some hints of the tension with philosophic gentleness or tameness, see bk. 3, 410b7–412a3. For their characterization as opposites, see bk. 2, 375c4. Although Socrates alludes subtly to this problem throughout the conversation, he is willing to articulate the problem clearly only toward the end (6, 503b3–d4). It might otherwise rob the conversation of much of its energy.

The reader should detect echoes between our discussion in ch. 2 of the cruelty of males and the gentleness of females and the present discussion of the hard (savage) and the soft (tame).

20. In bk. 1, Polemarchus offers this combination as his definition of justice. This is significant because Socrates tells us in passing in the *Phaedrus* (257b3) that Polemarchus was "converted" to philosophy. That is, a person devoted to philosophy shows himself to be inclined toward this rather savage definition of justice. At the same time, in Socrates' conversation with Polemarchus, he shows himself to be extremely gentle or docile. He is willing to be persuaded that one should do good to friends and harm to no one, except perhaps in war with foreign enemies (cf. 332d1–335e4 as a whole and esp. the end with 332d–e8). This would seem to embody precisely the kind of combination of gentleness and spiritedness the virtuous city requires. At the same time, it is also worth noting that Polemarchus was put to death when the Thirty Tyrants came to power in 404 B.C.E. Although he may well have been put to death arbitrarily, if he contributed at all to his death presumably it was due more to spiritedness than gentleness.

For the possibility that Socrates embodies perfectly this combination of gentleness and spiritedness, consider Alcibiades's portrait of him in battle in the *Symposium* 219e4–221b. As Grace and Thomas G. West have already implied in their notes to Plato's *Apology*, Socrates seems to display courage or bravery in retreat (*Four Texts on Socrates*, rev. ed. [Ithaca: Cornell University Press, 1998], 80n51 on *Apology* 28e). Although this may be sufficient for saving one's friends (*Symposium* 220e3) and for keeping one's head in battle (221b), one might doubt its sufficiency in the ruler of an actual city. Cf. Socrates' account of his decision to stay out of politics in Athens (*Apology* 31c3–33b).

21. The quintessential example of "what's one's own" in the *Republic* will prove to be the family. Like the dog's or wolf's pack, human beings are born into a family. Although parents are more willing to die for their young than perhaps anything else, our siblings are not always good. Our family is our own, but all of its members might not be good. Socrates or the philosopher treats the potential philosopher as his true offspring, preferring the good to his own. Cf. *Rep.* 549c4–d7 and *Phaedo* 60a.

22. Consider, for example, Socrates' opening visit to the Piraeus to view the Thracian festival of Bendis.

23. Again, cf. ch. 2 on cruelty and gentleness. This tendency in the guardians and in human nature generally is articulated clearly by Socrates only *after* he has established the Noble Lie—to persuade us to love the common good as our own private good—and *before* he recommends that the guardians be deprived of all private property. See 416a-c and context.

24. The alliance between desire and spiritedness is Glaucon's or the excessively ambitious man's problem (see 439d1-440a2).

25. That Plato cannot prefer the rule of the philosopher is evident from Socrates' intentional failure to prove *kallipolis* possible. Aristotle states clearly more than once the need for the rule of law to avoid the danger of tyranny. See *NE* 1134a32-b3 and *Pol.* 1282a43-b6, 1286a7-1287b35, esp. 1287a28-33.

26. As we have already seen, the division between character formation and instruction is not rigid, just as force and persuasion are, at least in this instance, not clearly distinguished.

27. Here I follow Mahdi's reading rather than Yasin's, though Yasin's reading as *mahiyyatin wahdatin* (very same essence) would not have a significant effect on my interpretation.

28. See Aristotle's claim in *NE* 1104b18, that punishment is like medicine. In other words, it has a rehabilitative purpose, not merely a deterrent purpose (1113b26). Certainly, while people are still young and their character has not become fixed, punishment can have a curative power (see the context of the quote at 1104b18). Still, there are profound limits to what can be achieved through punishment, at least with the genuinely vicious adult (1150b33). Perhaps in most penal settings it functions almost solely as a deterrent (1179b7-20).

29. Note the disagreement between Mahdi's translation (43, 32.9-17) and Yasin's critical edition (p. 81, sec. 48, end-49). The key issue is *juz'i* versus *harbi*.

30. For another context in Plato's thought, however, in which there is some precedent for such an idea, namely, the *Laws,* see the discussion of Alfarabi's *Summary* (disc. 3.4-6) in Parens, *Metaphysics as Rhetoric,* 64-66.

31. See, for example, *AH* 31, 25.5-7.

32. Aristotle's rejection of the *Republic* in the *Politics* is based on a quite literal reading of the *Republic*. Similarly, his rejection of the so-called theory of forms in the *Metaphysics* is based on a quite literal reading of the *Phaedo*. At times, it appears that Aristotle's disagreements with Plato are largely about the fitting way of presenting various philosophic teachings.

33. Of course, Aristotle envisions a society in which not only statesmen but also, above all, legislators should possess beliefs informed by philosophy through education. For the superiority of the legislator to the statesman, consider 1141b15-34. The basis of this superiority is that the legislator's prudence concerns universals. Universals here refer to the (hierarchy of) ends. The statesman's prudence is an excellence in deliberation about the fitting means or particulars. Although the legislator's grasp of the hierarchy of ends may not rise to the level of a full grasp of all of the discursive arguments for this hierarchy, his grasp rises above the mere good beliefs of the statesman.

34. On the theme of realization or attainment, see sec. 3 of this chapter; ch. 5, sec. 4; and the beginning of ch. 6 and sec. 1.

35. For which the reader should see Alfarabi's *Selected Aphorisms*.

36. I will offer a more detailed analysis of his treatment of deliberative virtue when we turn to the issue of the multiplicity of nations and religions in chapter 5.

37. See, for example, Maimonides, *Guide of the Perplexed*, II 32.

38. See chapter 5.

39. See note 6 for the sense of "theoretical science" in *AH* and sec. 34 for deliberation's reliance upon "theoretical virtue" for adequate arguments for the hierarchy of ends. Note that even practical science in the traditional Aristotelian account depends not only upon practical virtue (or prudence) but also upon theoretical virtue. In other words, "theoretical virtue," in *AH* at least, has a wider bearing than on theoretical science alone.

40. Here Alfarabi runs directly counter to Aristotle's concerted effort to separate theoretical virtue from politics, discussed previously.

41. See chapter 5, sec. 3.

42. See chapter 5, sec. 2.

43. This argument about natural virtue could also be viewed as adding additional weight to a point we have already touched on. When Alfarabi raised the possibility that there was a moral virtue powerful enough to bear the burden of supreme rule, we noted that this view has things in common with the revealed view of prophecy. Alfarabi ruled this out because of the inseparability of moral and deliberative virtue. The idea that natural virtue must lie at the root of supreme rule confirms our suggestion that there must be a natural, not only a miraculous, basis to such a ruler.

44. See chapter 6, sec. 1, for further discussion of this Arabic term and its translation.

45. In this respect, Aristotle echoes the structure of the *Republic* in his *NE*. In the *Republic*, Socrates first establishes the education for character formation or the common good in bks. 2–4, and only later the philosophic education or education for the private good in bk. 7. As part of an ascent, Socrates implies quite openly that the highest private good is in a sense higher than the common good, though it need not be at odds with it. Cf. also this distinction between private and public good as presented in the *Laws* (666e).

46. Moral virtue is superior, because it fixes the end, and prudence is inferior, because it fixes the means. The end is superior to the means in Aristotle's thought.

47. The division between practical and theoretical virtue is different from the division between practical and theoretical science, even for Aristotle. Practical virtue is deliberative. The power that makes practical science possible is not mere deliberation, however. This power is what Alfarabi refers to here as "theoretical virtue."

48. See note 33.

49. See the end of this chapter and chapters 5 and 6.

50. See *Rep.* 540a. Here I will merely allude to the conundrum of the fitting ages for the study of philosophy as opposed to rule, respectively. (To see the conundrum or problem, compare the final plan alluded to by Alfarabi [540a] with Socrates' initial plan [484d, 497d4–498c].) Alfarabi may have this problem in mind, since he mentions the fitting age for becoming a philosopher-king. The problem of the fitting age is simple. The young are best suited to the study of philosophy because they are flexible or soft. But the old are best

suited to rule because they are more moderate or, at least, inflexible or hard. Indeed, a young philosopher is bound to make nearly incalculable blunders due merely to immoderation. This problem is a subset of the general problem of combining the hard with the soft.

51. See Mahdi, *AH*, sec. 40n5.

52. The entirety of our account of the tension between prudence and wisdom in Aristotle can be viewed as an echo of the uneasy relations between Glaucon and Socrates in the third wave (see ch. 2). Here in *AH*, Alfarabi alludes to the same problem. If this problem made philosopher-kingship implausible in the *Republic,* then a fortiori this will prove a profound problem in Alfarabi's virtuous regime of the inhabited world.

53. Throughout the passage on the elect and the vulgar in secs. 50–53, Alfarabi elaborates upon Aristotle's discussion of the true meaning of wisdom. For Alfarabi, as for Aristotle, this discussion culminates in the recognition that the greatest competition for rule occurs near the top between wisdom and prudence. Cf. *AH* 53, 39.5–10 with *NE* 6, 1141a10–1141b2.

54. Of course, Alfarabi does not indicate that such exploitation should take the form of the Enlightenment effort to own and possess nature through its reconstruction. Indeed, his sympathy with Plato and Aristotle implies the contrary regarding nonhuman nature.

55. Mahdi, *PPA,* rev. intro., xviii–xxv.

56. Ibid., xxii.

57. Reading this as a cautionary tale is in some tension, however, with Mahdi's claims in some of his later writings that Alfarabi is focused, above all, on realization and in a way that his successors failed to emulate at all. I believe there may be something quasimodern or anachronistic about Mahdi's stress on realization. See chapter 6.

58. The following discussion of Mahdi's interpretation is an explication of ibid., xxi–xxii.

59. Ibid., xxv. Although Mahdi has tracked down innumerable connections between Alfarabi's arguments and those of Plato and Aristotle, for which all readers of Alfarabi are deeply indebted, I wonder whether he is sufficiently aware of the basis in Plato for this claim about the philosopher. As discussed earlier, Plato's account of why the philosopher is useless focuses, above all, on how much this lack of use is due to the ruled. I believe Alfarabi's odd claim about the unused philosopher remaining a true philosopher(-ruler) echoes this Platonic view. Philosophers such as Plato and Aristotle have been of the greatest use to politics by writing works with which potential statesmen and legislators can be educated. They did so without extensive political experience.

60. See chapter 6.

61. Up until this point, I am following Mahdi's lead. See *AFIPP,* 173–76.

62. I mean to question, then, whether Alfarabi's inclusion of political science in theoretical perfection is tantamount to a rejection of Aristotle's distinction between theoretical and practical science (Mahdi, *PPA,* rev. intro., xii, xiv), or is meant merely to represent the prevailing view of certainty within his own community (cf. *AFIPP,* 176).

63. Once again, I take my lead about the presence of the interlocutor and his limited grasp of the sciences from Mahdi (*AFIPP,* 175 ff.).

CHAPTER 4

1. In H. Diels and W. Kranz, *Die Fragmente der Vorsokratiker* (Zurich: Weidmann, 1952), 22B53.

2. Of course, I allude here to Hobbes's account of the state of nature as just such a state of war. In the opening of Plato's *Laws,* one of the Stranger's interlocutors, Kleinias, expresses this same view (652d–626c). In his pathbreaking book on war in Islam, Majid Khadduri stresses rightly that war was not viewed as the exception but the rule in ancient societies. In doing so, he cites not only the modern Hobbes and the ancient Plato (opening of the *Laws*) but also the more immediately relevant, late medieval Ibn Khaldun. See Majid Khadduri, *War and Peace in the Law of Islam* (Baltimore: Johns Hopkins University Press, 1955), 54n7, 72n47.

3. Such ambition manifests itself politically less frequently in modern society, for among other reasons, because of the sheer population size of modern states. When it does, however, it can take on an even more savage cast than in the ancient world.

4. See Parens, *Metaphysics as Rhetoric,* 65–66.

5. Khadduri, *War and Peace,* 63. As is implied here, Khadduri is well aware of the imperialistic epochs of Christian history. Judaism, though never a missionary religion on a grand scale, has had periods during which proselytization was considered acceptable—for example, Alexandria around the time of the translation of the Septuagint. Furthermore, Judaism does expect ultimate world recognition of the one God, even if only in the end of days at the resurrection of the dead.

6. Strauss, *What Is Political Philosophy?,* 164.

7. Cf. introduction, "Alfarabi's Life and His Influence."

8. Khadduri offers a profound analysis of why *jihâd* is not one of the pillars of Islam (except in Khârijî jurisprudence), yet is the most certain means of access to paradise. See *War and Peace,* 60–62.

9. See ibid., 69. It becomes the only fitting form of war, because no war among Muslims can be just; only war with non-Muslims can be.

10. The most extensive work on just war theory and its relation to Islam has been done in volumes written and edited by James Turner Johnson and John Kelsay. See Johnson and Kelsay, eds., *Cross, Crescent, and Sword* (New York: Greenwood Press, 1990); *Just War and Jihad* (New York: Greenwood Press, 1991); Johnson, *The Holy War Idea in Western and Islamic Traditions* (University Park: Pennsylvania State University Press, 1997).

11. See Abdulaziz A. Sachedina, "The Development of *Jihâd* in Islamic Revelation and History," in *Cross, Crescent, and Sword,* ed. Johnson and Kelsay, 36, 42–44. Sachedina is a bit fuzzy about the meaning of both "moral purpose" and "social order." Above all, he avoids relevant passages in which polytheism or associationism (*shirk*) is the main focus of Muhammad's ire. Cf. Khadduri's citations on polytheism in *War and Peace,* 75. Are polytheists to be eliminated solely because they undermine Muslim social order, or because their beliefs or opinions are incompatible with Islam? The animosity toward polytheism is, of course, not exclusive to Islam.

12. Sachedina, "The Development of *Jihâd*," 35–36, 44.

13. Indeed, the origin of the demise of "essentialism" is modernity itself. Although postmodernists often ascribe essentialism to modernity, they reveal their ignorance of their own pedigree when they do so. The great founders of modern biblical hermeneutics, Hobbes, Spinoza, and Locke, led the charge in repudiating the essence of biblical religion. Their purportedly scientific reading of Scripture imported modern scientific views and political teachings into the original. Without the injection of such a new essence, it would not have been possible for religious tolerance to take hold in the West. The most problematic inheritance of the new hermeneutic is that it came to be applied to all texts. Postmodernism is only the latest expression of the unlimited application of that hermeneutic.

14. In Judaism, the case is less obvious, above all, because of the relative weakness of the Jewish community. It is also less obvious because the relation between Israel and the other nations is understood traditionally on analogy to the relation of the priestly class and the rest of the nation of Israel. This analogy leaves it unclear as to what extent other nations are supposed to embrace the one God. Of course, prophetic books such as Isaiah are filled with hope for an end of days when all will accept God. The closing prayer of all Jewish religious services looks forward to the day when "every knee shall bend and every tongue swear loyalty" to God.

15. The reader may suspect that the rise of Hindu militancy in India would contravene this claim. I suspect, however, that the Pakistani Muslim effort to wrest Kashmir from India (whether justly or unjustly) has contributed mightily to a peculiarly late modern breed of religious militancy in contemporary India.

16. See Fred M. Donner, "The Sources of Islamic Conceptions of War," in *Just War and Jihâd*, ed. Kelsay and Johnson, 31–69, esp. 50 ff., and Johnson, *Holy War Idea*, 48, citing Majid Khadduri, *The Islamic Law of Nations: Shaybani's Sîyar* (Baltimore: Johns Hopkins University Press, 1966), 13.

17. Sachedina, "The Development of *Jihâd*," 38.

18. Ibid., 39.

19. We may thereby set aside the vexing question of whether the Qur'an's accusations against Medinese Jewry are intended to be generalized or not. We may also avoid confronting issues such as how temporary or permanent are the treaties of Muslims with protected peoples (*dhimmi*s), including Jews and Christians.

20. See John Locke, *Letter Concerning Toleration* (Indianapolis: Bobbs-Merrill, 1955), 41.

21. At least in "The Development of *Jihâd*," Sachedina is wholly silent about the connection between beliefs and *jihâd*. Because the jurists gave religious justifications for offensive *jihâd*, and Sachedina gives moral justifications for defensive *jihâd* (36, 39), Sachedina leads us toward a (possibly false) dichotomy between religious and moral justifications for *jihâd*. Whether he intends to (and he does seem to) or not, he makes it difficult thereby to justify war in the name of beliefs at all.

22. Though many will disagree with me, I believe that concern for the soul of one's neighbor has inspired religious strife nearly as much as explicit Scriptural sanction. Although some believing Christians will say that the Crusades were wholly defensive, I doubt

it. Of course, the New Testament does not give explicit warrant to either offensive or defensive war in the name of Christianity. Nevertheless, I suspect that the manner in which it threatens those who fail to accept Jesus as the proper path to God has served as a potent inspiration to those who have pursued offensive wars in the name of Christianity. I am well aware that the great thinkers of the Christian tradition, such as Thomas Aquinas, have opposed conversion by the sword.

23. The deep link between spiritedness and such a division is strikingly apparent in Plato's *Laws*. In one of his theological accounts, the Athenian Stranger distinguishes between a good and a bad god, in an odd echo of Zoroastrianism or Manicheeism (896a).

24. Sufi thinkers, as opposed to jurists, came to distinguish between these as the greater (internal) struggle and lesser (external) struggle.

25. Relatively extensive scholarship already exists on this theme. I would not address it here if I did not believe that I have significant additions and criticisms to make. Leaving aside the work of Dunlop and the various reviews of his translation, I will focus on Joel Kraemer's "The *Jihâd* of the *Falâsifa*," 288–324, and Charles E. Butterworth's "Al-Fârâbî's Statecraft: War and the Well-Ordered Regime," in *Cross, Crescent, and Sword*, 79–100. For the debates surrounding Dunlop's views and translation, see the footnotes of Kraemer's "*Jihâd*," esp. 311n71.

26. Here I follow Kraemer's apt account of Lambton's view in "*Jihâd*," 291n4. See previous note for Kraemer.

27. Ibid., 292–93. When one combines Kraemer's account of accommodation with his claim that Alfarabi uses terms for law and war with as little precision as did the Syriac and Arabic translators of Plato and Aristotle (ibid., 293–97), the result is that Alfarabi is always expressing the views of the philosophers, no matter what term he might use. The general result is that whichever views Alfarabi expresses are taken to be his philosophic preference. Because I do not take every view expressed by Alfarabi as his own preferred view, I cannot accept these hermeneutic principles.

28. Butterworth, "Al-Fârâbî's Statecraft," 94.

29. In this important respect, I view Alfarabi as a far more dialectical writer than Lambton or Kraemer. We must be extremely careful not to assume that any particular view he offers is simply his own. See chapter 1 for an account of Alfarabi's manner of writing; see chapters 5 and 6 for my interpretation of Alfarabi's approach to methods of argumentation, especially in *AH*.

30. Cf. Kraemer's claim ("*Jihâd*," 303, 319) that the "world state" mentioned in *AH* and *VC* is offered as Alfarabi's "ideal" with my claims in chapters 2 and 3, that they should be viewed more as a standard and cautionary tale. By the way, Kraemer himself cites a text from al-ʿÂmirî that supports the view that Muslim philosophers were well aware of the impossibility of the best regime (ibid., 288).

31. Although the Arabic here used for submit does not allude to the submission (*islâm*) of the Muslim, the verb used for the "call" is from the crucial Arabic word for the call of the Prophet (*daʿwah*).

32. Aphorism 67 in *Alfarabi's Political Writings: "Selected Aphorisms" and Other Writings*.

33. Kraemer, "*Jihâd*," 312.

34. Butterworth, "Al-Fârâbî's Statecraft," 84–85.

35. Kraemer, "Jihâd," 313.

36. Butterworth, "Al-Fârâbî's Statecraft," 83.

37. Kraemer, "Jihâd," 290, 312; 303, 319.

38. Butterworth, "Al-Fârâbî's Statecraft," 84.

39. With this reference to "erroneous opinion," I follow the lead of Butterworth's division and naming of the *Aphorisms*' parts. See Butterworth, trans., *Alfarabi's Political Writings: "Selected Aphorisms,"* 8.

40. See note 27.

41. Butterworth, "Al-Fârâbî's Statecraft," 89n31.

42. Ibid., 85–87.

43. Kraemer, "Jihâd," 314–16.

44. That Alfarabi uses the utmost care in his choice of words does not mean that each word has very restricted denotations. Rather, it means that Alfarabi chooses with care the word whose connotation offers the most food for thought. Sometimes the connotation can be jarring. I believe the translator does the reader a service when he retains awkward and jarring translations to flag the author's choice of a word with jarring connotations. Compare what I say here with the last paragraph of Butterworth, "Al-Fârâbî's Statecraft," note 31. Also consider Kraemer's criticisms of Lerner's translation of Averroes's commentary on Plato's *Republic* ("Jihâd," 295).

45. This section runs from Aphorism 6 through 29. I follow Butterworth's persuasive account of the division of the *Aphorisms*. Again, see Butterworth, trans., *Alfarabi's Political Writings: "Selected Aphorisms,"* 8.

46. Butterworth, "Al-Fârâbî's Statecraft," 90.

47. Ibid., 86, 89–90.

48. Here and in what follows, the reader should compare Alfarabi's account with *Nicomachean Ethics* 7.

49. Cf. Aristotle, *NE* 1144b7 and Alfarabi, *AH* 35–36. Note Alfarabi's repudiation of the term "natural virtue" for this predisposition in Aphorisms 10–11.

50. Aphorisms 16 and 74.

51. This humorous echo of Socrates' hyperbolic claim about philosopher-kingship being the *sine qua non* for the cessation of evils (*Republic* 473d) could be viewed as an encapsulation of the Aristotelian response in *NE* to this claim.

52. In the middle of my discussion of Aphorisms 67 and 79.

53. Although Butterworth does not discuss these aphorisms in "Al-Fârâbî's Statecraft," in one of the footnotes to his indispensable translation of these aphorisms, he refers to a Qur'anic allusion of relevance for our discussion. See Butterworth, trans., *Selected Aphorisms,* p. 47n44.

54. In my use of the phrase "erroneous opinion," I am drawing on Butterworth's title for this section of the *Aphorisms,* "G. The Divisions of Being and the Status of Happiness: Sound vs. Erroneous Opinions." See Butterworth, trans., *Selected Aphorisms,* 8, 44.

55. Other obvious choices might have been "divine" (*ilâhiyyah*) or "intellectual" (*'aqliyyah*). Compare, for example, the closing part of Alfarabi's *Philosophy of Aristotle*.

56. I will avoid descending into the details of the challenges surrounding these two aphorisms, because the essential point is unaffected by the choice between the Chester Beatty ms. or Najjar's preferred text, highlighted in Butterworth, trans., *Selected Aphorisms*, pp. 45n40, 46n41.

57. See Aphorisms 72–73 for clear indications that Alfarabi classes human beings among beings that can possibly be or not be.

58. Fazlur Rahman, *Islam*, 2d ed. (Chicago: University of Chicago Press, 1966, 1979), 34. For a start, see Qur'an 6:100, 18:50, 55:14–15.

59. The tension between the traditional characterization of the *jinn* as being made of a fiery substance and Alfarabi's allusion to them as "spiritual" highlights an important irony of evil and spiritedness. Anger, as a significant element in self-restraint, tends to ascribe either a "spirit" to dead matter or matter to the "spiritual." Plato alludes to this problem when his Athenian Stranger playfully admits a law expelling rocks that have harmed the inhabitants of Magnesia, as if dead matter could have a "spirit" (*Laws* 873e–874a).

60. Cf. Qur'an 2:35 with John L. Esposito, *Islam: The Straight Path*, 3d ed. (Oxford: Oxford University Press, 1998), 27.

61. Various advocates of relativism in early modern thought echo the premodern philosophic and theological claim that evil is an absence of being. But they couple with this the claim that, strictly speaking, evil is merely subjective. Something is evil when a particular individual finds it painful. Alfarabi rejects this claim explicitly in Aphorism 74, paragraph 5, in Butterworth's translation.

62. See Butterworth's discussion of this locution as a divergence from Qur'anic usage. Again, see Butterworth, trans., *Selected Aphorisms*, p. 47n44.

63. See ibid. As we will see later, Alfarabi does not accept the Mu'tazili notion that the innocent sometimes suffer here for the sake of a greater reward in the hereafter. Cf. Maimonides, *Guide of the Perplexed*, III 17.

64. Cf. Aristotle, *Metaphysics* E.2.

65. See Aphorism 9.

66. See Kraemer, "*Jihâd*," 314–16. Also Butterworth, "Al-Fârâbî's Statecraft," 85–87.

67. Sachedina, "Development of *Jihâd*," 39–40.

68. Ibid., 39–40, nn. 8, 9, and especially 11.

69. Again, as in Aphorism 67, the term translated as "submit" is not derived from the root for Islam. Rather, it is from the root for "accustoming or habituating."

70. Mahdi's translation does not pull any punches. Yasin's Arabic (p. 81) sticks closely to the questionable reading that appears in the existing manuscripts in which war fighting as a virtue is downplayed. The word "partial" (*juz'iyyah*) is repeatedly substituted for "war" (*harbiyyah*) because of the similar Arabic orthography of the roots *j.z.'.* and *h.r.b.* Thus we have oddities such as the "partial craft" rather than the "craft of war" and the "partial art" rather than the "art of war." Even Yasin's reading would not eliminate the central theme of the passage, established in the first sentence of the English translation, namely, the compulsion of the

conquered by means of arms. Cf. how a similar problem has crept into the reading of Averroes's allusion to the same passage in Alfarabi in Lerner's translation of *Averroes on Plato's "Republic,"* 26, esp. notes to ll. 19, 23.

71. See chapter 3.

72. Alfarabi does not even entertain the possibility of those scourges of the twentieth century, "brainwashing," "indoctrination," or "ideological training." He does not do so because the conjunction of instruction and compulsion that they represent would be completely antithetical to philosophy.

73. I have in mind the "double-formula," indicating belief in Allah as the one God and Muhammad as His Prophet.

74. See Lenn E. Goodman, *Islamic Humanism* (Oxford: Oxford University Press, 2003), 98, on the oddity that the most rationalistic part of the *kalâm* tradition, the *Muʿtazila,* should have descended into this fruitless endeavor.

75. See *Republic* 405a, 410a, 459e, and 541a. Also consider Averroes's allusions to Socrates' or Plato's exclusion of doctors from the city (*Averroes on Plato's "Republic,"* 36–38).

76. The closest that Socrates comes to envisioning punishment in the *Republic*'s virtuous city is a vague allusion to it as an unlikely possibility (464e–465a). On the lower focus of the *Laws* as compared with the *Republic,* see *Laws* 739a–e and Parens, *Metaphysics as Rhetoric,* ch. 4.

77. See the previous section on Aphorisms 11–16.

78. We have already seen evidence in the section on Aphorisms 11–16 of Alfarabi's familiarity with *NE* 7. This last discussion refers to Aristotle alone. I cannot prove that Alfarabi is familiar with these specific arguments about the incurable from *NE* 7 and compulsion from *NE* 10 in Aristotle. His familiarity with the meaning of the human types from *NE* 7 and of the relative worth of moral virtue and philosophy from *NE* 10 suggests that it is likely, however.

CHAPTER 5

1. Of course, "the ancients" refers most explicitly to Plato's *Timaeus,* which he goes on to cite (55, 41.5). See Mahdi's suggested passages (p. 140, sec. 55, note 7). It also refers, however, to the Chaldeans of *al-ʿIraq,* who a page or two earlier are identified as engaging in philosophy even before the Greeks (*AH* 53). In other words, philosophy is indigenous to the Islamic world, not foreign, as are "the ancients." For a similar line of argument in a different religious tradition, see Maimonides, *Guide of the Perplexed,* I 71.

2. Cf. *Alfarabi's Book of Letters* (*BL*), edited by Muhsin Mahdi (Beirut: Dar al-Mashriq, 1969), sec. 108.

3. Of course, the classic form of this claim about oneness and manyness is Plato's so-called theory of forms. The form or nature of a being is one. The particulars we see in the everyday world are imitations of those originals. See, for example, *Rep.* 474d–476d, 479a, and cf. 423a ff. and 551d.

4. Great scholarly controversy still abounds about the exact character of Latin Averroism. The most traditional view of thinkers such as Siger of Brabant and John of Jandun is that they believe it is possible for theology to prove truths that contradict the truths proven in philosophy. According to this view, they seem to imply no difference in rank of the respective truths.

5. It should be noted, however, that he never refers to these juridical differences. And the term for religion or religious community, *millah*, usually denotes something more substantial than these juridical distinctions.

6. On Alfarabi's use of "schematic" writing, see chapter 1.

7. An example would be the following: Christians have an easy time distinguishing their version of monotheism from that of Jews because of their dogma regarding the Trinity. To bear out the difference, Christians have their own testament, the New Testament. Of course, Christians claim the Hebrew Bible as their own Old Testament. Precisely because Islam's and Judaism's understanding of divine unity is similar enough, Islam could not similarly incorporate the Hebrew Bible.

8. Cf. Plato, *Republic* 562b–588a with Aristotle, *Politics* 1295a1–24. Once again, it must be stressed that, to our knowledge, neither Alfarabi nor any other medieval Islamic philosopher had access to the *Politics*. This does not detract from my comparison of Alfarabi's full-bodied discussions of domination with Aristotle's relative silence. Sometimes the best way to suppress a bad phenomenon is to remain silent about it; at other times, that path is not useful.

9. Of course, Socrates does mention the tyrant's proclivity to stir up foreign war to divert the attention of his populace (*Rep.* 566e), and Plato shows greater concern about external tyranny in his *Laws*. See Parens, *Metaphysics as Rhetoric*, 65 ff.

10. If Alfarabi makes such an argument, then his position is quite the opposite of most contemporary Muslim militants. And if so, he is likely to view a world filled with great religious diversity, perhaps including even irreligious nations, more favorably than such a homogeneous but purportedly pious world. Qualifications of this claim about the presence of irreligious nations will follow shortly in the upcoming discussion of the connection between diversity or multiplicity and virtue.

11. Although Aristotle criticizes the city in the *Republic* in his *Politics* (2.1–5), his own best regime, described in bks. 7 and 8, is surprisingly similar to Socrates' inaccessible *kallipolis*. Neither regime seems to be intended as a serious model for this world.

12. Cf. his similar discussion of nonvirtuous regimes in *Virtuous City,* Walzer, ed., ch. 15, secs. 15–20.

13. Fauzi M. Najjar's translation of *PR* in Lerner-Mahdi, eds., *Medieval Political Philosophy,* 31–57, esp. 41 ff. is most helpful in indicating these broader classes and subdivisions.

14. The first, indispensable city resembles Socrates' city of necessity, described in *Rep.* 2, 369b–372b. The third, base city resembles his city of luxury, described immediately following in 369d–373e. Here Alfarabi evinces his familiarity with bks. 2 and 8, in addition to his familiarity with bks. 6–7, which we have seen in previous chapters.

Philologically oriented scholars will attempt to show that Alfarabi's ordering reflects a poor translation to which he must have had access. I will assume that Alfarabi had an adequate translation (or possibly access to the original Greek) in no small part, because Averroes's *Commentary on Plato's "Republic"* recounts the order of decline of regimes in *Rep.* 8 quite accurately (see Averroes, *Republic* 80.13–23). True, Averroes and Alfarabi are separated by more than a century. Nevertheless, Averroes's willingness to follow Alfarabi's lead in his own account of the worse regimes suggests that he trusted Alfarabi as a source. Why shouldn't we as well?

15. Socrates' coinage "timocracy" is from the word *timê*, meaning honor. Timocracy is the rule of the honor lovers.

16. Note that the effort to hold the worst and best natures apart in *Rep.* bk. 8 is contradicted by the admission in bk. 6 that they are rooted in the same kind of soul (491b–e).

17. Socrates distinguishes among three kinds of desires, love of gain or money, love of honor, and love of learning. These parallel the three parts of the soul and of the city he makes so much use of throughout the *Republic*. At the same time, it should be acknowledged that Socrates allows *eros* itself to become identified with the tyrant (573b ff.).

18. See *PR*, Hyderabad, 68. "Despotic cities are more often tyrannical than timocratic (*Al-mudun al-taghallabiyyah hiya mudun al-jabbârîn akthar min al-karâmiyyah*)."

19. In a subsequent discussion of the third kind of city, the base or luxurious city, Alfarabi notes that there are two basic kinds of luxuriating peoples: those who are soft and those who are hard. The hard are driven by both their spiritedness and their appetites. The Arabs and Turks of the steppes (*PR*, 73) are his leading examples of the hard.

20. Although Alfarabi might recommend humility to most men, he acknowledges the place of high-mindedness or greatness of soul in the philosopher (cf. *Aphorisms* 18, *tawada'*, with *AH* 60, 45.2, *kabîr al-nafs*).

21. With this usage of tool, we come close to the disturbing if remote possibility inherent in the pursuit of the virtuous regime of the inhabited world through the "exploitation" (*isti'mâl*) of all beings, mentioned in ch. 3.

22. Also see the discussion of Alfarabi's treatment of this theme in his *Summary of Plato's "Laws"* in Parens, *Metaphysics as Rhetoric*, ch. 7.

23. I have altered Mahdi's translation because Alfarabi's Arabic does not make any reference to the will "making" the voluntary intelligible or the accident. He has introduced this because some sense of making is surely implied by the reference to "will." Yet to introduce "make" is to introduce a word that misleadingly suggests the third kind of activity apart from *theoria* (contemplation) and *praxis* (action), namely, *poiesis* or production or the practical arts. But what is at issue here is *praxis* or action.

24. In Alfarabi's parlance, "intelligible" is rooted in the intellect's ability to apprehend natures. Alfarabi's understanding bears little similarity to the notions of rational construction one finds, for example, in Spinoza's understanding of man's "idea" of himself or Locke's understanding of moral "archetypes."

25. Alfarabi gives no indication that he might envision a Pythagorean or protomodern notion of rational construction (on the model of mathematics) in human affairs.

26. Although Alfarabi never mentions the legislator by name here, his existence is implied by the task set at the beginning of part ii, namely, the realization of the four kinds of things leading the citizens of cities and nations to attain happiness (see *AH* 21–22).

Alfarabi's avoidance of explicit identification of the legislator parallels his avoidance of explicit reference to philosophy and the philosopher. Rather than argue early and often for the coincidence of philosopher and legislator, he, like Socrates in the *Republic*, puts off making such an explosive announcement until the last possible moment. He wants to lead his reader to feel the need for a character of such unparalleled virtue before identifying the philosopher as that character. Finally, Alfarabi does refer specifically to the legislative form of deliberative virtue or prudence, if not the legislator, as early as sec. 28 (22.2).

27. For evidence that thinking about accidents is the very essence of deliberation, see *AH* 26, 20.7. Cf. Aristotle's identification of its subject matter as the variable or contingent (*NE* 1112a23–b3 and 1139a5–15).

28. *Bilâd* has a more spatial meaning than *ummah* (a nation) or *millah* (a religious community). The latter two are kinds of what Aristotle means by "regime" (*politeia*). See my review of Mahdi's, *AFIPP*, in *American Political Science Review* 96:2 (2002): 410–11.

29. See Ibn Khaldun, *Muqaddimah*, Franz Rosenthal, trans. (New York: Pantheon Books, 1958), second through fourth prefatory discussions.

30. Here I have quoted Najjar's translation in Lerner-Mahdi Sourcebook, p. 32. *PR*, Hyderabad ed., p. 40.

31. Cf. Alfarabi, *BL*, secs. 114, 115, 122. The key term there is *fitra*, which is defined in turn in terms of *khilaq* (122, Mahdi, ed., p. 134, l. 21).

32. *BL*, sec. 118.

33. See *NE* 1144b5–15 and Alfarabi, *AH*, secs. 35–36.

34. As has been observed by others before me, he mentions such a society not only elsewhere in *AH*, as we already know, but also in *VC*. See ch. 15, sec. 2. Could it be that a regime of the inhabited world reflects more of a hope or an opinion of the members of Alfarabi's virtuous city (the subject matter of *VC*) than Alfarabi's own expectation? Certainly, *PR*, with its extensive discussion of nonvirtuous regimes, has a greater air of reality to it than *VC*.

35. Cf. *PR*, Hyderabad, 39, and *VC*, ch. 15, secs. 2–3. In *AH*, Alfarabi never states explicitly how big the regime that he envisions should be. He does discuss the necessity that the ruler should possess knowledge, especially deliberative virtue, covering "the inhabited earth" or "all nations." See 24, 19.13–18; 25, 20.2; 28, 22.4; 44, 33.5; 45, 34.13–15. For the importance of "cooperation" in Alfarabi's understanding of such a large regime, see Mahdi, *AFIPP*, 142–43. This theme of cooperation could be usefully linked to the issue of delegation, made explicit by Alfarabi in *AH*, sec. 48. Contrast Walzer's misleading renderings of the title of *VC* as *Al-Farabi on the Perfect State* (see note 37 for the full title) and of the suitability of the philosopher for rule over "the universal state" rather than "the whole inhabited world" (*al-ma'mûrah kulliha*). "State," and above all "universal state," implies a level of centralization of administration, to borrow a phrase from Tocqueville, that Alfarabi never intends.

36. I omit the distinctions that Alfarabi draws between the subsets of celestial bodies, namely, the outermost sphere, the sphere of fixed stars, and the inclined spheres. I will not trouble the reader with an account of the Aristotelian-Ptolemaic world system to which Alfarabi here appeals. For the purposes of climatic differentiation, only the inclined spheres are relevant, because the sun is among them.

37. The full title of *VC* is *The Principles of the Opinions of the Inhabitants of the Virtuous City* (*Mabâdi' ârâ' ahl al-madînah al-fâḍilah*).

38. For the philosophically rigorous basis of his schematic remarks on celestial bodies and climate in *PR,* see Alfarabi's *Philosophy of Plato and Aristotle* (in *PPA*), sec. 67, and sections preceding as far back as sec. 37.

39. See chapter 1, the section "Alfarabi's Manner of Writing."

40. See note 35 on "cooperation."

41. Admittedly, there appears to be a certain redundancy in treating deliberation as a part or a kind of prudence (since prudence is deliberating well). Here Aristotle uses "deliberative" in the ordinary, if narrow, political sense to refer to the kind of deliberation that takes place in a governing assembly.

42. Not that Alfarabi views religion as an issue of opinion alone. The central place of character and actions in religion is made quite explicit in the opening lines of the *Book of Religion.*

43. Even that discussion is not sufficient as philosophic training in the various methods of argument. It does, however, clarify the relative rank of the kinds of argument, left far less clear in *AH,* sec. 3. See chapter 6.

44. Mahdi has established the Qur'anic provenance of the very term "certain." See *AFIPP,* 176. Note the frequency in usage of certainty in secs. 2 and 3.

45. Perhaps the most striking feature of this passage is that Alfarabi does not mention "dialectic." This alone suggests that he seeks in *AH* to downplay this crucial, less-than-demonstrative aspect of the sciences.

For the disputes surrounding Alfarabi's inclusion of rhetorical and poetic forms as part of the Aristotelian logical canon and the possible connection to the Alexandrian classification, see the original version of ch. 4 of Mahdi's *AFIPP.* The original version contains questions and Mahdi's responses to them. See Mahdi, "Science, Philosophy, and Religion in Alfarabi's *Enumeration of the Sciences,*" in *The Cultural Context of Medieval Learning,* edited by J. E. Murdoch and E. D. Sylla (Dordrecht-Holland: D. Reidel, 1975), 146–47.

46. The main foci of this discussion are the relation between what is first for us in inquiry and what is first by nature in various sciences and the limits on our ability to acquire knowledge of causes in each science. See ch. 6 in this book, the section "Knowledge and Exploitation," on *AH.*

47. It is unclear in what sense similitudes can produce images.

48. In translating this as "if" rather than "provided," I am merely extrapolating from an observation that Mahdi has made about the use of *idhâ* at *AH* 24, 19.5, and 32, 25.12 (*AFIPP,* 184–85). I believe "if" conveys the conditional character of the statement better than "provided." Considering the consequences of the statement, it should be viewed as highly conditional.

49. I have not included more of the Arabic because Alfarabi's exact words about extracted sciences are not any more illuminating than the translation.

50. See Mahdi's comments on "unexamined common opinion," in *PPA, AH,* secs. 40n5 and 50n2. In sec. 33, Alfarabi seems to use "generally accepted opinion" as the marker

of the lowest form of opinion. It should be noted, however, that the *mashhûr* is the equivalent of Aristotle's *endoxa*. As such, it is a highly flexible term. It serves as the starting point of inquiry into moral and political affairs. As such, it should be viewed as containing partial access to the truth. See Larry Arnhart, *Aristotle on Political Reasoning* (DeKalb: Northern Illinois University Press, 1981). At the same time, such opinion is of lower rank in theoretical inquiries.

51. *AH* 55, 40.9–12, philosophy depends upon certain demonstrations; religion employs persuasive methods and imagines through similitudes.

52. Note the echo of *AH* 40, 30.15. This one claim alone helps explain why Maimonides put so much store in Alfarabi's writings. One of the central claims of Maimonides's *Guide* is that when Moses refers to God with corporeal imagery, he is speaking metaphorically about the incorporeal.

53. See Mahdi, *AH,* sec. 55n7, for passages in the *Timaeus* that Alfarabi likely has in mind.

54. See chapter 6 in this book, the section "The *Philosophy of Aristotle.*"

55. I do not mean simply that early modern philosophers chose to focus on certain causes because they sought to avoid conflict; I also mean that they saw the continuance of such conflict as evidence that these causes must not really be causes. In keeping with their commitment to what Machiavelli calls the "effectual truth," they focused on how to produce proximate effects rather than speculating on first causes. This sense of truth and this focus rest on a kind of harmony between utility and truth never entertained in the ancient or medieval periods—for reasons I cannot consider here. On the relation between utility and certainty in Descartes, cf. Richard Kennington, "Descartes and Mastery of Nature," in Richard Kennington, *On Modern Origins,* edited by Pamela Kraus and Frank Hunt (Lanham, MD: Lexington Books, 2004), 123–44, esp. 131 ff.

56. Admittedly, this portrait of Kant is based primarily on his handling of final causes in the first critique. Here I avoid descending into the details of Kant's complex and often mystifying treatment of teleology. That it came to play an increasing role in his evolving understanding of religion in the last decades of his life is obvious. I am inclined to believe, however, that Kant could not find a way to move beyond the view that religion either is the same thing as ethics or if independent then at best an instrument of ethics.

57. Most readers of modern philosophy will acknowledge without much disagreement that Hobbes repudiates any notion of formal causality. Many will not acknowledge it for Descartes and Spinoza, because both continue to use the language of "ideas." I am confident that I can show that neither admits anything akin to the premodern understanding of "idea." I must leave clarification of this point for another occasion.

58. Alfarabi's most telling divergence is the identification of "humility" (*al-tawâdu'*) as a mean rather than the Aristotelian disposition of character that we expect "greatness of soul" (*megalopsuchia*), the likely equivalent of Alfarabi's excess *al-takabbur*. Cf. how Maimonides follows Alfarabi's lead in this at *Eight Chapters,* ch. 4. Considering what a pivotal role Aristotle ascribes to this virtue (*NE* 1124a2–8), Alfarabi's shift is significant. See Herbert A. Davidson, "Maimonides' *Shemonah Peraqim* and Alfarabi's *Fusûl al-Madanî,*" *Proceedings of the American Academy for Jewish Research* 36 (1963): 33–50, on the relation between the *Eight Chapters* and the *Aphorisms.* Cf. Daniel H. Frank, "Humility

as a Virtue: A Maimonidean Critique of Aristotle's Ethics," in *Moses Maimonides and His Time,* edited by Eric Ormsby (Washington, DC: Catholic University of America Press, 1989), 89–99.

59. See note 3.

60. See Mahdi's claim that Alfarabi here offers Aristotle's response to the Platonic usage of forms or ideas (*AH* 22n1).

61. See also Parens, *Metaphysics as Rhetoric,* 145.

62. See, for example, Plato, *Rep.* 583c–588b.

63. For the reader who doubts this, I recommend a reading of the *Philosophy of Plato,* in which Alfarabi makes the Socratic-Platonic case for this way of life extraordinarily well.

64. Also see *BL,* Mahdi, ed., sec. 108.

65. See the first section in chapter 4.

CHAPTER 6

1. The most significant occasions on which he uses "realization" are the openings of parts ii and iii of *AH* (secs. 22 and 38). It should be kept in mind that there are not any such divisions in the manuscripts. Nevertheless, I find Mahdi's division of *AH* into four parts compelling and persuasive.

2. Mahdi, *PPA,* introduction, 1962 edition, pp. 9–10.

3. See *AFIPP,* ch. 3, the sections entitled "Political Philosophy and Metaphysics" and "The Question of Realization," esp. pp. 57, 61. Mahdi is highly critical of Alfarabi's followers, thinkers such as Ibn Bajjah, Ibn Tufayl, and perhaps even Averroes, for failing to adopt his focus on realization. I plan to argue elsewhere that the depth of Alghazali's influence in the Islamic world necessitated a different approach to political philosophy—albeit a highly indirect, attenuated approach. Contrast Mahdi's own reservations about the realization of the highest human aspirations for "theoretical perfection and right action" in *PPA,* intro. to rev. ed., xxi–xxv.

4. I must acknowledge that in sec. 22, Alfarabi joins with *taḥṣīl* the phrase *bi'l-fi'l* ("actually" or "in actuality"). Yet it should also be noted that this phrase appears in a question rather than an affirmation of what can be.

5. I remind the reader that this word in Arabic need not have the sinister tones it possesses in modern English. More broadly speaking, it means merely to "use" or "employ." It always suggests instrumentality, though it need not carry the sense of "oppression."

6. On the greater certainty attaching to mathematics, consider *AH* 10, 8.11 and 11, 9.18–10.12. In using the phrase "what is first for us and first by nature," I employ a contrast that Aristotle often draws when discussing the starting point of a science (see, for example, *NE* 1095b3). The most obvious example of this contrast is the difference between the human starting point of metaphysics, the study of the beings in our immediate experience as effects of the divine cause, and the basis in nature of that science, God. Aristotle's terminology seems more self-evident than Alfarabi's. Alfarabi uses instead the phrases often used

in the tradition of Greek commentary on Aristotle, "principles of instruction" and "principles of being."

7. On this divergence, see sec. 15. On the problems caused by such divergences, compare sec. 11 with sec. 8.

8. Cf. *PA*, sec. 74, where Alfarabi presents the Aristotelian account of the soul as belonging not only to animals but also plants. See *On the Soul* 412b, 413a32–b10, 18. The abstraction from plants in *AH* is in keeping with Alfarabi's haste in that work to turn to the metaphysical.

9. Cf. *AH* 19, 15.5–9 with *PA* 99, 130.12. This sense of transcending the categories should not be confused with the negative theology or even analogical theologies of the revealed faiths. Cf. Maimonides's *Guide* I 50–67 with I 68.

10. After his brief excursion into the first principle, he shifts from speaking of what one "should" know to the conclusion "having understood this" (*fa-idhâ waqafa*). Even though *idhâ* may not warrant translation as "if" here (cf. *AFIPP*, 184–85), Mahdi's "having understood" conveys too much confidence. The English fails to convey the dependency of the later clause on the earlier conditional statements.

Questions of grammar aside, *PA*'s concluding denial of our access to metaphysics must put everything stated in *AH* secs. 16 and 19 in a new light.

11. Again, one must be careful not to confuse the kind of journey of exploitation that Alfarabi has in mind and the kind envisioned by the founders of modernity.

12. In spite of a certain similarity of parlance in English translation with Foucault, one should not confuse Alfarabi's discussion of exploitation with post-Rousseauan critiques of same.

13. Mahdi, *AFIPP,* 186.

14. The relation between theoretical knowledge and practice in Alfarabi does not rest upon a modern epistemology in which theoretical knowledge is knowledge of proximate effects, which are in turn applied in medicine or manufacture.

15. The absence of adequate knowledge of divine and human purposes accounts for the fact that Plato, Aristotle, and Alfarabi (and, in their own way, the revealed religions) acknowledge the ultimate superiority of the rule of law over the rule of the best human being. And law, in turn, is a kind of mixture of reason (aristocracy) and consent (democracy) necessitated, at least in part, by the limitations of our knowledge.

16. Of course, the *Philosophy of Plato* appears between *AH* and *PA*. It would seem, then, that Plato has either somehow reconciled himself properly to the limitations of human knowledge or failed to strive vigorously enough for the highest knowledge. Alfarabi alludes to both possibilities without resolving the matter in the opening lines of *PA*. I cannot pursue this interesting issue further here.

17. Although Thomas Aquinas, for example, denies that Aristotle has achieved knowledge of the divine, he seems to argue as if Aristotle had deluded himself into believing he had achieved it. See *Summa contra gentiles,* bk. 3, chaps. 39 and 48. (Of course, we will seek to clarify to the extent possible the nature of these limitations in what follows.) It is a more convincing manner of defeating an opponent to ascribe to him high aspirations that he could not achieve than to ascribe to him more limited expectations. In general, Alfarabi has

led me to believe that many authors have overestimated what Aristotle believes he achieved. Following Alfarabi, I read Aristotle in a more dialectical and Socratic vein.

18. Strauss, "Farabi's *Plato,*" in *Louis Ginzberg Jubilee Volume,* edited by A. Marx, S. Lieberman, S. Spiegel, and S. Zeitlin, 375 (New York: American Academy for Jewish Research, 1945).

19. An interpretation with some plausibility seems to recommend itself, at least initially. One could claim that *AH* reflects Alfarabi's greater confidence in the adequacy of human knowledge once it has been the beneficiary of revelation. (Alfarabi's) Aristotle evinces less confidence only because he lacked access to revelation. There are two problems with this interpretation, however. Alfarabi does not appeal to revelation or prophecy in the establishment of his virtuous regime of the inhabited world in *AH.* And if he believed that revelation put him in such a privileged position, then should he not have given clear indication that *AH* belongs at the end of the trilogy because it answers what *PA* cannot?

20. It must be remembered that all of the evidence seems to indicate that the medieval Islamic philosophical tradition (as well as the Jewish one that developed from it) did not have access to Aristotle's *Politics.* Nevertheless, this fact about the *Politics* does not diminish the importance of my following argument.

I thank a dissertation advisee of mine, Daniel Silvermintz, for drawing my attention to this passage in Aristotle. His interpretation of this passage, in a paper he wrote for a Maimonides seminar I led, has influenced my own.

Mahdi highlights the contrast between the conclusions of Alfarabi's Aristotle and the aspirations of *Politics* 1.8 at *PPA,* rev. intro., xviii–xix. Mahdi also develops this contrast in his following pages in various ways to which I am indebted in these following pages.

21. See citation at previous note.

22. Once again, I do not mean to imply that the revealed religions justify the "exploitation" of nature in the spirit of modernity. What is required for that are plans such as those of Bacon and Descartes for the ownership and mastery of nature. It is significant that final causes do not play any role in that plan. The focus on proximate effects facilitates an unprecedented unleashing of "energy" in nature.

23. See note 40.

24. This second point is so obvious as not to require specific citations. Nevertheless, I must address a passage that could appear at first glance to challenge my first claim that the Qur'an presents man as the peak of Creation. Even though Qur'an 40:57 appears at first to lower man's rank, it does so only in relation to the rest of Creation taken as a whole. (See A. Yusuf Ali's edition of the Qur'an [Brentwood, MD: Amana, 1983] for an interpretation making the same basic point, 40:57n4431, p. 1278.) In other words, this is merely part of an effort to remind man of his place in relation to his Creator, which is my second point.

25. Review the opening pages of chapter 4.

26. See Aristotle, *NE* 1141a19–b2. As *Metaphysics* 12.8 makes apparent, Aristotle means to demote traditional Greek worship of the heavenly bodies themselves.

27. *NE* 1142b1–2.

28. The Arabic for "purpose" is the same throughout. N.B. the same word is used here as was used for the purpose of the philosopher-king, namely, the common good in the previous section on *AH*.

29. The ellipses in this paragraph are first an analogy for purpose drawn from the productive arts and second an analogy for purpose drawn from the relation of organs to the organism. The last kind will prove to be one of the most dependable kinds of final cause that Alfarabi's Aristotle identifies.

30. Here it is worth recalling that Alfarabi is self-conscious in using a hierarchical account of the cosmos to bolster the political hierarchy that he advocates for example in *AH*. See *VC,* Walzer, ed., chs. 6, 9–11, 15; *PR,* Hyderabad ed., pp. 16–20; *BR,* secs. 19–27.

31. With the help of Mahdi's excellent notes to his translation, we may trace Alfarabi's subsequent itinerary as the following: *Meteorology, On Minerals, On Plants, Parts of Animals, On the Soul* (secs. 75–78, 117.12), *Health and Disease, Youth and Old Age, Sense and the Sensible, On Locomotion, Parva Naturalia, On the Soul* (secs. 90–99, 130.24), *Nicomachean Ethics,* and a closing reference to the *Metaphysics.* The most noteworthy feature of this itinerary is the recurrence of *On the Soul.* The first appearance of *On the Soul* will give rise to or signal a crisis in the inquiry into final causes.

32. See David Bolotin's excellent discussion of how problematic the theme of place is in Aristotle (*An Approach to Aristotle's Physics* [Albany: State University of New York Press, 1998], ch. 4).

33. Of course, I do not mean that it is difficult to imagine how human beings might make use of rocks. Yet it is difficult to conceive of a convincing argument that rocks should have as their purpose such use by human beings. Obvious difficulties would arise, such as a vast overabundance of various kinds of rocks for human needs.

34. Review sec. 3, 68.13, and my comments on it after quoting the surrounding context.

35. See note 31. He highlights its pivotal character by returning to it, much as he returned to both metaphysics and political or human science in *AH*.

36. During the second discussion of soul, the soul will serve as potency, instrument, even "matter" for intellect as its actuality or form (90, 122.20–23).

37. Few issues fueled such endless debate in medieval thought as Aristotle's barely decipherable views on immortality in *On the Soul* 3.4–6.

38. Compare the account of practical intellect (sec. 91) with the opening discussion of the four human goods recognized by everyone (sec. 1, 59.10–15).

39. "Theoretical intellect" here must not be confused with "theoretical virtue," which played such an important political role in chapter 5, sec. 3.

40. Sec. 99 should be compared with the opening sections of *PR* and *VC*.

41. Compare this unusual usage with the more common "natural science" (*al-'ilm al-ṭabī'ī),* for example, at 17, 85.21.

42. On the inquiry in *On the Soul* as a subject of natural philosophy, see 402a5–8, 403a28–30, 403b12–16. *On the Soul* 3.4–6 has borne so much metaphysical weight because Aristotle barely discusses the soul as a first philosopher (that is, someone concerned with

that which is "separable" from matter) in the *Metaphysics,* except indirectly. See, for example, *Meta.* 7.10–11, esp. 1036b23–32.

43. Maimonides went on to develop this theme. Cf. Alfarabi's tempered view of what Aristotle really claimed to know about the interrelation of final causes in *PA* with Maimonides, *Guide* III 13 [22b–23b]. Alfarabi's and Maimonides' views should be contrasted with "what is sometimes thought, according to our opinion and our doctrine of creation," *Guide* II 13 [23b–24b]. All of these views should be contrasted with Spinoza's far more extensive attack on and abandonment of *all* teleology (*Ethics* I appendix and 2p40s1)—an attack sometimes conflated with Maimonides's Alfarabian limitations on teleology.

44. I have touched on this fact repeatedly in chapters 3 and 5. Mahdi's discussion of the pretheoretical understanding of certainty in his chapter on *AH* is the basis of this observation. See *AFIPP,* pp. 173–76.

45. As if to challenge those who traffic only in certainties, *PA* is the occasion for Alfarabi's introduction of dialectic (13, 78.7–79.19, 83.17–84.4; 20, 91.22–92.9). As I mentioned in chapter 5, he is completely silent about dialectic as a method in *AH,* most notably sec. 4—even though he employs some there, for example, part ii, sec. 31. See chapter 3, "Tension in the 'Unity of the Virtues.'" Any attention to dialectic in *AH* might have cast unseemly doubt on the air of certainty surrounding the hasty account of the sciences in part i.

46. Here he does so merely by implication while discussing dialectic.

47. Scholasticism has left the false impression that metaphysics should serve as both the ground and the starting point of the sciences. That false impression derives from the fact that Scholastics model their own accounts on the revealed model of the order of knowledge. Rather than beginning, as Alfarabi and others do, with human opinions about the good for human life, that is, with what is first for us, they begin with the affirmation of the fact of creation and therefore the Creator. This has fomented the mistaken impression that Western philosophy is rife with foundationalism.

48. Alfarabi spends less time discussing practical or political science in the *Philosophy of Aristotle* than in any other part of the trilogy. To my knowledge, the following are the only passages dealing with these themes: secs. 1–4; 15–16; 99, 131.1–132.2. As we have seen in earlier chapters, Alfarabi's adaptation of Aristotelian political science in *AH* is quite extensive.

49. Of course, like the natural sciences, according to Aristotle, political science concerns things that are "for the most part" as well. Sometimes interpreters of Aristotle's political science have lost sight of this similarity between natural and political science because (1) the former is a theoretical science and the latter is a practical science, and (2) because there is another layer of contingency added to the *object* of study in political science, namely, the contingency of the prudent or imprudent choice of the actor. As a result, a great deal of ink has been spilled on the scientific status of Aristotle's practical sciences, at least since G. E. L. Owen's seminal *"Tithenai ta phainomena,"* in *Aristote et les problèmes de méthode,* ed. S. Mansion, 83–103 (Louvain: Éditions de l'Institut supérieur de philosophie, 1961). See Aristide Tessitore, *Reading Aristotle's "Ethics"* (Albany: State University of New York Press, 1996), introduction and his references to related writings by Larry Arnhart, Carnes Lord, and Mary Nichols at 123n5. Also see May Sim, ed., *From Puzzles to Principles?: Essays on*

Aristotle's Dialectic (Lanham, MD: Lexington Books, 1999). For the most, perhaps too, detailed discussion of the subject, see Georgios Anagnostopoulos, *Aristotle on the Goals and Exactness of Ethics* (Berkeley: University of California Press, 1994).

50. Cf. this assessment of the relation between theoretical and practical science with Aristotle's *Metaphysics* 1.1. For Alfarabi's account of Aristotle's starting point, see Mahdi's footnote 2 to his translation of sec. 1.

51. There may be similarities between this version of political science and the first account of political science in Alfarabi's *Enumeration* (Amin, ed., 102–104). Yet even the account in the *Enumeration* seems far more scientific than this practical science.

52. Political philosophy, because of its more intimate affiliation with divine science (than political science), is more cognizant of the limits to human knowledge of human affairs, due to limitations on human knowledge of the whole.

53. See *AH* 18, 20; *PA* 99, 131.20–132.2; Mahdi, *PPA,* rev. intro., xv–xvi; Plato, *Apology* 20d7.

54. To the extent that we are children of modernity, we do not credit human prudence very much. The denigration of Aristotelian prudence that began with Machiavelli and came into full flower in Hobbes (*Leviathan,* ch. 13), along with the effort to substitute predictive science for prudence, has left us far removed from this dimension of the pretheoretical mind-set. Yet we are prone to substitute an overstated faith in the predictive powers of science, especially overstated in political matters, for this older faith in the semi-divine prudence of great rulers.

55. See Plato's allusion to the same phenomenon in the *Republic* (514b6–515c2, 516c5–d).

56. By the "good beyond being," of course, I allude to Socrates' suggestion at *Republic* 509b, which Neoplatonists were to make into the core of their teaching. Neoplatonists take this passage too literally by failing to attend to its role in the drama of Glaucon.

57. For Alfarabi's admission that God as First Cause transcends the categories, see *AH,* sec. 19. Also see note 9.

58. See *On the Soul* 3.4 and *Metaphysics* 12.9.

59. Again, see *AH,* sec. 19. To avoid the danger that anyone might suppose that his First Cause is the good beyond being or the object of mystical union, Alfarabi interposes the Active Intellect between human beings and God. The special role of the Active Intellect in Alfarabi's thought (as well as subsequent Islamic thought) is to account for prophetic access to the divine, while preventing conjunction (*ittiṣâl*) with the divine from collapsing into union (*ittiḥâd*) with God.

60. Aristotle, *Metaphysics* 6.2.

61. See chapter 4.

62. Although Aristotle claims that God or the Unmoved Mover is thought thinking itself, he is quite vague about the content of that pure actuality (*energeia*) (cf. *Metaphysics* 12.9 with 12.10).

63. See chapter 1 on "schematic" writing.

64. The reader should notice that *BR* presents its equivalent to the openings of *VC* and *PR* at the end, albeit in a far more schematic fashion. Alfarabi implies thereby that the political philosophy set forth in the previous pages establishes the groundwork for the closing theology. In contrast, the reverse appears to be the case in *VC* and *PR*.

65. See *Nicomachean Ethics* 1100b18–33, 1123b32.

66. Of course, I do not mean to insinuate that the prudence of things beyond our power does not affect us. I merely mean to suggest that for Alfarabi, as for Aristotle, what is up to us really is our last line of defense in life. Unlike the Stoics, neither Aristotle nor Alfarabi claims that "what is up to us" is the only thing we should really concern ourselves with, however.

67. Cf. Sachedina, "The Development of *Jihâd*," 44–47.

Bibliography

PRIMARY SOURCES

Alfarabi. *Alfarabi: The Political Writings: Philosophy of Plato and Aristotle* (PPA). (The trilogy includes the *Attainment of Happiness [AH]*, the *Philosophy of Plato [PP]*, and the *Philosophy of Aristotle [PA]*.) Translated with introductions by Muhsin Mahdi. New York: The Free Press of Glencoe, 1962; revised editions, Ithaca, NY: Cornell University Press, 1969, 2001. *Taḥṣīl al-saʿādah*. Edited by Jafar al-Yasin. Beirut: al-Andaloss, 1981. *De Platonis philosophia*. Edited by F. Rosenthal and R. Walzer. London: Warburg Institute, 1943. *Falsafat Arisṭūṭālīs*. Edited by Muhsin Mahdi. Beirut: Dâr Majallat Shiʾr, 1961.

———. *Alfarabi: The Political Writings: "Selected Aphorisms" and Other Texts* (including *Selected Aphorisms*, chapter 5 of *Enumeration of the Sciences, Book of Religion [BR]*.) Translated and annotated by Charles E. Butterworth. Ithaca, NY: Cornell University Press, 2001. *Fuṣūl muntazaʿah*. Edited by Fauzi M. Najjar. Beirut: Dar al-Mashriq, 1971. *Iḥṣāʾ al-ʿulūm* and *Kitâb al-Millah*. In *Abû Naṣr al-Fârâbî, Kitâb al-Millah wa-Nuṣūṣ Ukhrâ*, ed. Muhsin Mahdi, 69–76, 43–66. Beirut: Dar al-Mashriq, 1968. (Iḥṣāʾ [Enumeration] cited by Amin edition [Cairo: Dâr al-Fikr al-ʿArabî, 1949] page numbers because they are present in all translations and critical editions.)

———. *Alfarabi's Book of Letters (BL)*. Kitâb al-ḥurûf. Edited by Muhsin Mahdi. Beirut: Dar al-Mashriq, 1969. Partial translation forthcoming in *Alfarabi: Political Writings*. Translated by Charles E. Butterworth. Ithaca, NY: Cornell University Press.

———. *Al-Farabi on the Perfect State*. Literally, *The Principles of the Opinions of the Inhabitants of the Virtuous City* (Mabâdiʾ ârâʾ ahl al-madînah al-fâḍilah) (*VC*). Translated and edited by Richard Walzer. Oxford: Clarendon Press, 1985.

———. *Political Regime (PR)*. Partially translated by Fauzi M. Najjar. In *Medieval Political Philosophy*, was. Ralph Lerner and Muhsin Mahdi, 31–57. New York: The Free Press of Glencoe, 1963; reprinted Ithaca, NY: Cornell University Press, 1972. *Al-siyâsâ al-madaniyyah*. Edited by Fauzi M. Najjar. Beirut: al-Maṭbaʿah al-kâthûlîkiyyah, 1964. (Cited by Hyderabad [1346 A.H.] edition page nos. because they are common to Najjar's translation and critical Arabic edition.) Translation forthcoming in *Alfarabi: Political Writings*. Translated by Charles E. Butterworth. Ithaca, NY: Cornell University Press.

———. *Summary of Plato's "Laws."* Partially translated by Muhsin Mahdi. In *Medieval Political Philosophy*, ed. Ralph Lerner and Muhsin Mahdi, 83–94. New York: The Free Press of Glencoe, 1963; reprinted Ithaca, NY: Cornell University Press, 1972. Subsequently, complete Arabic text edited by Thérèse-Anne Druart. *Le Sommaire du livre des "Lois" de Platon (Jawâmiʿ kitâb al-nawâmîs li-Aflâṭûn)*. In *Bulletin d'Études Orientales* 50 (1998): 109–155. Translation forthcoming in *Alfarabi: Political Writings*. Translated by Charles E. Butterworth. Ithaca, NY: Cornell University Press.

OTHER PRIMARY SOURCES

Aristotle. *Metaphysics*. Translated by Joe Sachs. Santa Fe, NM: Green Lion Press, 1999.

——. *Nicomachean Ethics*. Translated by Joe Sachs. Newburyport, MA: Focus Publishing, 2002.

——. *Politics*. Translated by Carnes Lord. Chicago: University of Chicago Press, 1984.

Averroes. *Averroes on Plato's "Republic."* Translated by Ralph Lerner. Ithaca, NY: Cornell University Press, 1974. Hebrew edition in *Averroes' Commentary on Plato's "Republic."* Edited by E. I. J. Rosenthal. Cambridge: Cambridge University Press, 1960.

Ibn Khaldun. *Muqaddimah*. Translated by Franz Rosenthal. New York: Pantheon Books, 1958.

Maimonides. *Eight Chapters*. In *Ethical Writings of Maimonides*, ed. and trans. by Raymond L. Weiss and Charles E. Butterworth. New York: New York University Press, 1975; reprinted New York: Dover, 1983.

——. *Guide of the Perplexed*. 2 vols. Translated by Shlomo Pines. Chicago: University of Chicago Press, 1963.

Plato. *Apology*. Translated with notes by Thomas G. West and Grace Starry West. In *Four Texts on Socrates*. Rev. ed. Ithaca, NY: Cornell University Press, 1984, 1998.

——. *The Laws of Plato*. Translated with notes and an interpretive essay by Thomas L. Pangle. New York: Basic Books, 1980; reprinted by Chicago: University of Chicago Press, 1988.

——. *The Republic of Plato*. Translated with notes and an interpretive essay by Allan Bloom. 2d ed. New York: Basic Books, 1968, 1991.

——. *Statesman*. Translated by Seth Benardete. In *The Being of the Beautiful*. Chicago: University of Chicago Press, 1984.

——. *Symposium*. Translated by Seth Benardete. Chicago: University of Chicago Press, 2002.

SECONDARY SOURCES

Anagnostopoulos, Georgios. *Aristotle on the Goals and Exactness of Ethics*. Berkeley: University of California Press, 1994.

Arnhart, Larry. *Aristotle on Political Reasoning*. DeKalb: Northern Illinois University Press, 1981.

Bolotin, David. *An Approach to Aristotle's Physics*. Albany: State University of New York Press, 1998.

Butterworth, Charles E. "Al-Fârâbî's Statecraft: War and the Well-Ordered Regime." In *Cross, Crescent, and Sword*, ed. Johnson and Kelsay, 79–100. New York: Greenwood Press, 1990.

Colmo, Christopher. "Theory and Practice: Alfarabi's *Plato* Revisited." *American Political Science Review* 84:4 (1992): 966–76.

Donner, Fred M. "The Sources of Islamic Conceptions of War." In *Just War and Jihad*, ed. Johnson and Kelsay, 31–69. New York: Greenwood Press, 1991.

Esposito, John L. *Islam: The Straight Path*. 3rd ed. Oxford: Oxford University Press, 1998.

Goodman, Lenn E. *Islamic Humanism*. Oxford: Oxford University Press, 2003.

Johnson, James Turner. *The Holy War Idea in Western and Islamic Traditions*. University Park: Pennsylvania State University Press, 1997.

Johnson, James Turner, and John Kelsay, eds. *Cross, Crescent, and Sword*. New York: Greenwood Press, 1990.

Kelsay, John, and James Turner Johnson, eds. *Just War and Jihad*. New York: Greenwood Press, 1991.

Khadduri, Majid. *The Islamic Law of Nations: Shaybani's Sîyar*. Baltimore: Johns Hopkins University Press, 1966.

———. *War and Peace in the Law of Islam*. Baltimore: Johns Hopkins University Press, 1955.

Kraemer, Joel L. "The *Jihâd* of the *Falâsifa*." *Jerusalem Studies in Arabic and Islam* 10 (1987): 288–324.

Lambton, Ann K. S. *State and Government in Medieval Islam*. Oxford: Oxford University Press, 1981.

Mahdi, Muhsin. *Alfarabi and the Foundation of Islamic Political Philosophy (AFIPP)*. Chicago: University of Chicago Press, 2001.

———. "Al-Fârâbî." In *Dictionary of Scientific Biography*, vol. 4, ed. C. C. Gillispie, 523–26. New York: Charles Scribner, 1971.

———. "Al-Fârâbî's Imperfect State." A Review of Richard Walzer's *Al-Farabi on the Perfect State*. In *Journal of the American Oriental Society* 110:4 (1990): 691–726.

———. "Science, Philosophy, and Religion in Alfarabi's *Enumeration of the Sciences*." In *The Cultural Context of Medieval Learning*, ed. J. E. Murdoch and E. D. Sylla, 146–147. Dordrecht-Holland: D. Reidel, 1975.

Owen, G. E. L. "*Tithenai ta phainomena*." In *Aristote et les problèmes de méthode*, ed. S. Mansion, 83–103. Louvain: Éditions de l'Institut supérieur de philosophie, 1961.

Parens, Joshua. *Metaphysics as Rhetoric: Alfarabi's "Summary of Plato's 'Laws.'"* Albany: State University of New York Press, 1995.

———. Review of Mahdi's *Alfarabi and the Foundation of Islamic Political Philosophy*. *American Political Science Review* 96:2 (2002): 410–11.

Rahman, Fazlur. *Islam*. 2d ed. Chicago: University of Chicago Press, 1966, 1979.

Rosenthal, Erwin I. J. *Political Thought in Medieval Islam.* Cambridge: Cambridge University Press, 1962.

Sachedina, Abdulaziz A. "The Development of Jihâd in Islamic Revelation and History." In *Cross, Crescent, and Sword,* ed. Johnson and Kelsay, 35–50. New York: Greenwood Press, 1990.

Sim, May, ed. *From Puzzles to Principles?: Essays on Aristotle's Dialectic.* Lanham, MD: Lexington Books, 1999.

Strauss, Leo. *The City and Man.* Chicago: University of Chicago Press, 1964.

———. "Farabi's *Plato.*" In *Louis Ginzberg Jubilee Volume,* ed. A. Marx, S. Lieberman, S. Spiegel, and S. Zeitlin, 357–93. New York: American Academy for Jewish Research, 1945.

———. *What Is Political Philosophy? and Other Studies.* New York: Free Press of Glencoe, 1959; reprint Chicago: University of Chicago Press, 1988.

Tessitore, Aristide. *Reading Aristotle's "Ethics."* Albany: State University of New York Press, 1996.

Author/Subject Index

accidents (*a'râḍ*) or states (*aḥwâl*), 45–47,
49, 80, 85–87, 90–93, 100, 119, 120,
132n9, 145n27
Adeimantus, 14, 16, 23, 26, 36, 39, 130n37
Alfarabi, works of
Book of Letters, 87, 88, 142n2, 145nn31–
32, 148n64
Book of Religion, 7, 119, 120, 125n8,
132n12, 151n30, 146n42, 154n64
Philosophy of Aristotle, 50, 52, 53, 93, 98,
105, 108–18, 122, 126n1, 131n6, 141n55,
149nn8–9, 149n16, 150n19, 152n43,
152n45, 152n48, 153n53
Philosophy of Plato, 37, 99, 118, 122,
126n1, 133n16, 148n63, 149n16
Philosophy of Plato and Aristotle (the trilogy), 99, 103, 122, 126n1, 146n38, 146–
7n50
Political Regime, 6, 8, 9, 77, 79, 81–84,
87–90, 97, 120, 121, 125n1, 125n8,
132n12, 143n13, 144nn18–19, 145n34,
151n30, 154n64
Summary of Plato's "Laws," 5, 55, 134n30,
144n22
Virtuous City, 6, 29, 80, 87, 90, 97, 120,
125n8, 126n4, 131n3, 132n12, 139n30,
143n12, 145nn34–35, 146n37, 151n30,
154n64
Alcibiades, 6, 130n41, 132n 15
ambition: excessive, 83; of Islam, 1–2, 5, 7–8,
109, 121–3; of philosophers, 35, 63, 118;
political, 35, 118; of revealed religions,
109, 121–3; for world rule, 1–2, 5, 7–8,
55, 109, 121, 137n3; of the young, 3
analogy: animals and humans, 18, 19, 20;

boxer and city, 23, 24, 26; doctor and
ruler, 74, 75, 84; puppy and guardian,
40, 41
ancients, the, 12, 14, 77, 97, 126n6, 142n1
argument: the a fortiori, 8, 29–53, 77, 80,
86; degree of certainty of, 105, 116;
demonstrative, 6, 94–96, 116, 118,
146n45; dialectic(al), 6, 44, 94, 125n7,
149n29, 146n45, 149–50n17, 152nn45–
46; imaginative, 73, 96, 120; poetic,
45, 94, 95, 146n45; persuasive, 95–97,
147n51; rhetoric(al), 6, 44, 45, 90, 94,
95, 146n45; sophistic, 94; subdemonstrative, 94; various methods of, 53,
93–96, 105, 117, 122, 146n43
Aristotle: and Alfarabi compared with
Stoics, 154n66; Alfarabi's, 108, 112, 114,
117, 150n20, 151n29; his account of the
virtues, 39; medieval Christian interpretation of, 149–50n17 ; traditional
portrait of teleology in, 108
Aristotle, the works of,
Metaphysics, 48, 116, 134, 151n26, 151n31,
151–2n42, 153n50, 153n62
On the Soul, 112–15, 149n8, 151n31,
151n37, 151–2n42
Politics, 108–109, 134n32, 143n8, 143n11,
150n20
Arnhart, Larry, 146–7n50, 152n49
art(s): the, 44, 45, 48, 116, 117; the highest
practical, 51; the leading, 44, 45; practical, 51, 144n23; productive, 51,
151n29;
attainment (*taḥṣîl*), 5, 44, 94, 113, 114, 121,
133n18, 134n34

Index of Passages from Alfawarabi's
Attainment of Happiness

Mahdi (English) section numbers	Yasin (Arabic) page and section numbers where beginning of Yasin section coincides with that of Mahdi section	Pages in *Islamic Philosophy of Virtuous Religions* where this section is discussed
Part i		53, 104-105
1	49	44
2	49-50	53, 93, 105, 106
3	50	93, 146n43
4	51	53, 93
5	51-52 (4)	94
6	52 (5)	94
7	52-53 (6)	94
8	53-54	94
9	54-55 (8)	94
10	55-56 (9)	94, 105, 148-9n6
11	56-57	94, 148-9n6
12	57-58 (11)	94
13	58	94, 105
14	58	94
15	59 (13)	94
16	59-60	94, 105, 149n10
17	60-61 (15)	94, 105
18	61-62	52, 94, 105, 153n53
19	62-63 (17)	94, 149nn9-10, 153n57, 153n59
20	63-64 (19)	94, 131n6
21	64	94, 131n6, 144-5n26
Part ii		6, 93-94, 106, 144-5n26, 148n1
22	64-65 (21)	44, 144-5n26, 148n1, 148n4
23	65	85, 100, 132n9
24	65-67	43-45, 77, 85-87, 90-92, 100, 106, 132n9, 145n35, 146n48
25	67-68 (26)	43, 44, 91, 106, 145n35
26	68	43, 45, 145n27